Sign Talker

Captain Hugh Lenox Scott, Seventh U.S. Cavalry, in dress uniform, ca. 1895. Artist Frederic Remington thought he looked like a "college professor." From *Seventeenth Annual Report of the Bureau of American Ethnology to the Secretary of the Smithsonian Institution, 1895–96*, 224.

Sign Talker

Hugh Lenox Scott Remembers Indian Country

Edited by R. ELI PAUL

UNIVERSITY OF OKLAHOMA PRESS : NORMAN

This book is published with the generous assistance of the Wallace C. Thompson Endowment Fund, University of Oklahoma Foundation.

Library of Congress Cataloging-in-Publication Data

Names: Scott, Hugh Lenox, 1853–1934, author. | Paul, R. Eli, 1954– editor. | Scott, Hugh Lenox. Some memories of a soldier. Abridgement of (work)
Title: Sign talker : Hugh Lenox Scott remembers Indian Country / by Hugh Lenox Scott ; edited and with an introduction by R. Eli Paul.
Description: Norman, OK : University of Oklahoma Press, [2016] | Abridgement of: Some memories of a soldier / Hugh Lenox Scott. New York : The Century Company, 1928. | Includes bibliographical references and index.
Identifiers: LCCN 2015044256 | ISBN 978-0-8061-5354-4 (hardcover : alk. paper)
Subjects: LCSH: Scott, Hugh Lenox, 1853–1934. | United States. Army—Military life. | United States. Army—Officers—Biography. | Generals—United States—Biography. | Indians of North America—Government relations—Anecdotes.
Classification: LCC E181 .S416 2016 | DDC 355.0092—dc23
LC record available at http://lccn.loc.gov/2015044256

The paper in this book meets the guidelines for permanence and durability of the Committee on Production Guidelines for Book Longevity of the Council on Library Resources, Inc. ∞

1 2 3 4 5 6 7 8 9 10

Contents

Illustrations

Figures

Map

Preface

Time may be catching up with Hugh Lenox Scott of Princeton, West Point, and points west. Once a prominent figure of the first third of the twentieth century, Scott's stature has fallen sharply in the intervening decades. Clearly, modern historians of the U.S. Army have overlooked Scott, which may be surprising given the major general's rank and station. Military biographies of his late nineteenth- and early twentieth-century contemporaries abound—many of them on individuals who had shorter careers, fewer professional accomplishments, and less interesting lives but who participated, often accidentally, in events that still capture the imagination. Hundreds of books have been written about George A. Custer, the perennial attraction to authors of all stripes, and several more on the individual officers under his command. The zenith—perhaps the nadir—of their respective careers consisted of what they did or had done to them at the Little Big Horn. Fortunately Scott missed that debacle by a year.

More biographies cover the military leaders who, decades later in the early twentieth century, led a national army to fight in the First World War. As the U.S. Army chief of staff, in his day the pinnacle of national military service, Scott did his part by helping prepare the country for the war against Germany. John J. Pershing and his frontline division commanders, though, captured the public's interest in the afterglow of Allied victory and continue to do so among biographers. Yet no such published biography of Scott appeared in the intervening century.

Until that book is written, one has Scott's 1928 autobiography *Some Memories of a Soldier.* Presented here is an abridged version, newly entitled *Sign Talker* and meant to serve as that future biography's prologue and as another introduction of a remarkably fascinating historical figure. Scott's military career spanned decades, literally from the Little Big Horn—he helped rebury Custer's men in 1877, a year after the battle—to the Meuse-Argonne of 1918, where the "army of democracy" he helped form and send off to France saw ultimate victory. Chapter titles for this edition contain key words—"Red Cloud," "Nez Percés," "Fort Sill," "Chiricahua," "Buffalo Running," and "Buffalo Bill"—that illustrate in their obvious way the breadth of his frontier experiences and the richness of his reminiscences.

Scott was no Custer, though, no "cavalier in buckskin" and never fought in a pitched battle or skirmish of the Indian Wars. He fired few shots in anger. Although lacking the opportunity, truth be told, he also lacked the inclination, not from cowardice or fear, but from an aversion to needless violence, an abiding respect for Native peoples, and a deep empathy for the wrongs they had suffered by his race. They "never . . . broke a promise to me," he once wrote of American Indians. His reputation as a soldier-diplomat served him well in the American West but garnered him few plaudits from those looking beyond diplomacy to the brutal demands of the western front in 1917–18 and its human carnage on a global, industrial scale.

Scott's day for a serious reassessment may be coming, and this book is a start. From his time in Indian country and from his own words, we discover an intriguing person, one who stood distinctly apart from his fellow officers. As the dust settles on the spirited refighting of the Indian Wars by academics and avocational historians—and as today's policy makers critically examine our country's current foreign adventures—Scott's personal attributes and professional accomplishments, particularly his ability to communicate directly with them through the Plains Indian Sign Language, demonstrate his effectiveness in dealing with peoples of other cultures. This aptitude combined with compassion makes him a sympathetic, enlightened figure, a modern man, if you will. Any survey of his mentors and contemporaries finds few, if any, other candidates for such recognition. My reason in seeing this volume to print is to highlight these contributions and to return this man to the public's high esteem. In so doing we can learn much from Scott's life story.

This judicious excerpt from the larger memoir reveals why Scott is special and worth remembering, though the decision to abridge was not made lightly.

Lengthy conversations with my editor and my peers convinced me that buried in that intimidating volume was a far more interesting but separate story, one in danger of again being lost by simply reprinting the 1928 book in its entirety. It would do little justice to Scott's significant role in the history of Indian-white relations in the American West—or to modern readers—to present the whole memoir and doom the effort to exhume his career.

Another goal as an editor is to provide a sufficient, but not exhaustive, biography that will set up and provide the context for his narrative. I have tried to point out certain high points in the autobiography without being repetitive or spoiling Scott's own telling and also have allowed him, as is his right, to have the last word. His future biographer should be the one to offer that level of lengthy, detailed analysis and retrospect that his rich life deserves.

I gave an earlier, shorter version of the introduction that follows as a paper, "General Scott and the Indians," at the Ninth Fort Robinson History Conference on April 27, 2013. In lieu of the usual acknowledgments that accompany most book projects, I wish to thank my fellow founders, organizers, speakers, and attendees of the Fort Rob conference. Nine times during the span from 1995 to 2013 an interested—and interesting—group of scholars, history buffs, authors, academics, and natives of northwest Nebraska and surrounding states came together to listen to presentations and to discuss the following topics: "Material Culture of the Frontier Army" (1995); "Everyday Life of the Frontier Soldier" (1997); "Indians, Soldiers, and Bureaucrats: A New Look at Old Foes" (2000); "Indian War Leaders and Leadership" (2002); "A New Army for a New Century: Military Culture in Transition, 1890–1917" (2004); "Four-Legged Soldiers: The Horse and the Mule in the Plains Wars and Beyond" (2007); "U.S. Army Posts on the Central and Northern Plains, 1820–1890" (2009); "The Civil War in the American West" (2011); and, fittingly, to draw the curtain down on the entire series, "After the Indian Wars" (2013). Held on the grounds and in the period structures of historic Fort Robinson, Nebraska, the combination of relevant topics, memorable settings, learned experts, and enthusiastic participants proved educational, enlightening, and inspirational for furthering my understanding of the Indian Wars and, pertinent to this publication, the world of Hugh Lenox Scott.

In particular, I want to recognize Tom Buecker, Brent Carmack, and Jim Potter, who were there with me at the inception when we four at the Nebraska State Historical Society founded the conference. Tom and Jim continued on when two of us moved to greener pastures, and with Tom's recent death, a great loss, this great gathering has drawn to a symbolic and real close.

Fellow presenters at the Fort Rob conference include friends and colleagues to whom I owe much regarding my professional development and whose writings on the above topics fill my bookshelves: Kingsley Bray, Lori Cox-Paul, Brian Dippie, Jerry Greene, Jim Hanson, Paul Hedren, Paul Hutton, Bob Larson, Doug McChristian, Jack McDermott, Tom Powers, Frank "Mick" Schubert, Doug Scott, and Robert Utley. Some of these individuals attended one or two conferences, many of them all nine. All have been generous with sharing their knowledge.

Finally, I wish to thank the talented crew of the University of Oklahoma Press, led by Chuck Rankin, that helped me with this project, including Brittney Berling, Stephanie Evans, Amy Hernandez, Kelly Parker, and a trio of dedicated, anonymous manuscript reviewers. Collectively, they make working with this distinguished university press easy, enjoyable, and rewarding. Robert Pilk of Lakewood, Colorado, drew the map of "Scott's Indian Country," a land to which I look forward to returning and further exploring.

Sign Talker

Editor's Introduction

While preparing his 1928 memoir, *Some Memories of a Soldier*, General Hugh Scott recalled the moment, nearly three decades earlier, when he had an epiphany. As an officer in the Seventh U.S. Cavalry, Scott participated in the annual camp of instruction of the Department of the Missouri for 1889. As he looked over the vast training field, he saw the employment of large formations of infantry and cavalry, as copied from the large, standing armies of Europe, to which his superiors looked as their models. He also saw that "the day of Indian Wars was over." He realized, as he later wrote, that "most all my studies had gone toward warfare with the Indian," and this had all changed because "it was now for the soldier to protect the Indian from the white man." In that memorable year, when his attention reluctantly turned to the great powers of Germany, France, and England, said Scott, "I began to study civilized warfare."[1]

This observation was not the sudden, unexpected revelation of an inexperienced shavetail. Hugh Lenox Scott was thirty-six years old, thirteen years removed from West Point, and no novice to army theory and practice.

1. Scott, *Some Memories*, 137, 145; these references can also be found on pages 142 and 149 of this edition, hereafter designated as *Sign Talker*, with their new page numbers. The 1889 camp of instruction is mentioned in Merritt, "Report" (1890), 1:197. Scott's revelation came when a host of structural changes, "swift and sure," as a noted historian of the frontier military described them, swept across the entire U.S. Army establishment. McDermott, *Guide to the Indian Wars*, 105.

Major General Scott, U.S. Army chief of staff, Washington, D.C., 1915. Scott described himself as "a cavalryman from the Indian country." Library of Congress Prints and Photographs Division, LC-H261-5608 P&P.

He had spent over a decade on the American frontier, had served as an officer in the army's most celebrated cavalry regiment, and had become a recognized master of the Plains Indian Sign Language. This man, who considered himself "freer than any junior officer," still felt the daily demands and eminent threats of western service.[2] Yet this officer, who barely commanded a unit of his own, pictured something bigger when he studied that 1889 tableau. What Lieutenant Scott saw, he later wrote in his memoir, was simply the future.

2. Scott, *Some Memories*, 207 (*Sign Talker*, 205).

But how could this nineteenth-century man have foreseen the "guns of August" in 1914 and his subsequent role in that world conflict in 1917? How could this junior officer have anticipated taking charge of an American army that would ultimately grow after his tenure to more than four million men and women in uniform? Yet this wartime experience, his extraordinary, insider vantage point, and a decade's passage after the war still seemed to leave him incapable of shedding much light on that world cataclysm. A careful reading of his memoir reveals that apparently Scott was far more comfortable with and could make more sense of another time, another place, and a different set of characters—his time in the West working with Indian people—and that is the part of Hugh Scott's life and memoir presented in this abridged volume.

Hugh Lenox Scott had a long, fascinating military career. As an 1876 graduate of the U.S. Military Academy at West Point when the Indian Wars on the American frontier were at their peak, Scott could hardly have conceived of his future foreign postings. The brief war with Spain, the event that dragged him from his Indian studies, resulted in postwar duty in Cuba as the adjutant general of the Department of Havana (his rank in the Regular Army was still only that of a captain). His obvious skills in the successful governance of new American protectorates saw a promotion to military governor with his next assignment to the Philippine Islands. As he mentioned briefly in the foreword to his memoir, he assisted in the "subjugation" of its Moro, or Muslim, population, "laying the foundation" for their "civilization." His return home to America in 1906 brought new, more conventional duties: the superintendency of West Point for four years; promotion to general (1913); postings along the volatile Mexican border; and finally advancement to chief of staff (1914), the U.S. Army's most important position. The last stint was marked by his efforts, not always successful, in preparing the small American army for a European war. His departure from the ranks in 1917, when he reached the mandatory retirement age of sixty-four, was postponed due to wartime exigencies so that he could command one of the homeland's massive training camps. Scott formally left the army in 1919 and turned to personally rewarding work with the Board of Indian Commissioners and its efforts to better the condition of American Indians.[3] In this

3. Scott proudly provided the highlights of his military career in the foreword to his book. Scott, *Some Memories*, vii–ix. Brief biographical essays by others include Bell, *Commanding Generals*, 108–109; Harper, "Scott" (2000); Harper, "Scott" (1984), 969–72; Kehrberg, "Scott," 532–33; Paullin, "Scott," 651–52; Thrapp, *Encyclopedia of Frontier Biography*, 1281–82; and *Who Was Who in America*, 1094–95.

capacity, he made several subsequent inspection trips to Indian country; however, he only mentioned two such trips in passing in his memoir.[4]

A modern biography would help assess Scott's illustrious career, but none currently exists.[5] Clearly deserving, why he has not attracted one may seem on the surface puzzling. The amount of available historical materials at one's disposal is truly staggering. Scott's personal papers, an estimated forty thousand items, reside at the Library of Congress; another significant collection exists in the National Anthropological Archives of the Smithsonian Institution.[6] One can also add in his official correspondence on such subjects as Indian-white relations, the Spanish-American War, the Philippine occupation, the Mexican border conflict, the Russian Revolution, and the First World War. A biography, therefore, might only devote a chapter or two to Scott's years of frontier service. If obligated to recount his entire military career, a biographer might ultimately miss the underlying theme of Scott's life.

The discovery of his life's theme will not come from tracing a career arc that took Scott from the American West to the western front, as one follows with, say, John J. Pershing, whose career reached a crescendo with the American Expeditionary Forces. Scott's World War I years brought no similar acclaim, neither then by his contemporaries nor now by military historians. Frederic Remington, the western artist who shared a common friendship with General Leonard Wood, described Scott's bespectacled appearance as "disappointing" and that of a "college professor," which may be considered positive for anyone other than a warrior. Scott's failing hearing and reported habit of dozing off in meetings indicated a conspicuous lack of vigor. His colleagues considered the affable old soldier too relaxed, a man who lacked ruthlessness and acted too deliberately in a modern age of speed and rapid-fire decisions. Today in most academic circles, he is considered at the most charitable as a nondescript chief of staff, a seat warmer for the later, more

4. Scott, *Some Memories*, 82, 93 (*Sign Talker*, 96, 106).

5. The first attempt and, to my knowledge, the only biography of Scott is a 1968 PhD dissertation. Its author tried to cover Scott's entire military career and, in doing so, could devote but one chapter of thirty-two pages to the years from his youth to the Spanish-American War, essentially the span covered by this edition. Harper, "Hugh Lenox Scott."

6. Hugh Lenox Scott Papers, Library of Congress, Washington, D.C. (hereafter Scott Papers); Ethnographic Notes, General Hugh Lenox Scott, Manuscript 4641, National Anthropological Archives, Smithsonian Institution, Washington, D.C.

accomplished Peyton C. March.[7] One needs to look past the entire résumé and focus on a portion. One of Scott's later admirers astutely observed, "His career has taken him through every rank of the Army and to many diplomatic posts where his ability has been of inestimable value to our Government. Yet through his entire active life there has run like the theme of a grand symphony, his friendship, fidelity, and consideration toward the American Indian, which has brought him back time after time to the country he loves."[8]

Scott's story, therefore, requires a recounting based on his interactions with American Indians, which began in 1876, continued long after the conclusion of the Indian Wars, and ended only with his death in 1934. The purpose of this edition is to present the episodes relevant to that part of his career. My goal, therefore, is to introduce Scott, a historical figure of whom I have grown to admire, to his fellow Americans. Tim McCoy, a Hollywood cowboy star, fellow sign talker, and himself a great admirer, correctly wrote, "Today [1977] his name is close to unknown, though at the time I met him, General Hugh Scott was regarded throughout America as a truly unusual character and an intriguing combination of soldier, statesman, and scholar."[9] I hope that those in the twenty-first century well versed in the history of the American West, the American Indian, and the U.S. Army will consider this a reintroduction to this intriguing character.

What sort of person was Hugh Scott? What drove him? How do the Native peoples he encountered in the West figure in his life? To help with the answers, one could mine the mountain of aforementioned archival materials, or, as has been done here, let Scott answer those questions in his own words. Fortunately he left a testament that superbly documents his personal growth and, more importantly, the key to understanding him.

In early 1926, Scott contacted several trade publishers and settled quickly on the Century Company of New York, perhaps because this publisher, unlike its competitors, was willing to enter a contract before seeing a manuscript. Century paid him a two-thousand-dollar advance on royalties

7. Scott, *Some Memories*, 186 (*Sign Talker*, 187); Harper, "Hugh Lenox Scott," 224; Coffman, *Hilt of the Sword*, 40; Robert H. Ferrell, Indiana University, personal communication with the editor, May 13, 2005.

8. Scott Leavitt, U.S. Representative from Montana, "An Appreciation," program for Hugh L. Scott, Kiwanis Club, Great Falls, Mont., Aug. 20, 1929, Scott Papers.

9. McCoy and McCoy, *Tim McCoy Remembers the West*, 141.

with the expectation of a finished manuscript by year's end. The writing, though, continued through 1927, and a complete, edited manuscript did not reach the printer until February 1928. Preordered books and review copies soon reached readers, and initial reactions to *Some Memories of a Soldier* were favorable, enthusiastic from friends and respectful from reviewers. Well-wishers aware of Scott's longtime research interests expected this book to serve as the companion to another on the Plains Indian Sign Language.[10]

That book never materialized, and later scholars came to know General Scott primarily for his autobiography. This 200,000-plus–word tome has become something of a rare book, and, to my knowledge, has never been reprinted.[11] This is somewhat surprising since many western historians consider it part of the Custer/Little Big Horn canon, if only because it provided an eyewitness account by a Seventh cavalryman to the 1877 reburial of his fallen comrades.[12] As a primary source, it continues to be regularly cited in the literature of the frontier army.[13]

The primary reason for its lack of modern readers, as well as an accommodating publisher, may be the shear expanse of time that Scott covers. How does one say this politely? Scott has too many memories.[14] After he departs the frontier on page 209 of the original edition, a reader must wade through four hundred more pages on his participating in the war with Spain, serving in the military government of postwar Cuba, trying to govern the Moros in the Philippines, running West Point as its superintendent, negotiating with Pancho Villa, and finally serving as chief of staff facing the most ruthless, treacherous adversaries of all—Washington politicians.

10. Herbert Adams Gibbons, Princeton, N.J., to Hugh L. Scott (hereafter HLS), Princeton, N.J., Feb. 3, 1926; W. Morgan Shuster, the Century Co., New York, N.Y., to HLS, Feb. 6, 1926; Shuster to HLS, Feb. 26, 1926; Gibbons to HLS, June 1, 1926; Gibbons to HLS, June 4, 1926; Lyman B. Sturgis, Book Editor, the Century Co., to HLS, June 7, 1926; Shuster to HLS, Mar. 7, 1927; Sturgis to HLS, June 9, 1927; Sturgis to HLS, July 25, 1927; Sturgis to HLS, Aug. 27, 1927; Lamar Middleton, Book Editorial Dept., the Century Co., to HLS, Feb. 10, 1928; and Robert Bruce, New York, N.Y., to HLS, Nov. 18, 1929, all in Scott Papers, Library of Congress; Henry E. Armstrong, "General Scott Looks Back Along the Line of Duty," *New York Times*, June 3, 1928.

11. Original copies, especially those that are autographed, fetch handsome prices, but the book itself no longer is scarce since becoming available in its entirety online at the HathiTrust Digital Library (www.hathitrust.org).

12. Scott, Willey, and Connor, *They Died with Custer*, 99, 141, 159; Hedren, *After Custer*, 178–82.

13. As but one example in the abundant literature of the frontier army, incidents of Scott's participation in the campaign against Chief Joseph appear throughout Greene's *Nez Perce Summer.*

14. The *New York Times* reviewer described the book as "garrulous." *New York Times*, June 3, 1928.

Admittedly, had Hugh Scott not reached his high rank, few publishers would have shown interest. Written after the First World War presumably for an audience eager to learn more about any Allied military leader, the subsequent narrative had to wield a broad brush. Carefully read in its entirety, the writing is informative, revealing, and even enthusiastic—right up to when Scott leaves Indian country. Once he departed, so did his heart, and so did his verve as a writer. His experiences with American Indians are when his autobiography comes alive. Afterward, the narrative becomes almost perfunctory, picking up only occasionally when later Indian episodes pop into the narrative. Newton Baker described the early part of the book as containing "all the thrills" he had once enjoyed as a juvenile reader of "wild Western scenes." The former secretary of war was less effusive in his praise for the sections that discussed the war. A book reviewer for the *New York Times* largely ignored the war years and used several Indian incidents to characterize Scott's "wide range of services." Eminent military historian Edward M. Coffman, who perhaps wrote the best account of America's participation in the war, gently described Scott's memoir as "an accurate reflection of the old Indian fighter's personality" without commenting on its value to his study.[15]

For all these reasons that touch on the quality and quantity of the text, presenting an abridgement of the original edition, one confined to his frontier service, was in order. Arguably, it is the volume that should have been published. *Sign Talker* is a work that takes Scott from his birth to West Point and follows with his arrival to, service in, and departure from the West. The result of this volume stands as an independent, coherent narrative, one that now places the appropriate emphasis on his beloved Indian country.

◆ ◆ ◆

Hugh Lenox Scott wrote clear and engaging prose, and, regarding editorial procedures, my work as his modern editor has been to keep textual changes to the bare necessities. The major decision was to choose what to include. The first and only edition of *Some Memories of a Soldier* finally concludes on page 628. About a third of the text is reprinted here as *Sign Talker*—the first two chapters of the original ten total. Also included are three Indian country

15. Newton D. Baker, Cleveland, Ohio, to HLS, July 10, 1928, Scott Papers, Library of Congress; *New York Times*, June 3, 1928; Coffman, *War to End All Wars*, 379.

vignettes from the later chapters and a "memory" missing from the original work (see appendix). Scott proudly included several laudatory testimonials from his commanders and peers within the main body of the text, which collectively stall out his narrative, and these have been noted, summarized, and dropped.

My approach was to present a corrected when needed, consistently edited and annotated, stand-alone text without changing the author's original meaning. In all these pages, only a couple of brief, extraneous digressions of no more than a short paragraph were dropped, as they should have been in 1928. Obvious typos have been corrected. Many words that Scott hyphenated are presented in today's preferred spelling, either as one word or two. Punctuation follows the *Chicago Manual of Style*, particularly the use of commas. When writing of a particularly exciting incident, Scott breathlessly strung together several sentences joined by conjunctions, and I have broken many of those instances into their single sentence components. Likewise, some paragraphs were either reduced or enlarged in size to make for a more readable, articulate narrative. I found a few sentences that were clearly out of order and subsequently placed them where they logically belong. Within the chapters themselves, a series of section breaks may appear where none were placed in the original edition. Still, my hope is that the final product exhibits a light, thoughtful editorial touch that retains all of the author's original meaning.

Scott did a commendable job of explanation, and the number of notes I have added is rather limited. Often it was possible to make minor emendations—a person's full name, a title, a date, or some brief descriptor—within the text. These are necessary if for no other reason than to help in the modern indexing of the book. Brackets are my additions; words in parentheses are Scott's.

Although I argue that Scott was remarkably modern in his outlook, he followed many nineteenth-century writing conventions, and not just ones grammatical in nature. In his eighty thousand–plus words excerpted here, he used the term "half-breed" half a dozen times. He referred to the "Battle" of Wounded Knee, which today is referred to by all but troglodytes as a massacre, and he observed rather meanly the native speakers of the Athabascan family of languages as being "particularly ugly." Relatively few that they are, such insensitive occurrences can cause an editor-advocate to scratch one's head, even cringe, but the original observation remains for the modern reader to ponder and assess within its period context. Marks on that side of the slate are far outnumbered by the examples of sensitivity and empathy Scott exhibited throughout his narrative. Deeds, it seems, outweighed words.

The story began with Hugh Scott's birth in Danville, Kentucky, in 1853. His step-grandmother's brother was David Hunter, a Union Civil War general. It was a tenuous kinship link perhaps, except Hunter later secured young Hugh's appointment to West Point in 1871 through his friendship with U. S. Grant. Scott should have graduated in 1875 but was caught hazing an underclassman and was expelled for disciplinary reasons; he missed an entire year before being accepted back. This setback may have been fortunate since his original class included James G. Sturgis, who graduated, and John J. Crittenden, who entered at the same time but left West Point early, both becoming fatalities the following year at the Little Big Horn. Nevertheless, Scott did succeed in graduating on June 14, 1876, ranked thirty-sixth in a class of forty-eight, and was assigned to the Ninth U.S. Cavalry.[16]

On July 5 of that year, while attending the Centennial Exposition in Philadelphia, he learned about Custer and the fate of his former classmates. He immediately requested a transfer to fill one of the many vacancies, which he wisely routed through his Uncle David in Washington, who, in turn, rushed to the U.S. Department of War and secured the coveted transfer. Hunter also succeeded in getting Scott's commission backdated to June 26, 1876, a day after the Battle of Little Big Horn. Ordered to report to Fort Abraham Lincoln, Dakota Territory, Scott soon found himself in "the country of my dreams and the Seventh Cavalry my choice of all the regiments in the army." He further rhapsodized, "No matter how cold, how wet, how hungry I found myself during all the years of Plains life that followed, I felt that I was where I belonged."[17]

Scott wasted little time in acclimating himself. On day two, George D. Wallace, a Little Big Horn survivor, took him to the camp of the Arikara Indian scouts. Scott was drawn immediately to the Lakota language and wanted to learn it from the Arikaras, all of whom spoke it, but he soon realized his approach's inherent limitations. It was better to learn their sign language, he concluded, a far more inclusive means of communication, "an intertribal language, spoken everywhere in the buffalo country from the Saskatchewan

16. Entry 2628 for Hugh Lenox Scott, in Cullum, *Biographical Register of the Officers and Graduates*, 271–72. *Military Record of Colonel Hugh L. Scott*, Library of Congress classification of E181-.S42, also available in digital form on the HathiTrust website.

17. Scott, *Some Memories*, 30, 31 (*Sign Talker*, 46, 47).

River of British America to Mexico, east of the Rocky Mountains and west of the Missouri."[18] Scott also began the intensive study of tribal customs, particularly on how Indians could be influenced, a fateful decision considering the later incidents into which he was thrown. This became ultimately a great career move.

Lieutenant Scott did indeed learn the sign language, quickly absorbing it as no other army officer ever had, and became well-known for this valuable skill within the army fraternity. Eventually he became indispensable to senior officers such as Philip H. Sheridan and Nelson A. Miles, following an age-old tactic of smart, junior officers, that of employing the winning combination of "mentors and luck."[19] Regarding the latter, Scott possessed more than his share. In the late 1870s, he took the rare opportunity to observe the Crow tribe, lodged for an extended time in the tipi of Chief Iron Bull, and experienced in depth the daily life of a village. Once, he wrote, "wishing to know what a real buffalo horse was like, I got the Crow chiefs arguing as to who had the best buffalo horse in the tribe."[20] After they agreed on one, he borrowed the animal for a bison hunt! A detailed description of this very dangerous activity, and what an Indian pony actually was trained to do, followed, probably unique in the annals of the frontier army.

If this initiative did not impress his Crow colleagues, maybe a telling detail with connections to Scott's youth did—his expert use of their bow and arrow. Scott's father had died when the boy was eight years old, and his widowed mother moved the family to the ancestral hometown of Princeton, New Jersey, where Scott spent a fatherless but happy childhood. Scott inherited an equal measure of studiousness and caution from his mother and an absolute love of the outdoors from his father. He hunted and fished incessantly, studying in what he called "the very best school that could have been devised for a soldier." One formative childhood experience came when his protective mother forbade his use of guns. His response was a practical one; young Hugh made himself a bow and arrow, "with which," he wrote, "I became extremely skillful."[21]

18. Ibid., 32 (49).

19. Powers, "Warrior Petraeus," 40. The young David Petraeus provides a modern example of the ongoing effectiveness of this military career tactic.

20. Scott, *Some Memories*, 71 (*Sign Talker*, 86).

21. Ibid., 7, 8 (26).

Between the adventure on the buffalo pony and the prowess with the bow and arrow, could any other officer in the U.S. Army boast of such details on his military record? Scott considered these outdoor experiences essential to his development as—his term—a "field soldier," yet he never considered himself a gentleman sportsman, a type of frontier officer he rather disdained.[22] Moreover, what began as a way of satisfying his natural curiosity soon developed into a means of distinguishing himself from his colleagues, and later evolved into something much more, an aptitude for diplomacy. Examples of how he applied this knowledge abound, although he recorded in his memoir "only a few of the most vivid."[23]

For instance, Second Lieutenant Scott left the northern Plains and in 1889 reported for duty at Fort Sill, Indian Territory, where he now encountered the Caddo, Comanche, Kiowa, and Kiowa-Apache tribes of the southern Plains. Scott's mastery of hand talking and his sincere interest in learning about their cultures ingratiated him with the tribespeople. These interests helped considerably when he was later ordered to investigate the Ghost Dance after its sudden appearance on the southern reservations. To the uninformed, the ceremony seemed to be a prelude and pretext for an Indian outbreak. Scott spent the volatile fall of 1890 making observations, gathering intelligence, drawing some astute conclusions, and advising his superiors against disarming the Indians. Allow them to dance openly, he said, where they can be monitored, wait for the spring and the prophesied arrival of the Messiah, and let time take its course.

James Mooney, the great nineteenth-century scholar of the Ghost Dance religion, later wrote a telling testimonial: "Scott was eminently fitted for the work by his intimate acquaintance with the Indians and his perfect knowledge of the sign language. . . . He visited the various camps of the western tribes of the territory, attended a number of dances, and talked with the leaders." He did so, one might add, customarily without any sizeable escort. Mooney continued, "His reports on the Ghost dance are most valuable and confirmed . . . that no danger was to be apprehended and that the true policy was one of noninterference."[24]

22. Ibid., 8 (27).

23. Ibid., viii.

24. Mooney, "Ghost-Dance Religion," 900.

The dangerous season passed peacefully, Scott later boasted, "without the firing of a shot or the shedding of a drop of blood," even after everyone had learned of Wounded Knee.[25] To confound his job, he had to deal with at least one dangerously inept Indian agent eerily similar to Pine Ridge's Daniel F. Royer, the man sarcastically dubbed by a later historian "Young Man Afraid of His Indians." The tragic results on the Sioux reservations were not repeated on the southern Plains, although all the same ingredients were present. Scott's superiors, particularly General Miles, appreciated and acknowledged this and other Scott successes in negotiating solutions and resolving conflicts.[26]

While stationed at Fort Sill, Hugh Scott forged some of his most enduring friendships with American Indians, particularly with members of the Kiowa tribe. He also had a hand in two more emblematic events of the post–Indian Wars era. In 1891 he took command of one of the newly formed all-Indian U.S. Army units, specifically Troop L, 7th Cavalry. The recruits came predominantly from the young men of the Kiowa and Comanche tribes, and during its brief existence the unit won great praise. Scott always had to fight silly regulations, though, that contradicted tribal norms and common sense—for example, the restriction against Indian soldiers being married. Ultimately the experiment of Indians as enlisted soldiers received little endorsement from superiors and endured only a few years. Scott hung on, but his troop was finally mustered out on May 31, 1897, fittingly the last such Indian troop on the muster rolls. Of all the Indian companies, his was considered the most successful.[27] Scott noted proudly that several of his men returned to their tribes and took up positions of leadership. Twenty years later as chief of staff, he reversed the army's error by integrating them into white units. The contributions of Native Americans during the Great War were honorable and significant, if little remembered today.[28]

25. Scott, *Some Memories*, 148 (*Sign Talker*, 153).

26. Miles testimonials of Aug. 21, 1897, and July 8, 1902, in Scott, *Some Memories*, 209, 214–15. These and other "recognition" letters, as they are called in the book's index, are noted but not reprinted in *Sign Talker*.

27. Lee, "Warriors in Ranks," 263–316, provides the most thorough examination of this experiment, although it is presented with a northern Plains bias.

28. Scott briefly told of his efforts on the behalf of Indians as World War I doughboys in *Some Memories*, 563–64. More on his and the campaign by others can be found in Britten, *American Indians in World War I*; and Krouse, *North American Indians in the Great War*. These two academic studies are exceptions to a story largely overlooked by the general public.

Scott's other noteworthy association came as role of jailer for the seventy-one-year-old Geronimo and three hundred Chiricahua Apache prisoners of war, who were moved from their incarceration in Alabama to Indian Territory in 1894. Although this southwestern tribe did not use the sign language, Scott made clear his intentions for these Indians. He considered their previous treatment abysmal, a black mark against the government, and devoted himself to their welfare. Historian Robert M. Utley praised Scott highly for his efforts, which included appointing headmen to form up several small hamlets and establishing garden plots and cattle herds in order to create self-sufficient and stable communities.[29] This logical approach worked magnificently, so much so that tribal ceremonies and dances, which had all but disappeared during the band's exile in Florida and Alabama, soon revived, and Geronimo lived in peace well into the new century.

Entering the twentieth century, "the man who talked with his hands" was still talking and listening to Indians. In any major American newspaper in the century's first two decades, one encountered headlines such as "General Scott Is Pow-Wowing," subtitled "Army Officer Is in Conference with Navajo Chiefs over Uprising."[30] While traveling in the southwestern United States and trying to keep on top of the Mexican border problem in 1913, Scott received a telegram at Fort Huachuca, Arizona. It directed him to Gallup, New Mexico, near the Navajo reservation, then home to many thousands of Indians but, fortunately, to an actual problem that involved far fewer. The breaking news, from a nearby newspaper in Farmington, New Mexico, November 27, 1913, continued: "An Indian runner today arrived here with the first news of the movement of the Twelfth Cavalry, acting as escort for Gen. Hugh L. Scott, ordered . . . to subdue an incipient uprising. General Scott, accompanied only by an Indian interpreter, today left for Noel trading post, at the foot of Beautiful Mountain, the Indian stronghold, for a pow-wow with the Navajo chiefs. . . . The outcome of his conference will decide whether the Indians will surrender without a fight."[31]

Scott had to deal with yet another excitable Indian agent, who expressed his fear that the Navajos would do to Scott what the Modocs had done to

29. Utley, *Geronimo*, 250–51.

30. Emblematic of Scott's appeal to a widespread audience, this Nov. 13, 1913, headline appeared in the influential *Kansas City Star*.

31. Ibid.

General Edward R. S. Canby in 1873, which was to assassinate him treacherously during seemingly peaceful negotiations. Scott replied laconically that he "had to give the Indians a chance first. I could not go over and shoot them all without giving them an opportunity." Scott proceeded to the trading post, immediately dispatched a courier, and beckoned the aggrieved parties to come in. He waited patiently—he always waited patiently—and on the second day, seventy-five heavily armed men arrived, "jammed into the store," and "listened with perfect silence after they had once settled down." Scott began the parley with the group's leader, a Navajo elder, with these few words, "Now I want you to tell me what is the matter." The troubles poured forth from the man, and Scott, following his tried-and-true pattern, listened at length without interruption. "Then I told them I was too tired to talk any more that day. . . . I would talk to them again in the morning." Scott wrote sagely, "An Indian cannot be hurried. He needs time to gather and [sort] his impressions and allow them to soften him."[32] After dinner Scott met on more intimate terms with the Navajo elder. "I established him at the fire in an easy chair with tobacco and began to hunt for his weak spot," which turned out to be the old man's passion for sharing tales of the origins and history of the Diné or Navajo people. After he finished a lengthy exposition and departed for the evening, Scott commented to a companion, "We've got him bagged. He is coming our way when the time comes."[33]

Newspaper readers—in this case those in the Midwest—scarcely had to wait for a follow-up when the *Kansas City Star* soon proclaimed breathlessly, "The Indian War Is Over," then took a measured breath to add more modestly, "Rebellious Navajos Surrendered after a Talk with General Scott."[34] Negotiations had continued the next day, and Scott convinced the old man and his sons to give themselves up to the authorities. Their major crime, the one that had so outraged their agent, was bigamy. Scott wisely allowed them to make arrangements with their families, escorted them to Gallup, and personally argued with a federal judge for leniency, which happily resulted in an extremely light sentence served locally and not in far off Santa Fe, and so ended the Great Navajo War That Never Was of 1913.

32. Scott, *Some Memories*, 490–92 (*Sign Talker*, 217–18).

33. Ibid., 492–93 (219).

34. *Kansas City Star*, Nov. 29, 1913.

Hugh Scott left us with a marvelous memoir, although he failed to write his true magnum opus, his study of the Plains Indian Sign Language, despite having every intention of doing so. In late 1897, the golden opportunity arose when he was assigned to the Bureau of American Ethnology for that purpose, but the Spanish-American War intervened, followed by a succession of growing job responsibilities.

If Scott had succeeded, his book would have joined two classics: civilian ethnologist Garrick Mallery's treatise "Sign Language among the North American Indians," published in 1881; and Lieutenant William Philo Clark's book *The Indian Sign Language*, published posthumously in 1885.[35] Scott considered Clark the only army officer who had possessed a "reasonable degree of proficiency" in sign talking with Natives.[36] Considering Clark's somewhat sordid role in the 1877 killing of Crazy Horse, one wonders if that talent was wasted.[37]

The work of Ernest Thompson Seton followed Mallery's and Clark's publications. A celebrated American naturalist and prolific author in the somewhat strange but popular genre of animal fiction, Seton published a book in 1918 entitled *Sign Talk*. Even with the demands of a world war, Scott found time to extensively advise Seton with his manuscript on the nuances of the sign language in the manuscript.[38] In 1930, which postdated his memoir, Scott made a gallant effort to record via motion pictures the vanishing language. This late-in-life endeavor is a story in itself, and scholars are only now mining this unique film record. Yet no great monograph authored by Scott exists, although his eleven thousand note cards on the subject remain at the National Anthropological Archives, and he did succeed in contributing to the professional anthropological record of his day.[39]

35. Mallery, "Sign Language," 263–552; Clark, *Indian Sign Language*.

36. Scott, *Some Memories*, 217 (*Sign Talker*, 207).

37. After the fact, William P. Clark coldly pronounced Crazy Horse's death as "necessary" and that it would "save trouble." Such comments, along with his many surreptitious actions that undercut the chief's authority and confidence, revealed an approach, motivation, and personality in stark contrast to Scott's. Powers, *Killing of Crazy Horse*, 427, 445.

38. Seton, *Sign Talk*.

39. Davis, *Hand Talk*, 72–77. For examples of Scott-authored articles, see "Sign Language of the Plains Indian," "Early History and Names of the Arapaho," and "Kado or Sun Dance of the Kiowa." For modern examples of how Scott's anthropological fieldwork has contributed to our understanding of Indian history, see appendix A, "Little Bluff Calendar Text," in Greene, *One Hundred Summers*, 203–19; and Greene, *Silver Horn*. More recently and dramatically, though, the manuscript ledgers that Scott filled with

Maybe it is more important, though, that the true testament of his life's work was, as he phrased it, "the preservation of peace in the Indian country."[40]

Those historians who examine the Indian Wars generally define the era's conclusion as when Geronimo surrendered at Skeleton Canyon in 1886 or when the Lakota Ghost Dancers rode into Pine Ridge Agency in January 1891. We can only speculate how this era may have been defined if Hugh Scott, the self-described "cavalryman from the Indian country," had not possessed the knowledge, skill, and opportunity to peacefully resolve so many later conflicts during his long, illustrious career. A contemporary, quoting from an unknown source, wrote after his death, "In many way's he's the most extraordinary soldier who ever served in the United States—this grizzled old campaigner—this greatest American Indian fighter, who never killed an Indian."[41]

Modern readers can find much to admire about Hugh Lenox Scott: his innate curiosity about other peoples and distant lands; his disdain for willful ignorance, especially among those in the U.S. Army he termed "old captains . . . who were blind on the prairie"; and his deep affection for the American West, what he called "the love of my youth, spent among the Indians, the antelope and the buffalo, and whose history is dear to my heart."[42] I detect in Scott a surprisingly modern man, who possessed values many of us share, someone who warned against going into war needlessly; who, as an army leader, saw the value of having the American Indian and the American Negro (his term) in uniform during World War I; and who succeeded in placing the former in desegregated units and looked forward to the day when the same happened with the latter. But what should command our admiration is his empathy for others different from himself and his ability to listen and to be, as he described himself, "someone who understands both parties." He relished these one-on-one, multiracial, and

---

a vast amount of ethnographic data gathered at Fort Sill have been expertly edited and annotated by William C. Meadows. No other publication with ties to Scott better reflects his ongoing relevance and importance to our understanding of Plains Indian culture. Meadows, *Through Indian Sign Language*.

40. Scott, *Some Memories*, vii.

41. Ibid., 548. The "who never killed an Indian" observation appeared as an unattributed quote in the obituary that William Carey Brown wrote for his fellow West Point alumnus and veteran officer of the frontier army. Brown, "Hugh Lenox Scott," 102.

42. Scott, *Some Memories*, 96 (*Sign Talker*, 108); Scott, foreword to Spring, *Caspar Collins*, 11.

multicultural contacts, all of which provided the old soldier with "delightful memories."[43]

If we are to remember and celebrate this U.S. Army officer, let us do so based less on the many entries on a lengthy résumé and more on the modest line carved on his tombstone in Arlington National Cemetery. Four words, it reads, "Blessed Are the Peacemakers."[44] Bless you, General Scott.

43. Scott, *Some Memories*, 156, 628 (*Sign Talker*, 162).

44. Hugh Lenox Scott died on April 30, 1934, and is buried in Arlington National Cemetery, Section 2. For an obituary see *New York Times*, May 1, 1934. Although the origin of "The-man-who-talks-with-his-hands" came forty years before when he first met and spoke with members of the Comanche tribe, the name, a most appropriate and singular one, followed Scott to his grave.

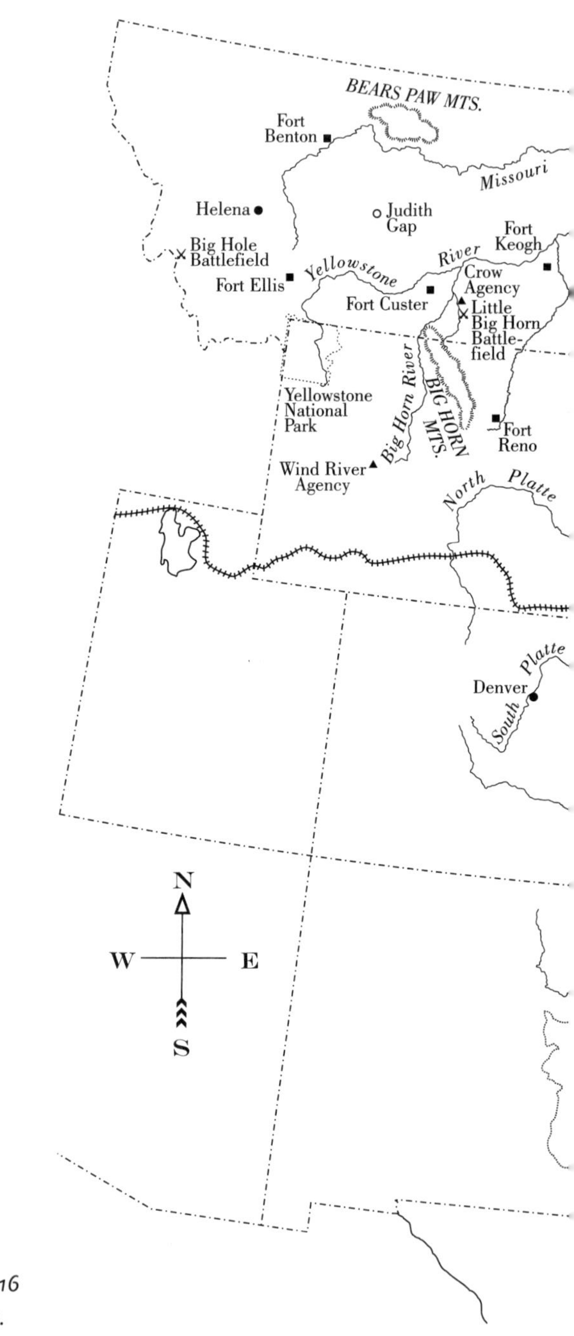

Scott's Indian Country, 1876–1898. Map by Robert Pilk. *Copyright © 2016 by the University of Oklahoma Press.*

Fort Buford
River
Fort
Totten
Devils
Lake
Agency
Red River
Fargo
Bismarck
Fort
Abraham
Lincoln
NORTHERN
PACIFIC
RR
Standing Rock
Agency
St. Paul
Mississippi
Deadwood
Pierre
Fort Meade
BLACK HILLS
Missouri
Pine Ridge Agency
Fort Robinson
Niobrara
River
River
River
dney
UNION
PACIFIC
RR
Omaha
River
Platte
Chicago
River
Fort
Leavenworth
Kansas
City
Fort Riley
Arkansas
Fort
Supply
River
Canadian
Fort
Reno
Kiowa,
Comanche
& Wichita
Agency
River
Washita
Washita
Battlefield
Fort
Smith
WICHITA MTS.
Fort
Sill
River
Red
Henrietta
STAKED
PLAINS
River

1

Boyhood

Looking back now upon a happy childhood surrounded by many friends and relatives, my memories, with a few exceptions of people and places in the Middle West, cluster about my grandfather's house in Princeton, New Jersey, where my father died when I was eight years old and my mother brought up her brood of three sons until they left the home nest. Life there seemed a matter of course, and it was only after getting out into the world and seeing that of other people that I was able to make comparison and appreciate its beauty. This quiet spot was, above everything, a home—a spacious, cultured home pervaded by a dignity and serenity, a hospitality and loving-kindness, that emanated from my grandfather and grandmother, in winter a place of light and warmth, in summer of cool shade and the hum of bees among the lindens, where friends and relatives and their children loved to congregate, where all found a boundless love and welcome. Small wonder the children looked back to it from the far corners of the earth, homesick to return.

The house was at its best at the time of the Princeton commencement when the great trees planted by my grandfather in his youth cast a grateful shade and the flowers were in bloom. Its doors were wide open to the friends who had graduated at college and seminary and were now returning from far and wide to renew the ties of friendship—and who looked up to my grandfather, as did the whole town, with reverence and admiration.

My grandfather was the Rev. Dr. Charles Hodge, for many years the head of the Theological Seminary at Princeton, the foremost theologian of his day in America.[1] He was born in Philadelphia in [December 27, 1797] 1798 and died at Princeton in [June 19,] 1878. My grandmother, Sarah Bache, whose mother was the sister [Catharine Wistar] of Dr. Caspar Wistar of Philadelphia, I never knew since she died at Princeton, December 25, 1849, before my birth. Her lovely character was attested by her children who all "rose up and called her blessed."[2] I was born at Danville, Kentucky, September 22, 1853.

Some years after the death of my own grandmother, my grandfather took a second wife, a widow, Mrs. Mary Hunter Stockton of Princeton, who was everything to me that any grandmother could be, and I always looked upon her as my own and upon her son Samuel, who married my aunt, as my own uncle. She presided over the large family with dignity and sweetness, admired and loved by all. Her father, Andrew Hunter, was the chaplain of the House of Representatives at Washington during the war with the British in 1812. She often told of the way he had hurried her and her two brothers out of Washington in a farm wagon to save them from the British when they burned our White House. She was always full of fun and humor, describing the men of note in the Washington of her day; and she often sang for me the Negro songs learned in Virginia in her youth. She told stories of the old times at Morven, the old Stockton place at Princeton, built in 1702, and the land title for which was obtained from William Penn.[3] Here much of her girlhood was spent, and I greatly fear that there was mischief afoot when she and her cousins, the sisters of Commodore Stockton, afterward Mrs. Mary Harrison and Mrs. Julia Rheinlander of New York, were abroad together. The death of Mrs. Rheinlander from a stroke of apoplexy during a visit to our house was a great shock to my youthful mind, and I was long afraid to enter the room in which she died or even pass the door after dark. Not long before this happened, Princeton's first murder about 1861 or '62 had stirred the town to its foundations and is talked of even yet. If you do not know all about the Rowen murder, you are not a real Princetonian. The horror of this murder long caused me to cling closely to my mother's skirts as soon as dusk fell.

1. This claim does not appear overblown. See Nichols, "Hodge, Charles," 98–99.

2. From Prov. 31:28.

3. Morven exemplified the social stature of the extended Scott family; the historic home survives today as the New Jersey Governor's Mansion.

When grandmother had become a very old lady, I asked her once to tell me the pleasantest episode of her life, and she said it was the summer of 1821, which she spent at West Point, her brother's last camp. Grandmother had a very great influence upon my afterlife, since it was at her instigation that her brother, General David Hunter, a friend of Lincoln and of Grant, secured for me from the latter the appointment to West Point, which was to shape my whole career.[4]

Uncle David was himself a graduate of 1822 and went, on graduation, to Fort Snelling, Minnesota, which it took him six months to reach. He was obliged to walk three hundred miles on the ice of the Mississippi from Prairie du Chien, Wisconsin. He was in the Fifth Infantry at Fort Dearborn at the mouth of the Chicago River in 1828. Fort Dearborn was a small collection of log huts surrounded by a high palisade, then the only settlement save the house and trading post of John Kinzie, the trader, whose daughter Maria my uncle married and whose family had been saved at the Chicago Indian massacre in 1812.

One night Uncle David heard someone calling from across the Chicago River and, borrowing a Pottawatomie Indian canoe built for one man, paddled across and found it was Lieutenant Jefferson Davis coming from West Point. Making Davis lie down in the bottom of the canoe, he straddled and sat upon him in order to get the center of gravity low enough to carry two men safely in a one-man canoe and ferried him to the other side. The two were warm friends until the Civil War.[5]

Uncle David pointed out to me once the place where he had slept on the floor of the White House guarding Lincoln with other friends of the president, who, fearing his assassination, had rallied about him at Springfield, Illinois, and come on with him as a self-appointed bodyguard to Washington for his inauguration.

My mother, Mary Elizabeth Hodge, was born in the old house in 1825 and died in Princeton in 1899. She married my father, the Rev. William McKendry Scott, upon his graduation at the Princeton Seminary and went to live with him at Danville, Kentucky, where he was a professor at Centre

4. David Hunter undoubtedly helped steer Scott's moral compass, along with his budding military career, with his expansive thoughts, deep convictions, and controversial actions on the subject of race. For numerous examples, see Miller, *Lincoln's Abolitionist General.*

5. This Hunter-Davis anecdote is confirmed by Davis, *Jefferson Davis*, 10–11.

College and pastor of the Presbyterian Church. Here their first four children were born: Charles Hodge, John Bayard, Mary Blanchard, and myself, born September 22, 1853, and named after my grandfather's brother, Dr. Hugh Lenox Hodge of Philadelphia. John Bayard and Mary Blanchard died in infancy at Danville. In 1856 my father was called to the pastorate of the Seventh Presbyterian Church at Cincinnati, where my brother William was born in 1857. In 1859 the Presbyterian General Assembly elected my father professor at the Northwestern Seminary at Chicago, later called McCormick Seminary. My father's father, William Scott, migrated from the north of Ireland in 1798 and settled on a farm at Mount Pleasant, Jefferson County, Ohio, where he raised a well-to-do family prominent in their section. He died in 1851 at the age of seventy-five.

My mother came from a family of students leading sedentary lives with indoor tastes and could never understand my passion for the outdoors and for hunting and fishing, inherited from my father, who during his youth in Ohio had been a very noted shot with the squirrel rifle. She looked upon me very much as a hen would look at a duckling she had hatched and upon my tastes as a tendency toward wildness, which ought to be suppressed until advised by a brother that I was following my strongest instincts in a perfectly innocent way and that by interfering she might divert me to something harmful. She was always afraid that I might shoot someone accidentally, and, although the gun was there, I was not allowed to use it until my fifteenth birthday when I was supposed to have arrived at some degree of discretion. So until that time I had to content myself with a bow and arrow made by myself, with which I became extremely skillful.[6]

I took no interest in boys' games and never played ball with the others except when drafted to help fight for the possession of the ball grounds of the college during vacations and defend them from another set. Every Saturday found me hunting or fishing somewhere at daylight, sometimes with some of my friends, more often alone.

This was the very best school that could have been devised for a soldier, as I found later on the Plains. It taught me to find my way about and take care of myself in the woods day and night and in all kinds of weather. I could hunt only on Saturdays during the school term and had to take the weather

6. Although he made little of it later in the book, Scott's boyhood skill with the bow and arrow no doubt surprised and favorably impressed members of the Crow tribe.

as it came or lose my weekend. So, many days in the dead of winter, I would be found starting a fox at four o'clock in the morning four miles from home with a strong, cold wind blowing and a foot of snow on the ground. We often chased a fox on foot ten miles along the ridge of Rocky Hill, covered with timber and heavy rocks as large as a small house, where no horse could travel, and night would find us eight or ten miles from home, hungry, wet, cold, exhausted, with clothes torn to rags and home to find in the darkness.

This bred a disregard of obstacles. It bred also the initiative and the optimism essential to the success of any enterprise, as well as the undespairing [undaunted] courage and the resolution never to give up a project without which no soldier can be a success. It brought in addition a practice in the arts of the field—swimming, handling a boat, riding a horse, shooting a gun—and it built up an enormous lung power and muscular force that has lasted to this day. I have seen so many come West brought up entirely to the life of the city, unhappy and helpless out of sight of the post, actually unable to command in the field and forced to go about with somebody else to guide and take care of them, without initiative of their own, and daunted before every obstacle. Not one of these has ever risen to eminence as a field soldier.

Shortly after our mother was left a widow, another widow, Mrs. [Eliza Getty] Ricketts of Maryland, came with her three sons and a daughter to live in Princeton, and the families soon became intimate. My own contemporary was the oldest son, who died early. While walking one day with the next oldest [Palmer C. Ricketts], who now for many years has been the honored president of the [Rensselaer] Polytechnic Institute of Engineering at Troy, New York, together with a boy who was larger than either of us, the latter began to tease the Ricketts lad, refusing to stop until I gave him a bloody nose.[7]

I encountered the offender in 1889 at Wichita Falls, Texas, where he was then mayor [Otis T. Bacon], and I was able to serve him by obtaining permission for him to hunt wild turkeys on the Kiowa and Comanche Indian reservation.[8] In 1908, Dr. Ricketts made a visit to me at West Point and asked me if I remembered the episode in our youth when the president of the Polytechnic at Troy was being annoyed by the mayor of Wichita Falls, Texas, who

7. Palmer Ricketts had a long association with Rensselaer. Ricketts, *History of Rensselaer Polytechnic*. From this telling episode and others, it is apparent that Scott abhorred bullies, more so when he himself was the perpetrator, as his punishment for hazing at West Point and subsequent shame demonstrated.

8. Hendrickson, "Wichita Falls, TX."

refused to stop until punched in the nose by the superintendent of the Military Academy at West Point.

My brothers and I attended the local schools at Princeton, my brother Charles graduating from Princeton College in 1868, leaving at once to take up a mercantile career in Pittsburgh. My brother William, after taking high honors at Princeton, Cambridge, and Heidelberg, became professor of paleontology and geology at Princeton. He now holds a high place among the scientists of the world and has taken every sort of honor belonging to his profession.[9]

After the school at Edge Hill was discontinued, my mother took me to Lawrenceville, the school presided over by Dr. Samuel Hammill for so many years, which developed into the present John C. Green Foundation at Lawrenceville [New Jersey]. Dr. and Mrs. Hammill were respected and loved by everybody, and, when in after years they traveled through the West, they found many of their old Lawrenceville boys in positions of trust who rose up everywhere to do them honor.

There was a younger son of one of our Princeton neighbors whom I had saved from drowning in the old mill pond at Stony Brook and whose mother felt that I ought therefore to be his guardian, and, although too young for Lawrenceville, he was sent there to be under my care. Shortly after our arrival at the school, he came upstairs late one night crying and said that he had been knocked down by one of the older boys. This boy was considerably taller than myself, and I lay awake all night thinking of the drubbing he was going to give me in the morning when I called him to account as I intended doing. We met going downstairs, and I asked him if he had struck my little friend. He acknowledged that he had, adding that my protégé had been teasing him. I then struck him across the bridge of the nose with the back of my hand by way of challenge. Instead of attacking me fiercely, as I expected him to do, he burst out crying, saying he could not fight, whereupon I told him that he must let little boys alone or he would have to fight. This episode, in spite of its pacific culmination, gave everybody to understand that we would fight if imposed upon, and we passed the rest of our course there unmolested. After becoming better acquainted at the school, we realized that

9. William Berryman Scott became an influential figure in the formative years of American vertebrate paleontology. His older brother must have exerted some measure of influence throughout the younger's life because William wrote an autobiography late in life as well, similarly and appropriately entitled *Some Memories of a Palaeontologist*.

our adversary had outgrown his strength and was really younger than he appeared.

I was quite homesick during the entire period of my stay at Lawrenceville and every now and then would climb out of my window after everybody had gone to bed, walk the five miles to Princeton, go around to see the horses and dogs, and look through the window at the people from the outside, afraid to go in for fear of a scolding for leaving school, then walk the five long miles back to Lawrenceville, stumbling along the road sound asleep for a hundred yards at a time, and climb back through my own window, at length, in safety. I often pass the old house in Lawrenceville now and look up at that window, in and out of which I crept more than fifty years ago.

In 1870, I passed all of my examinations for Princeton College, but, before the session began, I was informed of my appointment to West Point. It was thought best that I should continue with a tutor, studying both courses so that I might enter the sophomore class at Princeton without losing any time in the event of failure to enter West Point.

As I look back, I recognize that my mother would rather have had me choose some other profession. She thought the life on the Plains in a military post extremely narrow and dangerous and would have preferred that I follow her uncle, the celebrated Hugh Lenox Hodge, M.D., of Philadelphia, after whom she had named me. There seemed in those days to be no future in the army, and graduating into cavalry it seemed that my life was destined to be passed in the buffalo country far from civilization and culture. If I was fortunate, I might see a little of England and France on a four months' leave, but nothing more of the world.

On the contrary, however, I have been once completely around the world and twice more with the exception of the width of Germany. In addition, my duties have taken me into Canada, Mexico, and Cuba, as well as into every state in our Union, so that my life has been extremely interesting to me, and I consider myself most fortunate in that my profession and pleasure have gone hand in hand. I have had immense freedom in the Indian country given me by Generals Sheridan, Miles, Merritt, Ruger, and other commanders and have shaped my own service very largely by their help.

Many individuals of our race have been forced by circumstances to engage in professions distasteful to them, from which they find themselves powerless to escape. I shudder at times, reflecting upon what my life might have been had I allowed myself to be confined to a sedentary occupation along with the thousands craving freedom and adventure, condemned to go through life with their longing unsatisfied, square pegs in round holes, working today to get something to eat so that they may work tomorrow, seeing no deliverance, no future for themselves in this life.

The prospects for a lieutenant of cavalry, to be sure, were very poor for many years. I was nineteen years a lieutenant and five years at the head of the first lieutenants without gaining a single file [one step on the promotion list]. But this was never allowed by either my wife or myself to sour our dispositions, as some have permitted slow promotion to do, and we enjoyed our daily life on little money.

2

A West Point Cadet and Plebe Days

In May 1871, my Uncle David took me to West Point. He piloted me over the whole place, pointing out the changes since he had been a cadet in 1822, forty-nine years before. He had many stories to tell of the old days, describing the buildings which had disappeared, the foundations of which may still be discovered when the drought scorches the grass off the thin soil about them. He introduced me to the superintendent [Thomas H. Ruger] and the commandant of cadets [Emory Upton], as well as to his other acquaintances. He was a friend and contemporary of all the professors of that period—[Dennis Hart] Mahan, [Albert E.] Church, [Henry L. Kendrick] Kendricks, [Robert Walter] Weir, and many others—Professor Weir being a kinsman of my own through the Bayards.[1]

In those days, West Point professors were sure-enough professors, with a lofty dignity all their own and a uniform by which they were distinguished from afar at a single glance—a high hat, a swallowtail coat, and a waistcoat with brass buttons. They would take off their high hats to each other thirty feet away in the most ceremonious fashion, saying, "Sir, your most obedient sir," at the same time bowing and scraping with one foot in a way I have never seen either before or since, evidently a relic of the military etiquette of the past.

1. Scott often provided surnames only, and I have added full names, where known, at their first usage. This later becomes more difficult when the individuals mentioned are enlisted men.

There was no regular time for the retirement of officers for age in those days, nor for long afterward. While at West Point, General Grant signified his intention of placing Professor Mahan, who was then more than seventy, on the retired list. This news so preyed upon the professor's mind that, while on a trip to New York, he jumped off the *Mary Powell*, striking his head on a paddle wheel, and drowned [on September 16, 1871]. His funeral was the first military funeral attended by my class. Eugene Griffin, in after years the vice president of General Electric Company, marched by my side, and many years afterward I marched over the same ground behind a like caisson which carried his body to its grave [in 1907].[2]

Few of our people today are aware of the great part which West Point has played in the education of America. It was for many years the only school of engineering in the country, and its early graduates did most of the engineering work of the nation. Its textbooks, written by its own professors, were adopted by Yale, Harvard, Princeton, and other colleges. The names of Mahan's [*An Elementary Course of*] *Civil Engineering*, Church's [*Elements of the Differential and Integral*] *Calculus*, Church's [*Elements of*] *Descriptive Geometry*, and David and Legendre's *Algebra* [Adrien Marie Legendre and Charles Davies, *Selected Propositions in Geometrical Constructions and Applications of Algebra to Geometry*] were once household names all over America. Colonel Sylvanus Thayer, Father of the Military Academy, established the Thayer School of Engineering at Dartmouth, while another superintendent of West Point, Captain Alden Partridge, established the University of Norwich, and still another Military Academy superintendent started the Naval Academy on its way. Many of West Point's graduates who went into civil life became presidents and chancellors of universities. Hundreds became professors, and all made a deep impress upon their time.

Uncle David warned me on entering that I was going into a new world with strange customs, where it was expected that the new cadets would fag [or act as a servant] for the older, just as the newcomers did at Eton and the other great schools of England. This had been the custom at West Point since the beginning, and all the distinguished graduates, such as Grant, Sheridan, and Sherman, had complied with it. Since no insult would be intended, my uncle explained, it would be better for me to do likewise, and, if ever it

2. *New York Times*, Sept. 17, 1871. Griffin died on April 11, 1907. New York (State) Legislature, "Proceedings of the Fourth Annual Encampment," 59–60.

were meant to insult me, I would know it at once and should then draw the line hard and sharp.

My uncle left me to the tender mercies of Fred[erick Dent] Grant and Tony [John Anthony] Rucker, both sons of old army friends, about to graduate. George Anderson from New Jersey of the same class gave me his overcoat, dress coat, and many pairs of white trousers. In these days a low limit is placed on the number of white trousers allowed, for otherwise no laundry could cope with them, but we were allowed then as many as anybody would give us. Friends in different classes graduating gave me their trousers, and my turn five years later I left my cousin Charles [H.] Hunter many pairs.

President and Mrs. Grant came to West Point to see their son Fred graduate and were taken to hear the prima donna Christine [Christina] Nilsson sing in our mess hall. She rested after singing a while, and in the interim George Webster of '71 sang, "I Am Dying, Egypt, Dying." Then Miss Nilsson sang, "'Way Down upon the Swanee River" and "Home, Sweet Home." This was too much for the poor, tired, miserably homesick new cadets to stand, and they wept. I was no exception.

Miss Nilsson expressed her desire for a cadet bell button, and she soon had a bushel, although it is supposed to be a more or less great crime to give them away.

The West Point of 1871 was very different from the West Point of today. The entire corps was only a third of its present size and was quartered in the old barracks. The superintendent's office was a small ugly building with a mansard roof on the site of the present office. The old hospital academy building, chapel, and riding hall—the last built by Colonel Robert E. Lee when superintendent in 1855, at the time when Mrs. Scott's father [Lewis Merrill] was a cadet—were all very small. Winter afternoons, after recitations were over, were taken up in boxing, fencing, or dancing with other cadets to improve our technique. Our summers were spent mainly in outdoor drill, dancing, and swimming by night in the river. There were only a few horses, and all had to do duty in the riding hall, as well as in the battery. The enlisted men and horses were all quartered at the north end of the Post under the hill.

The class of new cadets in those days was placed under the charge of a few upperclassmen. Ours was under the first captain of the class of 1872. We thought he treated us badly but said nothing about it until he went too far in the mistreatment of one our number whom we considered unable to look after himself. A meeting was held at which it was decided that a challenge to fight should be sent to the first captain, and it was also thought that the challenge should emanate from me. This role had not been sought after by me, but, since it seemed the decision of the class, it was carried out. It developed that the captain did not propose to lose his position by fighting a miserable plebe, but his roommate, Jug [Abram Epperson] Wood, later of the Fourth Cavalry, said that "if that plebe wants to fight, I'll fight him." The second explained that nobody wanted to fight, and, if the proposed fight took place, it would do us no good. We held that all we wanted was justice for our classmate and that we would have to get it somehow. There was no fight, but the situation regarding our classmate was relieved.

There was a fight, however, after we returned to the barracks in September. The vacancies left after the general examination were filled during the summer by what we called the "Seps," who came into the corps in September after we old and experienced men of the same class had been hazed by the upperclassmen in June. It was the custom for us June men to haze the Seps mildly for a few days. During this process, a small man by the name of [Francis J.] Marrin from New York was knocked down a whole flight of steps by a big man from the West. A class meeting was held over this, and again the star part fell to me, and my challenge was carried by [Eli DuBose] Hoyle and [Harvey Walter] Isbell.

We met after reveille at Fort Clinton, one of the old forts of the Revolution, under the rules of the Marquis of Queensbury, each with two seconds before a referee or umpire.[3] My opponent [John C. Wickliffe] did not have so much skill with his fists, but he was a good head taller and twenty pounds heavier, and his rush was like that of a locomotive. He knocked me down twice, the last time by what is usually a knockout blow on the point of the chin, which dented the bone and stunned me so that I was almost counted out. He had been knocked down only once, and I was almost all in when happily I placed a blow on the point of his chin, landing him on the small of his back, and he was counted out just in time to save me from a Waterloo. He failed to graduate, and I lost sight of him for many years when one day I learned that he was a lawyer in New Orleans, instrumental in putting the Louisiana Lottery out of business. I wrote him a letter telling him I still had

3. At this point in his life, the young Scott apparently saw no contradiction between engaging in the West Point tradition of hazing cadets at one moment and standing up to a bully the next. Harper, "Hugh Lenox Scott," 4.

that pretty little dimple he had given me on the chin. He wrote back that that was "one of the things it was better to give than to receive."

Our lives crossed in another way, we found, as it was his father [Charles A. Wickliffe] who, as a congressman, brought into question the enlisting of 1,500 Negroes in the Civil War by my uncle, David Hunter.[4]

4. Congressman Charles A. Wickliffe of Kentucky created a national controversy in 1862 when he publicly criticized Hunter's emancipation of slaves and their enlistment as Union soldiers. Miller, *Lincoln's Abolitionist General*, 104–106. See also Smith, "Let Us All Be Grateful," 10–11.

3

Yearling Misfortune

Winter and spring [1872] examinations were safely passed, entitling me to become a yearling. We were all warned not to haze members of the new class, but we all disregarded this, giving them, however, a far milder hazing than we had received ourselves. As luck would have it, I happened to be the one caught.

It was set down in the drill regulations that the hands should be carried with the palms to the front, but in practice this was made to apply only to the new cadets. I told one to carry his palms to the front and, upon his failure to obey, caught him by the wrist and turned his hand around for him. He saw my name on my shirt and reported me for hazing him, for which I was suspended for one year and ordered to join the next lower class. I and my class were much aggrieved at this severe punishment for what had been a custom ever since the founding of the academy. Far rougher things were done in those days in civilian colleges as a matter of course, and no notice was taken of them.

I now, however, look back on the occurrence far differently. In the first place, West Point is a national school where men are being fitted to command armies for the defense of our country. Although hazing might be permitted in a mild way in a civilian college, it cannot be permitted at West Point, as all cadets have taken an oath to obey the orders of the president of the United States and of the officers appointed over them, who have forbidden this practice. Many old graduates who were well hazed in their times excuse hazing by saying that it does a plebe good, operating to cut his mother's apron string, as well as to give him a sense of discipline which he might otherwise never attain. This is eminently true, and I myself recognize the benefits received from hazing. But this is a mere sophistry which has nothing to do with the case.[1]

The facts are that the foundation of all military discipline is obedience to orders and that, therefore, since hazing has been forbidden by the proper authorities, it cannot be tolerated. To teach otherwise at West Point would go far to sap the foundations of the republic by producing a type of officer who could not be trusted at the critical moment to obey his orders. West Point furnishes the initiative, the directing and informing spirit of American armies, the leaven which leavens the whole lump, the standards of duty and honor without which an army is but an armed mob. Nothing should be spared to keep these standards of the highest quality and to cause them to be adhered to, for upon these in crucial moments depends the life of this republic, and certainly neither politics nor sentimentality should be allowed to interfere.

In those old days, many years before the beautiful swimming pool in the gymnasium at West Point, the cadets were allowed to swim in the Hudson River off Gee's Point. This is rather a dangerous place, for the water deepens rapidly, and the tide is apt to turn and carry one far out into the river, and in fact a number of cadets have drowned there, including a member of my class. The cadets were allowed to swim only in the late evening because the location was too public.[2]

Notwithstanding the danger, cadets constantly took advantage of this permission, and in the summer of 1871, while swimming away from the others, I kept going until I reached the other side, and I acquired much merit for crossing the river and returning. No doubt there have been many who have accomplished this same feat in the years both before and since, but nobody else had achieved it in our time.

A classmate of mine named Josiah [H.] King asked to swim over with me, which I always refused, telling him that, while I knew my own ability, I did not know his, and I did not wish to be drowned on his account. His

1. Scott had to return to the nagging issue of hazing, addressing it during his tenure as superintendent of West Point. Scott, *Some Memories*, 441–45.

2. The implication here is that cadet swimming—"in the late evening" and at a "public" location—occurred in the nude.

requests were renewed in the summer of '72 and became so insistent that I gave way to his importunity.

We swam out very comfortably, but suddenly the tide turned and carried us far down toward the railway embankment. King did not want to land and rest, as seemed best, and, when we were near the embankment, he started back without me. I was obliged to follow and catch up with him. We swam a long time against the tide, but it had become so dark by that time that we were unable to gauge our progress by anything on the banks. We seemed to be swimming out into infinite space and getting nowhere. This got on King's nerves after a while, and he announced that he was all in and could go no further and that I must leave him as there was no reason for us both to be drowned. I encouraged him to persevere and told him that I would never leave him under any circumstances. He struggled along for some time with assistance, but finally it became necessary for me to take him on my back, struggling all the time against the tide until at last we both got ashore.

It was the feeling of my class that the saving of King had offset this breach of discipline in turning the new cadet's hands around, but none of us knew how to present it to the authorities, who seemed indifferent to such matters, possibly because they did not wish to let the only fish they had caught escape through the net (although a similar case occurred about the same time at the Naval Academy where the cadet was forgiven). But those were not the days of forgiveness at West Point.[3] "Stand on your own feet!" "Behave yourself or take the consequences!" "Work out your own salvation!" and "Root, hog, or die!" were the sentiments which dominated there. While a good many did die metaphorically, there is not a doubt that those who survived were a hardy band and fully earned their commissions.

◆ ◆ ◆

Those old superintendents, whose character it was that governed the spirit of the West Point of that day, were imbued with the doctrine of rigid discipline

3. In 1897, Scott received a letter from the War Department that officially recognized his "act of heroism." Arthur L. Wagner, its author and then an assistant adjutant general, had witnessed Scott's feat as a fellow cadet. Wagner wrote, "I think you must have sustained him [King] for at least half an hour." Arthur L. Wagner, Adjutant General's Office, Washington, D.C., to H. L. Scott, Washington, D.C., Dec. 31, 1897, reprinted in Scott, *Some Memories*, 20–21.

inherited from the British Army. Although they were just as hard on themselves as on everyone else, their methods in dealing with the young subordinates may see a bit unfeeling to this more humane generation.

As a specific example of their inflexible attitude, a mother of a cadet who had graduated before the Civil War once told me that she would never forgive a certain superintendent because, when her son asked for a permit to go home as his father was dying, the superintendent said, "Young man, the government is your father and mother both. If you feel badly, you can trot around the parade ground once or twice, and you will feel better."

In the old days the superintendents did not want any outsider to come on the Post, nor any insider to go off. It had been the custom in the classes before ours for the yearlings to purchase some rowing shells from the graduating class for their use on the river, but, when we made application to purchase them in our turn, we were met with a firm "no," and the shells remained at least four years in the boathouse without being used. We thought that it was because Fred Grant's class had been too undisciplined. Whenever discipline gets below the standard at West Point, the War Department sends some case-hardened superintendent who pushes the pendulum of discipline to the opposite extreme. That is what happened to us. Conditions were much harder in our time than they have ever been since. Nowadays there are many sports and other alleviations unheard of and unthought of in those days. Whereas we look back upon the old gray barracks as a jail where we served four years at hard labor, the great majority of present-day graduates leave the academy with actual regret.

Aside from the more sympathetic trend of present-day discipline, the entire modernization of barrack facilities has much to do with this new attitude of graduating cadets. No longer does the plebe struggle up four flights of stairs carrying water, nor is he obliged to trudge down icy halls in the middle of the night and across the area knee-deep in snow or to steal hot water out of the radiators for shaving, to be punished if caught. Neither is he restricted to the two baths a week "permitted" formerly. He goes down heated halls into a tiled bathroom in the basement and takes as many baths as he likes with warm water and in warm air. Thirty years after my own graduation, I replaced with hot and cold water on every floor the ancient hydrant at which old [Pvt. Louis] Bentz, the bugler, who called Cadet U. S. Grant and others of fame to recitations before my time, used to wash out the "nails" those bad cadets put in his "pugle." Bentz, by the way, lies out with the other honored dead in the cemetery above the river. His "pugle" is shown to visitors in the museum, where, the moment I laid eyes on it, I recognized the patches where his faithful fingers had worn through the metal.

I have heard old graduates groan over this "coddling of cadets," which they claim is carrying West Point straight to the dogs at a rapid stride. But no deterioration was evident in France [during the World War] that was ever directed to my attention. It is very easy for the old to think that the young are retrograding if things are not run for them in exactly the way to which they themselves were brought up. But association with the armies of England, France, Russia, and Rumania has convinced me that our regular army officers are the peers of any. From my own experiences at West Point, covering eight years both as boy and man, supplemented by various inspections made as chief of staff and numerous visits since as an alumnus, I have become firmly assured that there is in our venerable military institution a constant evolution upward. Every time I go back, I note some new improvement and ask myself, "Why didn't I have the wit to do that long ago?"

So far as the slackening of the iron bands of the old-time discipline goes, one hears nothing any more of "butter riots," nothing about the reveille gun being brought up to take a shot at the quarters of the superintendent, nor of a companion to the ancient ditty:

> Seventy-three, seventy-three,
> They fired the gun in the a-ri-ee!

Instead, in these saner, more wisely directed days, surplus energy is expended in baseball, football, lacrosse, hockey, polo, and other athletic games unknown in our time. Tactical officers, instead of rushing distractedly about in the middle of the night to forestall some nefarious plot, are like Shakespeare's men o' substance who "sleep o' nights all to the glory of God and the good of this commonwealth."[4]

4. Although Scott seemingly attributed this quote to Shakespeare, I have found no variation of it in the various databases of his work.

4

Service on the Plains

I witnessed the graduation of the West Point class 1875 with deep sorrow and bade good-by to my roommate George L. Scott from Oregon. I saw him only once again in after years, and there were others, too, I have never seen again.

I myself graduated on June 14, 1876, ranking thirty-six in the class of forty-eight, but high enough for the cavalry, which was my ambition. If I had missed the cavalry, I would have considered that all my toil at West Point had resulted in failure. I asked for an additional second lieutenancy in the cavalry in preference to being assigned to a full lieutenancy in any other branch.

We were marched into the old chapel to receive our hard-won diplomas from General W[illiam] T. Sherman, commanding the army, and paid about as much attention to his words of admonition as do other classes, members of which are mainly intent on donning civilian clothes and getting down to New York in a hurry. Whenever I have since had to speak at a West Point graduation, I have remembered Father Isadore, the old Belgian priest in charge of the Kiowa Indian Catholic school at Anadarko, Oklahoma, who said that, when those little folk were seated at the dinner table, he could see their hungry eyes fixed on the bread and gravy and made his grace very short.[1]

I was assigned to the Ninth Cavalry on the Arizona border, then a quiet sector. There was only one vacancy available for our class in the Seventh

1. This is Father Isidore Ricklin. M. Ursula, "Sources for the Study," 346.

Cavalry, then operating on the Yellowstone against the Sioux of Montana, since one of the only two vacancies had gone to a civilian as a political appointment, and the first had been obtained by my classmate, [Ernest A.] Garlington, who graduated some four files above me. He, because of the Custer fight, joined the regiment as first lieutenant, but I was glad to be admitted into any cavalry regiment and returned home a free man for a while, rejoicing to see my family.

With my brother William I went down to see the Centennial in Philadelphia, where I first met and grew to know that splendid old soldier and my lifelong friend Colonel Dan[iel] Appleton, afterward colonel of the Seventh Regiment of New York. The Corps of Cadets and the Seventh Regiment were both camped there, but discipline was somewhat stricter in the cadet camp, as was very natural. Any soldier who got into one of the company streets of the Seventh Regiment was in for a strenuous time. Each tent floor had a small cellar under it, filled with ice, champagne, roast chicken, and other delicacies. A passerby would be hauled into those tents, one after another, and, with the cellar door opened wide, he would not be allowed to leave until some duty called his hospitable hosts elsewhere. There were no such cellars under the tents of the cadets.

I met one of my friends from Princeton on July 5 in the street, who told me that Custer and all his men had been killed in battle with the Sioux. I answered that I did not believe it. He suggested that I get a newspaper, and I soon verified the news. Custer was killed on June 25, and it had taken ten days for the news to get to the nearest telegraph station, Bismarck, Dakota [Territory], first coming downstream on a steamboat on the June rise, the fastest possible way for it to travel.

After recovering somewhat from the shock of the tidings and the death of my classmates [James G.] Sturges [Sturgis] and [John J.] Crittenden of '75, I began to see that there were many vacancies now in the Seventh Cavalry and hurried back to Princeton to consult with my uncle, Sam[uel W.] Stockton, who had been a captain in the Fourth Cavalry, as to the best means of securing a transfer. He told me to sit down at once and write an application and send it through our Uncle David in Washington, who knew everybody in the War Department. I demurred at this haste, as jumping for the shoes of those killed in the Little Big Horn before they were cold, but I was advised not to delay.

Our uncle got my letter at breakfast, went at once to the War Department, where they were then making out the transfers to the Seventh Cavalry, and saw to it that my name was included in that fighting regiment, much to my satisfaction. Things were now coming my way, and I would soon be in the Indian country.

It took some time for my transfer to the Seventh Cavalry to be effected with the making out of a new commission as second lieutenant of cavalry, which was dated June 26, 1876, the day after the Custer fight. At length, however, my orders came to report at the headquarters of the Seventh Cavalry at old Fort Abraham Lincoln, Dakota, across the Missouri River and five miles away from Bismarck—not to be confounded with the new Fort Abraham Lincoln of this day on the Bismarck side of the Missouri.

Bismarck was very crude in those days. The houses were mainly board shanties, few in number. It was for long the end of the Northern Pacific Railway and the jumping-off place of the Northwest. One might go a thousand miles west or travel north to the Arctic Circle with the probability of not seeing a human being. That country was the home of the buffalo and the wild Indian, a land of romance, adventure, and mystery, and I had carried it in mind during those five long years at West Point, fitting myself for service within its borders.

No boy ever left home with brighter anticipation or with more affection and love from those left behind. Going out from the East, I stopped at Pittsburgh to see my brother [Charles] and his new wife, again at Chicago, the headquarters of General [Phillip H.] Sheridan, who commanded all the Plains country, and at Saint Paul where General [Alfred H.] Terry commanded the Plains of the Northwest clear to the Rocky Mountains. Saint Paul was not then the great city we know now. Mrs. Scott and I have lately been in Saint Paul again, and about the only thing we could recognize of that early time was the Mississippi River.

Staying at the old Merchants Hotel on Third Street, I explored the town, not then a lengthy process, and saw tall, straight Chippewa [Ojibwa] Indians, wrapped in their blue and scarlet blankets, striding about in a very dignified way, giving me the feeling of proximity to the frontier which, however, was still far to the west. All Minnesota then was up in arms, aflame with excitement over the chase after the James and Younger brothers from Missouri, who had attempted to rob the bank at Northfield, Minnesota [on September 7, 1876], and had killed the cashier. Some of the gang had been killed, and the body of one [Charlie Pitts] was exhibited in the window of a store on Third Street, Saint Paul. Bob Younger had been wounded, and Jesse James wanted the brother, Cole Younger, to kill Bob so as to facilitate their escape, but Cole refused. Both were captured and served a long sentence in the penitentiary at Stillwater, Minnesota. Frank and Jesse James escaped and reached their asylum in Missouri, to which they always returned after some deed of iniquity in other parts of the country, and received protection as heroes.

At the Merchants Hotel, I met captains Frederick [W.] Benteen and [Thomas M. McDougall] MacDougal of the Seventh Cavalry, fresh from the Yellowstone and Missouri after the Custer fight. Benteen was then the hero of all America, credited with saving the remnant of the Seventh Cavalry. They both gave me a cordial welcome to the regiment and were strong friends of mine as long as they lived.[2] With them was Texas Jack (John Omohundro), just off the Yellowstone, with long hair, dressed in buckskin, on his way east to join the new show of Buffalo Bill. I was to see him again in the Nez Percé war in the confines of the Yellowstone Park, but at that time he was the first of his kind that I had met.

Leaving Saint Paul, I stopped a few days at Fargo on the Red River of the North, where a friend of Benteen's furnished me with a boat in which I had my first duck shoot in the Northwest. I had brought out a pointer and a setter from home, given me by friends, and saw my first live prairie chicken not far from Fargo. From Fargo two hundred miles west to Bismarck, the end of the track, I did not see a house until I reached the Missouri River, except those of the section hands along the railroad. The passengers got their meals at Jamestown in a freight car standing on the sidetrack. We arrived at Bismarck after dark, the train having taken the entire day to come from Fargo. Trains did not run then at night, and it required three days to make the run from Saint Paul to the Missouri River.

I drove down to the Missouri the next morning and sat on the bank, waiting for the ferry, as I was to do many times in the years to come. This was my first sight of the wild Missouri, and I looked at it with deep interest. Nowhere is it described so fitly and beautifully as by Francis Parkman, the great historian of the North, in his *Conspiracy of Pontiac*, which I carried, with the report of Captain Raynold's expedition of 1859[–60] through the Northwest, in my pack basket for ten thousand miles and read again and again, as I still do at intervals with perennial pleasure.[3]

2. Scott admired the older Benteen immensely: "I found my model early in Captain Benteen. . . . I never once heard him raise his voice to enforce his purpose. . . . Often I watched his every movement to find out the secret of his quiet steady government, that I might go and govern likewise. . . . Benteen's police . . . paid me large dividends." Scott, *Some Memories*, 454.

3. Parkman, *Conspiracy of Pontiac*, 2:261–62; Raynolds, *Report on the Exploration of the Yellowstone*.

Reporting at the headquarters of the Seventh Cavalry, I found Major Marcus A. Reno in command, Lieutenant George D. Wallace, the adjutant, of the class of 1872, and many classmates and friends from other classes at West Point. I received a genuinely warm welcome and was assigned to the Gray Horse Troop [Company E] of the Seventh Cavalry with Lieutenant [Charles C.] DeRudio in command. Our captain, Charles Illsley, was then away on the staff of General John Pope at Fort Leavenworth, Kansas. I looked rather askance at Reno, whose reputation was being pulled apart all over the United States, and my impression of him was not improved by observation.[4]

The regiment had got back to its post from the Yellowstone only a short time before and was in process of reorganization, with thirty new officers, some of whom had reported before me, while others were still to come in one at a time. Five hundred new recruits and five hundred new horses had just been received from the East. It was in the air that we were to take the field again in a short while. The only property we each had was a saber, a trunk, and a roll of bedding, to which I added a couple of dogs, two shotguns, and a Henry rifle. No one thought it worthwhile to acquire any furniture for the short period we would be able to use it.

Wallace and [Charles A.] Varnum took me in with them to sleep in the drawing room of the quarters just vacated by Mrs. Custer, who had gone east.[5] Eight of us slept on the floor in our field bedding until the regiment started off on a new campaign. Thus the house that Custer had left with such bright hopes the spring before was my first habitation on the Plains of the West. The first subscription in the Seventh Cavalry I was asked for was in the purchase from the government by the officers of the Seventh of Custer's horse, Dandy, to be sent to Mrs. Custer.

Fort Lincoln at that time was the station of headquarters and eight troops of the Seventh Cavalry and of two infantry companies that took care of the post in the absence of the cavalry, the latter living in what was called

4. Reno famously became the scapegoat for Custer's defeat at the Little Big Horn and the source for spirited debate ever since. See the following classics: Graham, *Reno Court of Inquiry*; and Graham, *Custer Myth*. In the latter compilation Graham included an undated newspaper story by Scott, "Custer's Last Fight: Notes by Gen. Scott; Facts He Gathered Led Him to Believe the Tragedy Could Have Been Avoided," in which the old soldier weighed into the controversy. Graham, *Custer Myth*, 113–14. The story appeared in its entirety in *New York Times*, Jan. 6, 1935.

5. Besides sharing quarters with Scott, officers Wallace and Varnum could also have shared stories of how each had survived the Custer fight. See Mackintosh, *Custer's Southern Officer*; and Carroll, *Custer's Chief of Scouts*.

the Upper or Infantry Post on a high hill a mile distant from the Lower or Cavalry Post. The Seventh Cavalry had come in from an expedition on the Yellowstone in the autumn of 1873 to find its winter quarters still unfinished and had turned-to and nailed shingles in order to get some place to live before winter, which sets in early in the Northwest and usually rages with great fury. North Dakota is where the blizzards reach us out of Canada, straight down from the Arctic Circle, and a winter out of doors is not to be looked forward to with pleasure.

The constructing quartermaster was enabled, partly through this voluntary labor of the Seventh Cavalry, to save thirty thousand dollars from the appropriation made for construction. Although he did not finish the post, which never was completed before it was torn apart and destroyed, he thought he would acquire merit for economy by turning this thirty thousand dollars back into the Treasury as a saving, leaving successive garrisons, who had to live in an unfinished post, to execrate his memory. General Pope at Fort Leavenworth heard of this saving and went to Washington, where he induced the quartermaster general [Montgomery C. Meigs] to spend the sum on a road between Leavenworth and Fort Leavenworth, Kansas.

The country began to roll just behind the post, the brakes [breaks] and ravines of the Missouri dotted with little oak groves containing deer and the river bottoms full of prairie chickens beginning to pack for the winter. This was the country of my dreams and the Seventh Cavalry my choice of all the regiments in the army, which I would have chosen had I graduated at the head of my class. The great Sioux Agency of Standing Rock was only sixty miles down the river, and we were on the Sioux reservation.

Francis Parkman wrote:

> The Indian is a true child of the forest and the desert. The wastes and solitudes of nature are his congenial home. His haughty mind is imbued with the spirit of the wilderness, and the light of civilization falls on him with a blighting power. His unruly pride and untamed freedom are in harmony with the lonely mountains, cataracts, and rivers among which he dwells, and primitive America, with her savage scenery and savage men, opens to the imagination a boundless world, unmatched in wild sublimity.[6]

6. Parkman began *The Conspiracy of Pontiac* with this as the opening paragraph of his two-volume history.

Here then before me was this primitive America for which I sought, and here was I with a spirit attuned to understand it and to rejoice in becoming a part of its life.[7] Many of my contemporaries were children of the East, always looking eastward and longing to get back. But no matter how cold, how wet, how hungry I found myself during all the years of Plains life that followed, I felt that I was where I belonged.

7. Scott's use of the word "primitive" here and later appears to mean "preliterate," "nonindustrial," or "unsophisticated."

5

With the Indians

Wallace, who commanded the Sioux and Arikara scouts at that time [1876], took me down into their village on the second day of my sojourn to make their acquaintance. There were always a few scouts kept there to carry despatches in the Indian country and to guide detachments out from the post. When an expedition was on foot, there would be a large number of scouts brought from their agency to scout the country in front of the command, guide it through the country by the best route, and show where water could be found. The tribe from which they came would be chosen according to the country in which we were to operate and the tribe we were to operate against, taking advantage of their knowledge of the country where they had been brought up and of their enmity against their neighbors. Now and then there would be some willing to combine against their own tribe.

Realizing that the Sioux tribe was the largest and most powerful in the Northwest, I thought that their language must be the court language of that section, especially as the Arikara scouts all spoke it, and I made arrangements to have them teach me Sioux.[1] I thought that a knowledge of the tongue would help me in getting command of the scouts, a position sought after by the more adventurous lieutenants with no troop of their own. The position was

1. Unnamed here, many of these men must have been those included in Libby's *Arikara Narrative of Custer's Campaign*.

analogous to that of an aviator of today; one could always be ahead of the command, away from the routine that was irksome, and sure to have a part in all the excitement.

I soon found that the Sioux language was quite limited in the scope of its usefulness, but that the sign language of the Plains was an intertribal language, spoken everywhere in the buffalo country from the Saskatchewan River of British America to Mexico, east of the Rocky Mountains and west of the Missouri. I began the study of this at the same time with the Sioux and have continued its study down to this very day.

Through my mastery of this means of communication with the Natives, I soon became known to commanders of every grade, clear up to Generals Sheridan and [Nelson A.] Miles, who befriended me as long as they lived. They gave me a freedom and scope I have seen extended to none else in the Indian country, perhaps because I was satisfied there and took pleasure in carrying out work they might have for me.[2] Generals Ruger and [Wesley] Merritt did likewise, and, in fact, I came and went as I pleased without question, but I always pleased to be on deck when I was wanted.

I began then an intensive study of every phase of the Indian and his customs, particularly as to how he might best be approached and influenced, a knowledge that has stood me in good stead many times, has doubtless saved my life again and again, and has also been used to the national benefit by different presidents of the United States, by secretaries of war and of the Interior.

It was the custom in those days for the cavalry to spend the greater part of the year in the saddle, either in pursuit of hostile Indians or in holding in check the semi-hostile. This was so much a matter of course that no officer could obtain a leave of absence, except under the most exceptional circumstances, until after the return of the annual expedition from the field. The longest time the cavalry might expect to spend at the post would be the few months in the dead of winter, and often this was not possible.

When operating in the Big Horn country, we had scouts from the Crow tribe, who lived generally along the base of the Big Horn and Pryor Mountains and hated the Sioux with a mortal hatred. The scouts were kept always in advance, often ten, twenty, or thirty miles ahead, watching the whole

2. General Sheridan promoted the research of a cadre of young, smart, ambitious officers in various areas of American Indian culture. Hutton, *Phil Sheridan*, 254, 334, 341–42.

Scott demonstrating the Plains Indian Sign Language. His loss of fingers from a Philippine War wound caused no impediment. National Anthropological Archives, Smithsonian Institution, 01311000.

country with a glass from the tops of high landmarks, themselves unseen. A bird could scarcely fly over that country without their knowledge, for they knew of certain lookouts that commanded views of wide areas. Lying on top of one of these points, his head screened by a bunch of grass or sagebrush, a keen young Sioux, Cheyenne, Arikara, or Crow scout, eager for the fame only to be gained by military prowess in war, seeing a raven fly up suddenly or a wolf or a coyote run up out of a ravine, stopping now and then to look backward, or a band of antelope or buffalo suddenly begin to stampede, would know that something had frightened them and would not leave his place until he had ascertained the source of the fear. Then he would turn back down out of sight on the reverse side of the hill and make his signals to the other scouts far in the rear.

While traveling with the scouts, I lived just as they did and allowed no custom of theirs to go unnoticed, never resting until I found the motive, which they were often unable to formulate themselves, although they were always the very soul of affability, anxious to impart information wherever possible. I know that I have been a sore trial to the patience of thousands of friendly Indians of different tribes by boring away at a subject which they were unable to elucidate, attacking the matter from every angle until they were worn out or I had attained my object. They must often have felt that I had been sent to them for their sins or would have had they thought they had any sins for which to be punished. But the idea of sin is the white man's invention and is foreign to the Indian.

6

Into the Field

Everybody in the Seventh Cavalry was feverishly engaged in training the "green" men and horses for the new campaign that everybody felt was imminent [1876]. I soon got an order to go down the Missouri, twenty-five miles to old Fort Rice and bring back some artillery harness and make a battery out of some muzzle-loading guns with cavalry soldiers and condemned cavalry horses unfit to ride. Long before these new men and horses were properly trained and disciplined, orders came to cross to the east side of the Missouri. We were ferried across the river and went into camp on the Missouri bottom, my first night in the field with the Seventh Cavalry. [Luther R.] Hare, whom I had known well in the class of '74, took command of the battery as my superior, as well as of his own Troop I, to which I had been transferred from E. We tented and messed together from that time on whenever we were in the same camp.

I was awakened in the middle of the night by a fearsome sound, which to my tenderfoot mind could only be caused by an attack on the camp by the whole Sioux tribe and aroused Hare to help defend the camp. This caused Hare much merriment, for his longer experience had taught him that those incredible sounds were caused only by the ardent efforts of one lone coyote to impart his sorrows to the moon. I have since heard this sound times without number and always with pleasure. Although he is proscribed and hunted by men, I have the same friendly feeling for the coyote that actuates the Indian.

We were joined in this camp by our colonel [Samuel D. Sturgis] and headquarters and remained here several days. No one knew where we were going or against whom we were to operate until orders were received to go down the Missouri River to disarm and dismount the Indians at the various Sioux agencies below, who had been sending ammunition, rifles, and supplies to the hostile camps of Crazy Horse and Sitting Bull near the mountains.[1] The Indian Department [the Office of Indian Affairs at this time] had at last awakened to the advisability of ending the traffic in arms and ammunition with the hostile camps.

Although there was a strong probability that the Sioux would resist having their arms and horses taken from them, we were going to attempt it with a force composed largely of new men and horses that had not had time to become half disciplined and instructed. My battery was the least efficient of all because of the wider scope to be covered by instruction. I kept instructing them every day, but I well knew that my efforts and ability were inadequate if we were going to fight. However, it was the best that could be done under the circumstances. I was too young and reckless to worry much. What bothered me infinitely more was that I had come west to be a flying cavalryman, to be free and far ahead with the scouts, and instead my adverse fate had nailed down my coattails to a battery that had to travel at a walk behind the column. I had not undergone five years of toil at West Point to come out to the Plains to be a wagon soldier, and my spirit chafed at the idea. I made every effort to get away from the battery to travel with the scouts, who broke camp and were on their way before daylight, covering the country far in front as carefully as pointer dogs in search of quail.

We were furnished with that bane of the soldier's life, "contract transportation," that was continually breaking down on the road, by reason of which the command was often without its tents and dinners until one o'clock in the morning, wearing out men and animals uselessly. The battery, however, was allowed to keep its wagons and its guns and not in the quartermaster's train. Whenever one of our wagons got stuck in the mud, a four-horse battery team would soon jerk it out. We saw to it that, whenever we reached camp, our wagons would be with us, and we soon had our tents up and dinner ready. Seeing our colonel waiting for his, we would always invite him to dine

1. The operation against the Lakota at Standing Rock occurred in late October 1876. Sherman, "Report of the General of the Army," 37.

with us, and it happened that he dined at our mess more frequently than at his own. The procurement of game made him more willing to let me go ahead with the scouts. I would come into camp laden with chickens, snipe, and ducks for our mess and his. It soon became a matter of course for me to leave the battery with Hare, my superior, in command and go off with the scouts before daylight every day.

As we approached Standing Rock, the signs of excitement among the Sioux began to be frequent. Every now and then we would find a travois—a litter made of two lodge poles drawn by horse or dog, the rear ends dragging on the ground—lying on the ground where the owner had left it on learning of our approach, cutting the lashings, allowing it to fall to the ground, then jumping on their horses and getting away in flight, abandoning all their property. This carried small message of danger to my tenderfoot mind. The efforts of the Arikara scouts to make me join the others, motioning me back with their hands, saying, "You go home, Sioux kill him—Sioux kill him—*Ktepi Ktepi!*" made as little impression.

While I traveled carelessly along with my orderly, we saw in the middle of the river bottom some Sioux bodies lashed on high platforms and went to examine them. We had seen a long line of Indian heads skirting the edge of the timber, watching our movements, but that made no difference to us until the orderly, looking up, called out, "Hurry up, lieutenant. They are going to fight!" We saw the eight troops of the Seventh Cavalry coming front into line at a gallop over the bluffs and Hare going into battery on a high knoll, while we were out in the middle of the bottom, halfway between the two forces. We thought we had better join our battery in a hurry to take part in anything that was going to happen.

After a short time, some Indians started toward us. Old Two Bears, long chief of the Yanktonai Sioux, approached with several followers.[2] He was dressed in buckskin, covered by a scarlet blanket with a broad band of beads across the center of the back, his face painted a deep red, and he carried a large redstone pipe on his arm.

The colonel told him what he had come for. This caused the old man great excitement, the perspiration popping out through the greasy paint. He tried to make an argument, but the colonel told him he was there under

2. Biographical information on Two Bears appears in Waggoner, *Witness*, 40, 143, 148–49, 618n21.

orders from higher authority and was compelled to carry them out, whether he wanted to or not. There was no use in discussing a matter which had been determined in Saint Paul or Chicago.[3] It was not in his power to alter the arrangements, and it would be best for all if Two Bears were to give up his horses and arms quietly and cheerfully because he would take them anyhow and greatly preferred to do it without bloodshed. Two Bears agreed finally to give them up quietly and went back to the other Indians in the brush. Although several hundred Indians had been seen, nobody knew how many more there were in the woods.

The colonel and staff rode forward near the edge of the woods, and I went along uninvited in an unostentatious position in rear. After a long wait Two Bears came out with some of his headmen and laid an old broken cavalry saber with half a blade down at the feet of the colonel's horse, stepping back with a grand flourish as if saying, "There! See what I am doing for you!" After another long wait, probably utilized in hiding the good guns, a rusty old muzzle-loading rifle without a hammer was laid down beside the saber, then a Hudson's Bay fuke [or Northwest gun], without a flint, and some other guns equally as serviceable.

Although the proceedings were very ceremonious and the conditions highly tense and dangerous, I was obliged to hold on to my saddle to avoid falling off my horse with laughter. The colonel's temper began to give way, and, thinking that he was possibly being spoofed by wild Indians, he directed some detachments to dismount and search the lodges hidden for a long distance among the willows up and down the river. I joined one of these detachments. We searched the lodges up the river with a lot of other ignorant tenderfeet, some of whom acted very rudely and had to be severely checked. Looking back now, I perceive that we were all in great danger of being killed, especially in view of the insulting mien of some of the recruits.

We gathered up a number of rifles and some carbines that showed by their numbers that they had been taken from Custer, but most of the good rifles had been hidden away earlier in the day and were never found. It is more difficult, however, to hide a horse, and some three thousand were taken here and at the Cheyenne River Agency and driven to Bismarck.

3. The military headquarters of the Department of Dakota was located in Saint Paul, Minnesota, and, up the chain of command, that of the Division of the Missouri was located in Chicago.

The colonel attempted to swim a bunch of horses across the Missouri and desisted only when he had succeeded in getting forty of them mired in a quicksand out of reach of help, where they were slowly sinking out of sight in the cold water in which a cake of ice would now and then float past. We had no boat with which to go to their assistance, and I asked permission to shoot them to put them quickly out of their misery, as their slow drowning was a heartrending sight to a cavalryman. I was told that certainly I might shoot them, if I wanted to, but that I must first pay their market price in Saint Paul. I had to go away in helpless sorrow.

Another sad thing happened here. I was sitting at headquarters when a Sioux chief named Mad Bear brought in a letter signed by General [Alfred] Sully in 1862, commending Mad Bear for saving a white woman at the Sioux massacre in Minnesota, having led her along by the hand, carrying her child on his back.[4] When the colonel finished reading the letter, Mad Bear asked if he were going to take his rifle and horse away, treating him just as he did the wild Sioux who were at war with the soldiers half the time. The colonel told him that he had no authority to make any distinction and would have to take them. This embittered me beyond words. Had I had my way, I would have given Mad Bear his horse and gun, making an example with ceremony to draw the attention of all the Sioux and would have gone to the mat afterward with Saint Paul by telegraph, but I was powerless to take any action.

Orders came from the secretary of the Interior [Zachariah Chandler], through the War Department, to drive the horses to Bismarck and then to Saint Paul to be sold in that market. Every second lieutenant well knew the futility of trying to drive three thousand horses four hundred miles to Saint Paul in the snow and cold of a Dakota winter. The consequence was that, when the snow melted in the spring, the passengers on the Northern Pacific Railway saw the road lined with the carcasses of horses on both sides of the track for four hundred miles to Saint Paul. It was impossible to properly guard so many horses in a snowstorm on the open prairie, and large bunches were stolen at night along the way, a bare remnant of those starting from Bismarck reaching Saint Paul, nothing but skin and bone, to meet a dead market. Under the circumstances, it would have been far more humane and less expensive to shoot every animal before leaving Bismarck. If the taking

4. For information on Mad Bear, a Yanktonai contemporary of Two Bears, see Waggoner, *Witness*, 305–307, 659n1.

of the horses had been postponed until the grass started in the spring, all would have been saved.

◆ ◆ ◆

Riding along one day with the scouts and the celebrated guide and interpreter F[rederic] F. Gerard, we stopped for lunch near Blue Blanket Creek, and Gerard gave me my first taste of beaver tail, that celebrated prairie delicacy.[5] It looked and tasted to me like tender, cold roast pork and was very much sought after in the Northwest by mountain men.

The Seventh Cavalry arrived once more opposite Fort Lincoln on November 11, 1876. Hare and I, being at the head of column, got across on the ferry with our troop and battery among the first with a few others, the crossing ending at dark. The river froze over that night, and, as the ice was too thick for the ferry and too thin to carry cavalry, half the command were prevented from crossing for a week until the ice was strong enough to bear them.

5. Gerard may have been "celebrated" for having narrowly survived the Custer fight. Libby, *Arikara Narrative of Custer's Campaign*, 171–75; Wagner, *Participants in the Battle*, 107.

7

Troubles at Home

The winter of 1876–77 was a cold one in the Northwest and was made more so for us by mismanagement at Saint Paul, where the wood contract was not made in time to season the wood as usual. We had to burn green cottonwood all winter. The cottonwood is full of sap, and it was only with the greatest difficulty and with the help now and then of a dry stick that we could keep the fire alight.

The weather was usually too cold and stormy to drill out of doors. The men had not been sufficiently disciplined and instructed on their arrival, having had to take the field too early. Now, after an expedition, they considered themselves veterans and never did become thoroughly disciplined. They were a rough lot who had enlisted in cities under stress of the excitement caused by the Custer fight and were called the "Custer avengers."[1] Many of them were criminals that were got rid of by court-martial from time to time during the winter and discharged.

I succeeded to the command of I Troop for the winter during Hare's absence on leave, for our captain was away for a year abroad. Fifteen or twenty of the men would run away at night, crossing the Missouri, the boundary of

1. More details on these individuals can be found in McChristian, "Custer's Avengers," 2–10. Scott's low opinion of this "rough lot" does not square with the relatively high marks the men received from McChristian.

the reservation, on the ice to a small village maintained just off the reservation, where they could not be reached and where whisky and depraved women were to be found in plenty. Here they would get drunk and fight. Now and then one would be murdered or infected with a disease. There was no legal way to stop it. Some fell down drunk on the road at night and froze to death.

I was officer of the day on Christmas and responsible for order in the post.[2] Just as I sat down to our Christmas dinner, someone whispered in my ear that the prisoners had procured whisky in the guardhouse and were battering down the door with the cordwood sticks given them to burn. I rushed down to the guardhouse at once and heard pandemonium going on inside. The guardhouse was divided into two parts by a driveway through the center, with the prison room on one side and the guardroom on the other, both raised a foot from the ground. There were fifty prisoners altogether, some of them in for murder and robbery, all in one large room, lighted by a few candles. They were still pounding on the door with cordwood sticks, and the noise inside was so great that they could not hear my orders to desist.

The door by that time was hanging only by the outside hasp and the upper hinge. I formed the guard with loaded rifles in front of the door and, freeing the hasp suddenly, saw two drunken men standing on the floor a foot above me, engaged in breaking down the door. Before they got over their surprise at the sudden opening of the door, I jumped up on the floor between them and threw them down, one after the other, on the floor outside, where the guard jumped on top of them, handcuffed them, and put them away in a cell to sober up. One of the sergeants then went around inside with me to cull out the worst cases to be locked in cells.

It has always been a surprise to me that some of them did not blow out the few dim candles and stab us there in the dark where no one could tell who did it, but things happened too quickly, I suppose, for them to think of it. They were none too good, however, for they formed a conspiracy the same week to knock the sergeant of the guard on the head when he opened the door. All were to rush out and escape, but the sergeant was too careful for them and had the door unlocked by a member of the guard, standing himself below the entrance with a cocked revolver in his hand. When the door opened, he saw a man poised above him with a club about to crush in his

2. This is Scott's only mention of Christmas, normally a holiday that generated warm memories of one's frontier service. See Cox-Paul and Wengert, *Frontier Army Christmas*.

skull, and he killed him with the revolver before he could strike the blow. That ended the conspiracy for the time being.

The dead man had been a member of my troop, and it was at this juncture that I made my debut as a chaplain. There was no regular chaplain at the post to bury the man. I had to do it myself, reading the Episcopal service for the dead as I have had to do a number of times since.

Shortly after a payday in the middle of winter, I rode alone to Bismarck to buy a chair and a student lamp and found the town full of intoxicated soldiers. The mayor had telegraphed to the commanding officer to send over and "get the Seventh Cavalry," some three hundred of whom were shooting up the town. Lieutenant [Jonathan] Williams Biddle, a very fine young officer from Philadelphia whom I had known at Princeton College was sent over with fifty men to bring back those who were there absent without leave and making a disturbance. When I ran across Biddle, he was in great distress. He had dismounted his troops in the middle of the street and had gone into a saloon to bring out the men he was after, putting them under charge of his guard while he went after some more. When he came back again, guard and prisoners were all gone. I volunteered to help him, one to catch and the other to hold. He soon went off with the "Seventh Cavalry," and I went back to make my purchases.[3]

Returning to the post alone, I found a soldier dead drunk, lying in the snow with his arm through the bridle of his horse, which was standing over him, by far the more intelligent of the two. He was more than a mile from any house. I tried to lift him up on his horse, but he was totally without intelligence. I could lift him up against the side, but he would slip down like a sack of wheat when I tried to change my hold to lift him higher. I worked at it in a sort of desperation, for there was no help in sight for miles. He was certain to freeze to death if I left him to summon an ambulance from the post. Finally I had to give up trying to get him on his horse, and, working myself down underneath him, pulled his arms forward over my shoulders and stood up with him on my back, his legs hanging down as limp as strings. I then put my arm through both bridles and staggered along, carrying him on my back for more than a mile and leading both horses until I reached a log house occupied by a depraved woman, on whose floor I threw

3. Biddle was killed the next year in the Nez Percé war. Greene, *Nez Perce Summer*, 275.

him and left him for her to take care of, too angry to care much what became of him, so long as he did not die.

I was much occupied during the winter with Blacksmith [Gustave] Korn of I Troop in taking care of the horse Comanche, a survivor of the Custer disaster left on the battlefield. He was brought down on the steamboat with the rest of the wounded, with nine shots through him. He had been ridden into the fight by Colonel [Myles W.] Keogh, then captain of I Troop, who was killed. Comanche was one of the original mounts of the Seventh Cavalry, purchased in 1867 in St. Louis, and was a very fine cavalry horse.

We nursed him all winter and finally got him well and strong. Our colonel issued a regimental order that he should never be ridden again and should be paraded in all his regalia with the headquarters of the regiment at all ceremonies, led by a member of I Troop. [Henry Wadsworth] Longfellow heard of this and wrote a poem about him. The noble animal marched with the regiment to the Black Hills in 1879, south to Fort Riley, Kansas, in 1888, to the place where he began service in 1867. He was a great favorite in the regiment, and he died years afterward at Fort Riley. Professor [Lewis. L.] Dyc[h]e of the University of Kansas at Lawrence, "set him up," and he may be seen now at Lawrence, just as he used to look during his valiant life.[4]

Toward spring, my colonel sent for me and said he wanted to send a batch of prisoners to the military prison at Fort Leavenworth, that no batch had ever left Fort Lincoln from which some of the prisoners had not escaped and that he had selected me to take this batch, in the belief that I would get them all through.

There were ten in the batch with long sentences. One man in particular, named [Pasavan] Williamson, seemed to have a mania for cutting people, having tried to cut Lieutenant [Donald] McIntosh on the Yellowstone and having succeeded in cutting a wagon master on Powder River.[5] After that episode, he had deserted with several others, but eventually they had all been picked up near Fort Lincoln in a starving condition. They made the boast now that they would all escape before getting to Leavenworth.

When it came time to leave, I had them shackled in pairs, left leg to left leg, so that should they start to run in a crowded station, where they could

4. Scott might be pleased to know that Comanche remains on display in the University of Kansas Natural History Museum in Lawrence.

5. Wagner, *Participants in the Battle*, 102.

not be fired on for fear of hitting innocent people, joining the shackles would trip them up. I warned them that this was the only talk I was going to make to them and that at the first attempt to escape they would get a bullet without warning.

The Northern Pacific Railway did not run at night, and the prisoners had to be put in jails at Bismarck, Fargo, and Saint Paul. At Brainerd, Minnesota, the lockup was too old and rotten to be trusted, and I hired a large room in the hotel in which to spend the night. Passing through a dark hall at dusk, Williamson and his shackle partner started to run into a side door, but, hearing the click of the revolver being cocked, they threw up their hands and begged for their lives just in time.

The members of my guard were all strange to me but one, who got drunk, and I was afraid to trust any of them. I told them to go to bed. I would watch all night. The prisoners slept on the floor at one end. I sat up with my revolver handy at the other, as far away from them as I could get, lest they make an attempt to rush me. I took a knife away from Williamson at Bismarck, at Fargo, and at Omaha; he always begged for them. The others would steal hairpins on the train with which to unlock their handcuffs. I took them away at every stop. I handcuffed them, four together, in addition to shackling them, two and two, when going through crowded stations. It took a week, but we finally all got to the military prison. I got my receipt for them.

Later, Williamson cut a companion with a shoe knife in the shoe shop and was then put in the Federal Prison at Leavenworth, where he committed suicide. He never carried out his threat to come "up the creek" (Missouri River) to take care of me when his time was up.

I did well in not trusting my guard, for the sergeant returned to Fort Lincoln, where he was sergeant of the guard in charge of a very important prisoner. He was bribed to allow him to escape, and they both deserted together. They were recaptured up near the British line, brought back, and tried by court-martial. The sergeant, among other things, was sentenced to be drummed out of the service.

Drumming out of the service was a custom inherited from the British Army. The whole command was paraded, and the prisoner under guard brought to the front and center, where all his buttons and insignia were cut off and the order read. Then the prisoner was brought to the right of the line with a placard tied around his neck marked, "Deserter," "Thief," depending upon his crime, and started down the line from right to left, preceded by the drums and fifes which played the tune for this refrain:

Poor old soldier, poor old soldier
Tarred and feathered and sent to hell
Because he would not soldier well!

At the left of the line, he was turned loose and told to get off the post. The sergeant of my guard was drummed out of the service at Fort Lincoln in the summer of 1877. This was the last case of the kind in the American army.

8

The Annual Expedition

Shortly after my return from Fort Leavenworth, preparations were begun for the annual expedition. We crossed the Missouri on May 3 [1877] and went up to Fort Buford at the mouth of the Yellowstone—eleven troops of the Seventh Cavalry and no battery. The grass had not started yet, and the nights were cold. After the first rain the burned prairies were covered with grass, plover running about everywhere in pairs, and the big sickle-billed curlew were innumerable. Their shrill whistle would be heard at all hours of the day. They would frequently hover overhead, stationary enough to be killed with a rifle. The little green and purple anemone was the first flower to make its appearance, but soon the flowers were everywhere in great banks of every hue.

We crossed the Missouri at old Fort Union, then went up the Yellowstone to Sunday Creek near the cantonment [Tongue River Cantonment] of logs with dirt roofs, where General Miles had wintered with the Fifth Infantry.[1] I went from here with my captain, H[enry] J. Nowlan, and his Troop I up the Yellowstone, crossing above the mouth of the Big Horn, then up the Big Horn to the mouth of the Little Big Horn, where the Fifteenth Infantry had come to begin construction of Fort Custer. Here we met Colonel Mike

1. Miles's founding of the two nearby establishments, Tongue River Cantonment and later Fort Keogh, figures significantly in Greene, *Yellowstone Command*, 57, 73, 77, 155.

[Michael V.] Sheridan, military secretary to his brother, the general. He was to go with us to get the bones of Custer and all his officers whose bodies were recognized, except Crittenden, whose father wished him to be buried where he fell—he lies there yet. Custer is buried at West Point, Keogh at Auburn, New York, and the others at Fort Leavenworth, Kansas, where tablets to their memory were placed by the Seventh Cavalry in the post chapel. Captain Nowlan was a close friend of Captain Keogh, both Irishmen, and he loved the government horse Paddy, ridden by Keogh up to the fight, when he changed to Comanche.

We borrowed a skiff here and swam the horses and mules across the Big Horn, then at the June rise and ice-cold from the melting of the snow in the mountains and very swift. The horses were towed by their lariats, six at a time, across the Big Horn behind the skiff. The lariats were thrown loose near the opposite shore to facilitate catching the horses on landing. Nowlan's orderly failed to take off the iron picket pins of Paddy and his own horse, and the current wound the ropes around the legs of both horses in an inextricable snarl, drawing the head of the orderly's horse under the water and drowning him. The current here, twenty feet deep, carried both horses up against a cutbank, where it swerved in near the mouth of the Little Big Horn, right against the bank. I ran down and caught Paddy's headstall, wrapping my legs around a stump and was nearly pulled apart by the current, hauling on the two horses until some men came up and relieved me. I was very angry at the orderly for his neglect and ordered him to swim down and cut his dead horse loose. He began to cry, saying he could not swim. Nobody else wanted to volunteer. Since it was impossible to order anybody into such a place lest he be unable to swim well enough and be drowned, I had to strip and go down myself.

The water was ice-cold and dark below with mud, so that nothing could be seen. I first cut the dead horse loose and let him go. Then I had to go down nine times alongside of Paddy in the darkness to cut him free from the knotted and tangled lariat that tied his hind legs together and fastened in some way his front legs. He was held up by his headstall with no footing below. Every now and then he would make spasmodic efforts with all four feet to get a footing, and this was extremely dangerous in the darkness, but finally all the tangles were cut away. He was eased down to the mouth of the Little Big Horn and led out, none the worse for his experience.

The horse of one of the men went down with the current and landed on a little island in the Big Horn. The man swam over and got him and brought him back. Many years afterward, he wrote asking me to get him a Medal of Honor for his conduct in getting that horse. He said he was exhausted before reaching the island and had already commended his soul to God, fully expecting to drown when he struck a bar and waded out. He said, "What the lieutenant done was noble, but what I done was heroic." But the hard-boiled medal board to which his letter was referred would have none of him.

◆ ◆ ◆

We picked up Colonel Sheridan and all the Crow scouts that had gone with Custer the year before, went out fifteen miles to the battlefield, and were there on June 25, exactly a year after the fight.[2] The valley was a different sight. Whereas the year before it had been thick with dust from drought and the trampling of innumerable hoofs, now the grass grew luxuriantly, higher than the stirrups, and flowers were everywhere.

Nowlan had a chart he had made the year before when he was quartermaster for General Terry. The chart showed where each officer was buried. A piece of a lodgepole about five feet long was driven at the head. As both pole and chart were marked with the same Roman figures, it was easy to find them all. Nowlan and Sheridan worked all the morning, while I kept the camp. I was to go out to work in the afternoon, but the work was finished sooner than expected. I went out with a detachment to bury all the others [the enlisted men] I could find. There was no time to dig deep graves, and I was told to cover the bones made up into little piles where they were lying. This I did, but the soil was like sugar, and I have no doubt the first rain liquefied it and exposed the bones later. We had neither the force nor the time to rebury the whole command in deep graves as we were obliged to join the main command.

We left about noon next day for the Big Horn River. I went out to count the sites of the Sioux lodges and had counted more than fifteen hundred when I had to stop and leave with the troop. There were very many willow wickiups in addition occupied by Sioux, who were out there from the agencies without their families. The lodges were crowded with sometimes four and five men in one. It was said there were nearer seven thousand men than six thousand in the various villages.[3]

2. Actually the Sheridan party reached the battlefield on July 2. Greene, *Stricken Field*, 22–24.

3. All students of the Battle of the Little Big Horn ultimately engage in the exercise of estimating the number of Indian warriors that Custer faced. Obviously, the "sites" of Indian lodges meant that Scott used evidence of tipi circles and/or campfires, not lodges, in his count, remnants of which may have predated

Shortly after leaving the neighborhood of the battlefield, the Crow scouts rushed in, saying that the Sioux were out there thicker than the grass on the ground. Half Yellowface [Yellow Face] and Curly had run off to the camp of the infantry at the site of Fort Custer, afraid of another Custer disaster. We squared off at each other, getting ready to fight, until it was discovered through the glass that there was a cavalry officer among the Sioux. We soon got together and found that it was Captain [Calbraith P.] Rodgers of the Fifth Cavalry with a large band of Sioux and Arapaho scouts, who had taken some packtrains to General Miles at [the] Tongue River and was on his way back to the [North] Platte [River]. After a little talk we left him, continuing our march to the Big Horn.

We recrossed the Big Horn in a skiff, swimming the stock again, and next day marched to the Yellowstone. Two days before, the Crows had killed one thousand head of buffalo in the Big Horn Valley, above where Hardin [Montana] now stands. There is today a bridge across the Big Horn, and from this bridge last year I pointed out to Mrs. Scott where I had had to cut the ropes from Paddy. It was six hundred miles from the railway when it occurred, and Mrs. Scott, then a young girl at Fort Lincoln, never expected to see that country.

The Great Crow camp was at the mouth of the Big Horn, composed of all the Mountain and River Crows, together with fifteen thousand horses. They had been held there by General Miles for a steamboat to take them over the Yellowstone and give them rations and ammunition. The thousands of buffalo and horses had tramped the valley into dust, and the verdure was all gone.

Our transportation was very short, and I had only a little bit of a tent of white canvas, which let the sun through and burned my face. When left open, it filled with flies. When shut, the heat was unbearable. Every little puff of wind would fill it with dust.

I wandered into the huge buffalo skin lodge of Iron Bull, head chief of the Crows, passing at once into a new world. The hide lodge cover was well smoked from the fire, and the sun could not penetrate. There was a dim religious light inside that discouraged the flies. Beds of buffalo robes were all

---

the fight. His ratio of four to five men per lodge also was high. See Paul, "Counting Indians," 27. For more on estimates of Indian fighting strength at the Little Big Horn, see Anderson, foreword to *Crazy Horse Surrender Ledger*, xii–xiii.

around the wall, and the floor was swept clean as the palm of one's hand. The old man, attired only in his breechclout, was lying on his back in bed, crooning his war songs and shaking his medicine rattle. He was the picture of comfort in that cool, dark lodge. I said to him, "Brother, I want to come and stay in here with you until we leave." He and Mrs. Iron Bull made me very welcome.[4] Theirs was the largest and finest lodge I have ever seen. The cover of twenty-five skins was in two pieces. The poles were twenty-five feet long and five inches in diameter. It took six horses to drag them.

The Crows crossed the Yellowstone in a steamboat before we could and went down the river. We crossed some days after, swimming the stock as before. One of our fine mules got loose will all his harness on his back. We saw him carried down by the current out of our sight around a bend of the river and bade him good-by, never expecting to see him again, but three days afterward we found him peacefully grazing out in the middle of a river bottom, far below, with all his harness intact.

We had a very unpleasant hailstorm on Froze-to-Death Creek, with hailstones one and a half inches in diameter, and there was great to-do to prevent our horses from getting away.[5] When struck in the head by hailstones, they think they are being beaten and become frantic. The year before, some of the horses had got away in a hailstorm, with saddles, bridles, and carbines, and were never seen again.

This storm was very general in the Northwest, the hailstones breaking more than a thousand panes of glass at Fort Lincoln and destroying the gardens, but the greatest damage was caused on Porcupine Creek, where the Crows were camped. We passed through there next day and found that the Crows had lost seven hundred horses, some of which had stampeded over a high bluff into the Yellowstone. Their dead bodies floated down the river past Fort Keogh for days. Many horses and colts were killed, where they stood, by chunks of ice larger than half a brick caused by the freezing together of several large hailstones in the upper air.

We went on down the river and joined the Seventh Cavalry on Sunday Creek. The whole of the Northwest seemed very peaceable, and the talk of the Seventh Cavalry was that we should soon go back to Fort Lincoln. Everybody built sunshades over their tents and generally made themselves comfortable.

4. Iron Bull was well known for his hospitality. Hoxie, *Parading through History*, 83.

5. This hailstorm was described in detail in Scott, *Yellowstone Denied*, 137–38.

I went over to Fort Keogh, the old log cantonment, several times and took dinner with my classmate [Oscar F.] Long of the Fifth Infantry, as well as with Captain and Mrs. [Frank D. and Alice B.] Baldwin and General and Mrs. [Mary Hoyt Sherman] Miles.

While here, Generals Sherman, Sheridan, and Terry came out.[6] One day a telegram arrived, telling of the killing of my classmate Sevier [M.] Rains of the First Cavalry, with fifteen of his men, by Nez Percé Indians, far on the other side of the Rocky Mountains in Idaho.[7] I had little dreamed that those Indians hundreds of miles away would ever affect me.

General Miles sent for me soon after and said that there were Sioux war parties from Sitting Bull's camp in Canada operating over on the Musselshell and directed me to take ten men and thirty-five Northern Cheyenne scouts and go over and see what they were doing.

Among the Cheyennes were Two Moons, Little Chief, Hump, Black Wolf, Ice (or White Bull), Brave Wolf, and White Bear—some of the cream of the Northern Cheyennes who had fought against Custer the year before and had surrendered to General Miles from the hostile camps but recently.[8] My friends cheerfully advised me not to go with them, saying that they had just surrendered and that they had only to shoot me and run over the Canadian border to Sitting Bull, where they could not be punished. If I went with them, the chances were I would not come back. But I never felt that way toward them. They were all keen, athletic young men, tall and lean and brave, and I admired them as real specimens of manhood more than any body of men I have ever seen before or since. They were perfectly adapted to their environment and knew just what to do in every emergency and when to do it, without any confusion or lost motion. Their poise and dignity were superb. No royal person ever had more assured manners. I watched their every movement and learned lessons from them that later saved my life many times on the prairie.

We did not, however, see any Indians or a recent trail. After our return Captain Benteen was sent with his Troop H over to the head of the Minipusa or Dry Fork of the Missouri on the same errand. A number of us were allowed to go with him to run buffalo. We were sitting one day on top of a

6. The visit was in July 1877. Greene, *Yellowstone Command*, 223–24.

7. Rains was killed on July 3. Greene, *Nez Perce Summer*, 60–66.

8. Two Moon(s) surrendered in March 1877. Greene, *Yellowstone Command*, 192–97.

high peak that overlooked the country in every direction for twenty miles on all sides. Everywhere we looked, the prairie was full of buffalo. Benteen thought that we could see at least three hundred thousand buffalo in one view, and, if we could see that many, there were many thousands more out of sight in the ravines and hollows. I have ridden in after years through a pasture of Indian Territory thirty miles square, where one hundred thousand counted cattle had been turned loose, and did not see more than five hundred, the others being hidden away out of sight.

While sitting on the bank of the Yellowstone one day waiting for the ferry, I heard the jingle of sleigh bells on the trail coming down from the tableland above. Soon some Northern Cheyenne came down and asked if they might cross with me on the ferry. I noticed an extra horse with a bloody scalp tied to its bit, and, asking whose horse it was, learned that it belonged to White Bear, who had been separated from the others on the tableland above, where he was attacked by seven Sioux. He got into some brush, killed and scalped one Sioux, and took his horse. The others, not daring to go into the brush after him, got tired and went away, leaving him alone.

White Bear had a great scar across his face that made him look very savage. He was sitting at the opening of a skin lodge in the Cheyenne village, inside which some medicine ceremonies were going on one day, when I came along with Tom [Thomas Ewing] Sherman, whose father General Sherman had asked me to show his son the Cheyenne camp. Tom started to go into the lodge, where he was not wanted lest he "break" the medicine going on inside. Not understanding the refusal, he persisted in trying to enter until White Bear flourished a knife about a yard long in his face. The combination of the knife and White Bear's face was more than enough for him.

9

After the Nez Percés

I had no sooner got rested on Sunday Creek [in 1877] than I was ordered to take a wagon train to Fort Custer. The empty wagons were each hauled by a six-mule team, the driver riding the off-wheel mule, managing the team with a jerk line, a long single rein. I put my saddle in the wagon and drove the lead team for a hundred and ten miles so as to learn to drive with the jerk line. This knowledge has since stood me in good stead many times.

Coming back with one wagon and a few men below Porcupine Creek on the Yellowstone, I cut across a high prairie and saw someone riding alone at a distance. Such things had to be inquired into in those days. Getting near, I was astounded to meet an officer of the Seventh Cavalry out there all by himself. We sat down together on the prairie to exchange the latest news, our horses being held at a little distance by my orderly.[1] I asked him what he was doing there alone and where he was going. He said that Lieutenant [Gustavus C.] Doane of the Second Cavalry, with DeRudio of the Seventh and E Troop, were out of sight on the river bottom, going to the Judith Gap [Montana] to fight Nez Percés. He was going to join them in a few minutes. He said the Seventh Cavalry was still on Sunday Creek, and he bemoaned his fate in having had to give up a poker game and come away.

1. Scott referred to his orderly later by his surname only; this was Seventh cavalryman John McKenna. Wagner, *Participants in the Battle*, 67.

It flashed on me that since that poker game was so dear to his heart, I might suggest a temporary transfer, which would let me go to the Judith Gap and let him go back to his game. The orderly was holding the horses about thirty feet away, and I called, "McKenna, how would you like to go and fight the Nez Percés?"

He answered quickly, "I'm wid yez."

It was soon arranged for me to go down to the regiment on Sunday Creek and get the authority and catch up with them. Their mess needed a bottle of walnut pickles and a tin bucket, which I promised to bring if I could get away.

We took the trot and went twenty-five miles, camping opposite the old cantonment on the bluffs above the Yellowstone. McKenna went down to the regiment twelve miles to get permission to exchange and bring back my extra horse, while I went across to get the permission of General Miles, who then commanded the District of the Yellowstone. McKenna returned with the permission next morning. I got the walnut pickles and tin bucket and sent my clothing and bedding roll to the regiment, intending to exchange it for the other fellow's roll as I had no other transportation than our saddle horses. But I never saw my property again—my overcoat, underclothing, boots, extra clothing, and six silk buffalo robes I had picked out of four thousand robes that a trader had bartered from the Crows at the mouth of the Big Horn for six cups of brown sugar apiece, holding his big thumb all the time in the cup. He charged ten dollars apiece for a blanket, and I traded my blankets for robes—and never saw any of them again.

We took the trail and trotted forty-five miles to the Big Porcupine and reached camp as they were sitting down to dinner. About the middle of dinner, we saw a steamboat coming down around the bend and fired a shot across her bows. She turned into the bank, the officer led his horse aboard, and I was not to see him for three months during which I traveled more than a thousand miles.

We went up to the mouth of Froze-to-Death Creek, where eleven Crows had frozen sometime in the long past.[2] We fed the last of the oats here. Grain is very bad for the morals of a horse or mule, though good for his body and strength. It will seduce the morals of any mount, no matter how reliable he

2. The "Froze-to-Death" place name has been attached to a mountain, a plateau, a lake, and this particular creek within the Beartooth Mountains of south-central Montana.

may be otherwise. Next morning we marched forty-five miles up Froze-to-Death Creek, one of the most exhausting marches I ever made. The creek was dry above, and the heat was terrific. The buffalo had eaten off all the grass. We passed antelope that stood and let us go by not more than thirty yards away, when the wind was right, for all animals are tame when running among the buffalo. They were probably unable to distinguish us from buffalo by sight but were exceedingly quick to get away when the wind was toward them. We reached a small lake up on the divide, about six inches deep, where we watered the stock and took care of the animals, but we were all so exhausted that we lay down on the ground and passed the night without cooking dinner or making camp.

The next morning seven pack mules were reported missing. It was thought that some Indians had run them off, but I said that I knew where they were. They had gone back to the Yellowstone where we last fed grain. The sergeant was sent to look for them, and sure enough there they were, howling for grain. The poor sergeant had to make that grueling march with his detachment three times, all on account of the grain fed on the Yellowstone.

We got breakfast and went over to the big Crow camp then at the Big Bend of the Musselshell, where we remained for some time, moving camp with them once a week to find grass for their immense horse herd. They ran buffalo once a week with savage ceremony. All Mountain and River bands of Crows were in that village of more than three thousand persons and needed a great deal of meat. Those Crows were rich in everything an Indian required to be happy. They wore wonderful dresses of primitive style, buckskin ornamented with beads, porcupine quills, and ermine. A thousand dollars would not pay for one of those costumes new.

The camp had meat drying everywhere. Everybody was carefree and joyous in a way we do not comprehend in this civilized day. All the life of a nation was going on there before our eyes. Here the head chiefs were receiving ambassadors from another tribe. Following the sound of drums, one would come upon a great gathering for a war dance, heralding an expedition to fight the Sioux. Or one came to a lodge where a medicine man was doctoring a patient to the sound of a drum and rattle. Elsewhere a large crowd surrounded a game of ring and spear on which members of the tribe were betting everything they owned; the loser lost without dispute or quiver of an eyelid. In another place a crowd was witnessing a horserace with twenty-five horses starting off at the first trial and no jockeying back and forth to wear out the opponent's nerve. The stakes were two piles of goods, one the property of each side, the victors to take both and divide the winnings. All day and far into the night, there was something happening of intense interest to me.

We were once sitting at dinner when we heard a great shooting of guns and thought it must be an attack by the Sioux. We all rushed out to see. It was the return of a war party with Sioux scalps taken along the Powder River. They dashed into camp, firing off their guns, and their wives and sweethearts ran out to receive them with the utmost joy, while a wail for the dead went up from their relatives.

I was completely fascinated with the life in that great village of skin lodges, the color, the jollity, the goodwill and kindness encountered everywhere. Getting into camp sometimes before the train, I would pick out our camp, unsaddle, put my rifle belt of ammunition on it, with field glasses, and go visiting all around the village, without seeing my property for hours in the midst of that camp of more than three thousand wild Indians.

The Crows were very primitive in those days. All they had of the white man's manufacture was a few blankets, beads, guns, and some saddles made by Main & Winchester of [San Francisco] California. Many rode saddles of their own make, but there was not a wagon nor a white man's suit of clothes among them. My rifle, ammunition, and field glasses would have been a fortune for a Crow, but I never lost so much as a cartridge in that village, although I left my belongings unguarded for hours. I wonder how long one of their beaded fire bags would last if left on the pavement in one of our large cities.

The buffalo runs were under control of the soldiers, who had the management of the whole village.[3] Buffalo runs were allowed only on certain days agreed upon among the chiefs. The herds were carefully watched by the young soldiers to note the direction they were moving, and none was allowed to shoot a gun on an off day or disturb the herds, under pain of being "soldiered," i.e., punished by the soldiers. If men had been allowed to shoot any time they wished, the buffalo would soon have been driven far away from the village, and the people would have gone hungry. It was a severe

3. The Crow word for "soldier" was *issachi*, and Scott's explanation of these camp marshals revealed an extension of responsibilities beyond simple military ones that the word implies. The Sioux tribe employed the *akicita*, a similar set of male enforcers of good order.

punishment for the aged, crippled, and wounded to have to move frequently to keep up with the buffalo. In order not to frighten the animals and prevent them from going far away, the soldiers would select a small bunch far from the main herd to avoid alarming them. Everybody who wanted meat would go out under the direction of the soldiers and drive them away so as not to scare the others and would kill every one if possible.

Sometimes a family would get out of meat, and the man would get stubborn. The soldiers would see him tying up several pack ponies in front of his lodge. On an off day that would mean that he was going after meat. A soldier would quietly cut the ponies' ropes and drive them out of camp, while the owner was inside his lodge. This would put him in a fury. He would then take his packs somewhere out of sight and saddle and get out of camp, thinking he was unseen. He would kill an antelope or buffalo, and the soldiers would come up out of a ravine, break his gun, and maybe slit his lodge cover into ribbons and beat him with a quirt. This was not the act of an individual but the act of the tribe for the protection of its food, a tribal punishment, and was called soldiering—to soldier a man. To soldier-kill was not a murder but a tribal act.

I once knew of an officer sent out on the range with a large band of Indians who were out to make meat. He went with them to prevent complications with white men. He was told not to hunt on an off day, but he announced that he was the commander there and would do as he pleased and would not be told by Indians what he might or might not do. He started out on an off day to kill an antelope and, seeing one, first looked all around to make certain he was alone. He saw no one, but, as soon as he fired at the antelope, Indians began coming out of ravines, seemingly from under the ground. They gave him a good beating over the back with their bows and told him that a second offense would mean his death.

This action was far different from that of Lieutenant G[ouverneur] K. Warren in 1855, who went on an exploring expedition west of the Black Hills of Dakota. He was met by a band of Sioux under their chief Bear's Rib, who told him that they were holding the buffalo between the Black Hills and the Big Horn Mountains until their robes were in proper condition, that the buffalo were their shelter, food, and clothing, and, if he went up there, he would likely drive away and scatter their winter food. Bear's Rib said he was a friend of the white men but did not believe he could control his warriors if their food were interfered with. Warren replied that those were their buffalo, and he certainly would not interfere with them but would turn back, going through to the east side of the Black Hills, thence north, and out of the way of the buffalo. If all white men had been as considerate of the Indian as Lieutenant Warren, we would never have had such bloody clashes.[4]

Lieutenant Doane, although of the Second Cavalry, with only five men of his own troop, was put in command by General Miles of DeRudio's Troop E of the Seventh Cavalry.[5] He had been with the "lost tribes of the Second Cavalry," the squadron stationed at Fort Ellis, Montana, ever since 1868, and he was a thorough plainsman, able to do everything anybody else could do on the prairie except interpret.[6] I modeled myself on him as a soldier, watched him carefully, and learned from him how to set up an *aparejo* [packsaddle] and to throw the diamond so that, if the packing should be delayed, we two would pitch in to help pack ourselves and get the command out of camp in a hurry. There was no delay, for no one loitered where we were in the train. We could put our hands to anything and show others how it was done. I was by that time an interpreter in a small way, knowing enough to get about, but not yet able to interpret in council.

We left the Crows on the Musselshell and marched up the Swimming Woman Creek toward the Snowy Mountains and the Judith Gap. We spent two nights of clear moonlight on the banks of the Swimming Woman. Nearing the Judith Gap next day with Jack [Collins John] Baronett, the scout, a blacksmith, and one other whose name I forget, we were about two miles ahead of the troop. Jack looked up and said, "There the Nez Percés are now!" We could see a party of twenty Indians in the gap.[7]

The blacksmith said, "Let's charge them!" I did not want to charge them a little bit, but I was very green and thought that if a blacksmith was willing to charge, it would not do for a second lieutenant to demur. So we galloped right at them, revolvers drawn. They did not seem at all disturbed. When we

4. Warren encountered Bear's Rib in the Black Hills in 1857, not 1855. Hanson, *Little Chief's Gatherings*, 165–66.

5. For another perspective of the travels of Company E, Seventh Cavalry during the campaign, see Scott, *Yellowstone Denied*, 158–73.

6. Scott's favorable opinion of Doane appeared early in the biography by Bonney and Bonney, *Battle Drums and Geysers*, xxii–xxiii.

7. Greene's *Nez Perce Summer* serves as the standard narrative for this Indian war and the main source for identifying the persons, places, and events Scott documented in this chapter. Conversely, Scott's *Some Memories of a Soldier* provided some essential, reminiscent details for Greene's comprehensive account.

got almost within shooting distance, Jack called out, "They're River Crows!" Had they been Nez Percés, as we thought at first, they would have killed us as dead as Julius Caesar, which would have served us right for being such fools.

Two railways now run through the Judith Gap, and, passing through on the train lately, I had the pleasure of pointing out to Mrs. Scott the place I once nearly lost seven years' growth from fright, while charging twenty men with four.

When we were camped in the gap, watching for Nez Percés to come along, an Indian came in with a despatch giving us the news of the battle of the Big Hole, far westward from us, between Joseph, the Nez Percé chief, and General [John] Gibbon with the Seventh Infantry.[8]

Doane had told us where the Nez Percés were going to go a month and a half before they actually went. He knew that country and the habits of the Indians so well that he could predict everything they did. He saw that our supplies were too low to wait for Indians to travel all that distance from the Big Hole [battlefield], and so we went into Fort Ellis to reshoe and refit. Colonel [Jirah Isham] Allen and Doane had been trying to get up a Crow war party to go with us to strike the Nez Percés somewhere west of Fort Ellis. The Crows refused to say anything except that "the Nez Percé heart was Crow, and the Crow heart was Nez Percé," showing their friendship for their own color. Despairing of getting any Crow scouts, we started off without them.

At our camp that night, we heard many small parties coming singing on the prairie. The next morning there were two hundred Crows in camp, ready to go to war with us. It was their custom to rendezvous at the first camp out at night and to come singing across the prairie so we would not mistake them for enemies and fire on them in the darkness.

As soon as we could refit and draw rations at Fort Ellis, we loaded a number of wagons and started for the Yellowstone Park, where Doane said he was going to intercept the Indians.[9] We took our packtrain also, intending to send our wagons back from Gardiner's River, for there were no roads beyond.

8. The Battle of the Big Hole, a stinging defeat of Gibbon's command, lasted through August 9–10, 1877, and allowed for Chief Joseph to begin his epic flight across Montana Territory.

9. Doane and Scott left Fort Ellis on August 27. Greene, *Nez Perce Summer*, 192.

The Crows began to drop out before we had gone far, parties leaving in the night, each morning seeing fewer and fewer, until we had only twenty left, who stayed with us to the end.

Going through the second and third canyons that lead down to Cinnabar Mountain with its red streak, called the Devil's Slide, we could see a column of smoke far in the distance.[10] Soon the Crows came rushing in back behind the troops, saying that the Nez Percés in front were as thick as the grass on the ground. They threw off their saddles, painted their faces, put on their warbonnets, and came rushing to the front again, riding bareback. Soon Jack Baronett and Colonel Allen came back, reporting that the smoke we saw was at [Sterling] Henderson's ranch on the Yellowstone, set afire by the Nez Percés [on August 31]. Jack announced his intention of going back there, and I announced mine of going with him and asked Doane's permission. He said I could go if I would take ten men. The troop would come along as fast as it could behind. I told him I didn't want ten men; that was just enough to get us all killed as Rains was killed by these same Indians with fifteen men in July. They were not enough to make a fight with, and I could not leave them, whereas Jack and I could at the first sign separate in the brush, where Indians would not follow and get away. But Doane said, "You can't go without them."

"Get them out then," I said, "in a hurry," and changed my saddle to my best horse, ready to go. We were away in less than ten minutes, leaving the troop to follow with the train.

It seemed that there were three men and a boy staying in Henderson's ranch on the Yellowstone near the mouth of Gardiner's River. Two had gone down to the Yellowstone to fish, three hundred yards from the house, leaving one man lying on the bed and the boy working about the place. After a while the man arose, walked to the door, and looked up the road. Seeing eight Nez Percés Indians charging down toward the house, he called to the boy, and both seized all the rifles and ammunition and ran to the other men fishing. All hid behind the bank, watching. The Indians came up behind the house, got the horses out of the corral, set fire to the house, and went back to join ten others who had stopped, watching from the hillside. Then the eighteen went back, driving the horses up the river. The white men put us on the

10. The Devil's Slide, located in present Park County, Montana, received its distinctive name in 1870 from white explorers of the Yellowstone River valley.

Indian trail at once, and we pushed them hard enough to get back nineteen horses. We rounded a point and at [James] McCartney's cabin in a side gulch found a white man [Richard Dietrich] lying dead at the door, not yet cold. He had been standing in the doorway, looking out, when one of the Indians we were chasing rounded the point and shot him. He had plunged forward on his face and been shot again, the bullet going the length of his body.

The trail led past the base of an extinct geyser cone called the Liberty Cap, near where the hotel is now.[11] I proposed first to follow it and bury the dead man afterward, but Jack, who had spent his life in that country and knew it better than I, would not hear of it. He said we could be ambushed from a nearby ridge at twilight, and we must get right back, lest a larger force get us all. It was too dark anyway to follow the trail. I depended largely on Jack's superior experience and judgment, and we went back to find the troop camped on an irrigating ditch in which we could lie with access to water and make a good fight if attacked by a large force.

That night Doane told me to take twenty men next morning to go to Baronett's Bridge and see if the Indians had crossed there and to set fire to the grass coming back to burn the Indians out of the Yellowstone Valley. The Crows could not be induced to go ahead, and I paid one named "Full up to His Throat" to ride with me, thinking he would be apt to hear or see something in one of the copses I might miss along the trail and give us warning. He rode along by my side every day for more than a month.

They wanted me to go on the trail down Blacktail Deer Creek, but I refused to follow any trail, knowing that, if the Indians were there, they would hide in the quaking aspen copses along the trail and give us a blizzard of bullets as we came along. We did not go over a ridge until we were assured all was safe beyond. With great difficulty in getting the horses down and up, we crossed the deep, narrow box canyon on Blacktail Deer Creek, where there was no trail. The edge of the canyon was held by ten men to hold back any Indians, who though unseen by us were doubtless watching us all the time, to keep them from coming up on the edge and killing us all like rats. The other ten went down with me, and we climbed out on the other side. Then we held the canyon edge for the others. I felt very uneasy at putting the canyon between me and the command but had to carry out my orders.

11. Liberty Cap, so named by 1871 explorers of the future Yellowstone National Park and part of the Mammoth Hot Springs complex, is a geothermal feature known as a "hot spring cone."

After crossing the canyon, we went on to the bridge, which was still intact. It had been built by Jack Baronett at the mouth of the East Fork of the Yellowstone and was the first bridge ever put over the Yellowstone River. We set fire to the grass as ordered and started back to camp, having seen no Indians. There were Indians there, however, even if we could not see them, for we picked up two of General Samuel D. Sturgis's scouts, [John J.] Groff and [J. S.] Leonard, who had come across the mountains and were going down the river, traveling on the trail I would not use in order to avoid just what happened to them. They were fired at from one of the quaking aspen groves. Their Warm Spring[s] Indian boy was killed with all the horses and Groff shot through the neck. Groff and Leonard had scattered into the brush. We took them into camp with us, where the surgeon dressed Groff's wound. Later they were both killed by the Nez Percés.

I found on my return to camp that night that a party of our men had gone to McCartney's cabin at Mammoth Hot Springs to bury the man there—named Dietrich from Helena, Montana—and had seen Indians following along behind the crest of the divide, watching me all day.

That little chase the day before after the eighteen Nez Percés had momentous consequences we little dreamed of and surely never intended since with us it was mostly a lark. None of us had thought that with ten men we could beat the Indian force that had nearly overcome the Seventh Infantry. We had only wanted to drive in their advance guard and maybe get back the horses, if we were quick enough, and we actually were quick enough to get back nineteen. It was months afterward that I learned what had really resulted.

Chief Joseph, on various occasions since, has repeatedly told me that they had intended to go out to the buffalo country down the Yellowstone Valley, leaving the mountains where the river turns northeast, now the site of the town of Livingston, Montana. But they were diverted by seeing us in front. They had been surprised by General Gibbon and the Seventh Infantry in their front at Big Hole and had caused General Gibbon to fortify after he was shot in the leg. They would have killed the entire command, corralled as it was away from water, if General [Oliver O.] Howard, following their trail, had not raised the siege. The Nez Percés had enough to think about with General Howard on their trail, and they did not wish to encounter any more troops on their front, with the risk of being caught between two forces.

The eighteen we chased back were Joseph's scouts, feeling far in his advance, who returned and reported meeting troops down the river. No one could imagine that we would chase them that way unless we had a strong support behind us. The Yellowstone Valley here is hemmed in between high mountains with little room to maneuver. If both ends of the valley were closed by troops, the Indians could never hope to save their women, children, and horses. So, instead of trying to go on down the river, as originally intended, they crossed the Yellowstone at the Mud Geysers just below the outlet of the Yellowstone Lake and went up Pelican Creek, across the mountains and down Clark's Fork of the Yellowstone, which they recrossed at the mouth of Canyon Creek, just above Billings. This change from crossing at Livingston put them more than a day's march nearer General Miles at Tongue River, thus losing them several days, without which it would not have been possible for General Miles to overtake them as he brilliantly did within a day's march of the British line. White Bird, one of their chiefs, escaped Miles, finding shelter with Sitting Bull across the border. I was first told of this by Joseph in 1877, and his information was confirmed by a signed statement obtained by the Nez Percé agent at Nespelem, Washington.[12]

I will speak of Miles later in this narrative, for I was to know him better some years afterward, but chronologically more than passing reference belongs to him at this juncture. Then colonel of the Fifth Infantry, commanding the District of the Yellowstone, his capture of the Nez Percés was one of the most brilliant feats of arms ever accomplished by the American army, considering the immense distance he had to travel through primeval country. He was a remarkably manly and handsome officer. The first time I had seen him was the summer before at Fort Keogh, sitting on a cracker box on the north side of the Yellowstone, whittling a stick, where he called me "Scott," which caused me to swell visibly with pride. We once rode together from Fort Buford to Fort Stevenson, where he took an ambulance and a small escort from my troop and drove the seventy-five miles into Bismarck in one day.

When we returned to camp that night, Doane put a cordon of Cossack posts around the camp.[13] DeRudio had the one on the trail. We were awakened in the middle of the night by a great commotion, and DeRudio came in, bringing a Negro [Benjamin Stone] he had caught coming down the trail,

12. Greene's later conclusions on the significance of this "chase back" differ from Scott's. Greene, *Nez Perce Summer*, 192–93, 436n88.

13. A "Cossack post," in the military parlance of the time, consisted of four men.

each taking the other for a Nez Percé in the darkness. A clash was only prevented because both heard some English.

The Negro told us that he and Dietrich were from Helena and had been with a party in the Yellowstone, ignorant of any Indians in the vicinity. The Nez Percés had surprised their camp in the Firehole [River] basin, captured a man and his wife [George F. and Emma Cowan], with her sister and brother [Ida and Frank D. Carpenter] from Helena, and were bringing them along the trail, all mounted. Reaching the foot of a steep hill not far from Mary's Lake on the divide, an Indian rode up and shot the husband with a small pistol, striking him on the head with a soft bullet that flattened and failed to penetrate the skull. He fell off his horse. His wife took his head in her lap but was dragged away. She believed her husband dead. He lay for a long time in a faint, but, coming to, he rose on his elbow. A passing Indian shot him again, making a wound in his hip, throwing him into another faint. When he came to, the Indians had all gone by. He traveled on his hands and knees for a while and then was picked up by Howard's scouts. He and I [later] occupied opposite corners of a room on Boteler's ranch [of the brothers Frederick, Henry, and Phillip Boteler], where I was sick with pleurisy for a while.

His [Cowan's] wife was taken forward with her brother and sister until Chief Joseph sent his young men back to take mules from General Howard, and then Joseph generously used the opportunity to give the man [Frank Carpenter] and his two sisters horses and let them go home. They reached Helena safely, the woman under the impression that her husband was dead. She was overjoyed to find that he was alive at Boteler's ranch on the Yellowstone and came after him in a carriage.

But Dietrich had escaped from the Nez Percés and came with the Negro to McCartney's cabin. The boy hid in the grass and eventually reached Virginia City [Montana]. Citizens came to McCartney's to get the wounded man and wanted Dietrich to return with them, but he refused, fearing to leave the hiding boy alone. So they left him. The eighteen Nez Percés were later seen approaching, and Dietrich and the Negro climbed a tree back of the house and saw the war party of eighteen loot the cabin and go down the river to Henderson's. Dietrich got tired and climbed down out of the tree, leaving the Negro still there. When I chased the eighteen back, they came suddenly around a point and killed Dietrich in the doorway. The Negro remained in the tree until night. Then, starting for Helena afoot, he ran into DeRudio in the middle of the night and finally reached home in safety.

No Indians ever waged war as humanely as the Nez Percés.

We planned that night to go forward to meet the Nez Percés the next day, not knowing that our presence in the Yellowstone Valley had caused them to leave it at the foot of the lake. Others of our scouts reported Indians up Gardiner's River. A courier, however, brought a despatch from Colonel [Charles C.] Gilbert, Seventh Infantry, ordering us to await his arrival with L Troop, Second Cavalry. General Sherman, who had lately been in the Yellowstone, authorized Colonel Gilbert to take over General Howard's command, if he desired to give it up, since he was now outside the limits of his department. Gilbert arrived next day. Doane begged him with tears in his eyes to go forward the following day, but he refused, saying that he was only trying to reach Howard and did not want to be delayed by a fight and miss him.

If he had gone forward as Doane advised, he would have met Howard that day at Baronett's Bridge, but instead he turned back down the Yellowstone thirty miles to Tom Miner's Creek, up which he went on an old Bannack [Bannock] trail over to and up the West Gallatin [River], striking the Madison [River] eight days after Howard had passed. He had no idea of marching cavalry. Fearing to separate his command, although away from the zone of operations, he camped two troops and two packtrains without grain in a mountain pocket, where there was grass for only half the number. The animals whimpered all night for food, although there was another pocket half a mile away. The animals of that command were starved until they became too weak to carry a man. We piled up twenty-five saddles on the West Gallatin and left them there, unable to transport them, and we sent twenty-five horses down the Madison by easy stages to Fort Ellis to recuperate. Gilbert took Jack Baronett and our best horses, trying to catch up with Howard but never reached him. We started back through the park, traveling slowly down the Yellowstone so that our animals might recuperate.

My horse and my orderly's got too weak to carry us. We made fifty miles over Mount Washburn in two days and a half, walking and leading our horses.[14] One would have to pull a horse uphill, and the other would push and then go back for the other horse. I got caught in my shirtsleeves in a sleet storm on a mountain—in August—and got a bad case of pleurisy. I had a tent fly for shelter, open at both ends, which allowed the sleet and rain

14. Mount Washburn is part of the Washburn Range, which is located within the boundaries of Yellowstone National Park, Wyoming.

to enter. They waited for me one day, my orderly giving me the most tender care. He put his extra socks on my feet and put hot stones at them. We had no wheeled vehicles and had to go on, so I was lifted on my horse and bandaged in the saddle, with my knees almost under my chin. Every step of the horse would stab my lungs like a knife, but we had to travel until we reached Boteler's ranch and could get some food for the men.

Nearing the divide at the head of Trail Creek on the road to Ellis, I saw a mountain sheep drinking about two hundred yards away. He ran up on a point and stopped to look at us. I wriggled out of my bandages and got my rifle from my orderly, who had been carrying it during my illness. I wounded him at the first shot, though he did not move. I was so excited, never having had a chance at a mountain sheep before, that I then missed him twice. He ran about ten feet and fell over dead from the first shot. I felt so elated that it cured me. I straightened up and rode the rest of the thirty miles into Fort Ellis, throwing away my bandages.

10

Buffalo Running

Traveling up the Musselshell one day during this Nez Percé expedition [1877], I was a couple of miles ahead of the troop with several men. Looking across the Musselshell, which ran between perpendicular banks twenty feet high, I saw what I thought was a claybank pony, standing with his head down among the rosebushes.[1] I called out, "There is a lost pony." But it was a magnificent bull elk, which, hearing me call, raised his head out of the rosebushes, showing a beautiful set of antlers, then, running toward me, jumped down into the riverbed, here covered with gravel, and joined a band of eight or ten elk, clattering up the stream. The river is very crooked here, winding from side to side of its valley. I rode out on the prairie to cut off a couple of its bends, then came in again ahead of the elk, dismounted, and waited for them to break out of the brush. A great number came out quite close to me, but they were cows and calves or bulls with small horns, and I let them go until I saw a large bunch break some distance away from me, one splendid set of horns showing above the group. I fired from the ground and turned out of the herd a bull with poor horns. Then I mounted quickly to get the finer bull. In the meantime elk were breaking out all around me,

1. Scott was particularly acquainted with claybank horses since Comanche, the Little Big Horn survivor mentioned earlier in the memoir, was of that dull yellowish color. Lawrence, *His Very Silence Speaks*, 44–48.

and I found myself running in the middle of a large herd of elk. I forced my way up to the great bull and killed him with a revolver and soon got five in all. Then I suddenly found that my saddle had become loose, and I was riding on the horse's haunches uphill and on his neck going down. I stopped to tighten it. The horse was very much excited. By the time I got on him again, the elk were a mile away. Sending for some pack mules, we soon had my kill butchered and meat despatched to the troops. It was very exciting to be running in the middle of a band of six hundred elk.

We got a despatch on the Musselshell, saying that the whole regiment was marching up the Yellowstone about parallel with us, going up the Musselshell probably forty miles away. The regiment stampeded the buffalo, which came over our way in countless numbers, running for dear life. When a big herd came down, going to the river as into the small end of a funnel, they jumped over the bank and down into the river. I dismounted on the bank to kill a calf for supper, but the buffalo, climbing up the bank, separated on both sides of me about ten feet away, a long string of them going past my horse, which was swinging me from side to side, trying to get away in mortal fright. I could not use my gun because the troop was in front of me and the packtrain behind, but they began to shoot into the buffalo from both sides, not seeing that I was among the herd. I howled at them as loud as I could, but the din was so great no one could hear me. After the buffalo had gone by, I expected to see at least a dozen on the ground, but there were none there.

During our visit at the Crow village, wishing to know what a real buffalo horse was like, I got the Crow chiefs arguing as to who had the best buffalo horse in the tribe. The argument waxed hot, but finally it was agreed by the council that Iron Bull had the best buffalo horse. I borrowed it at the next run. He did not have to be fought with like our horses. All he needed was to be pointed at the animal selected. Then he would take one so close that one could put his hand on the buffalo's back if one wished. He would lay alongside "a little abaft the beam," as the sailorman says.

The buffalo is very heavy forward and turns differently from a horse, which has to be pulled up and pivots on his hind feet, while the buffalo pivots on his forefeet like a shot without pulling up. His hind quarters swing around in a flash when his forefeet are planted. If you are too far forward, his head is under your horse's belly, throwing horse and rider twenty feet, with the horse's belly perhaps ripped open. In the running [rutting?] season in July an old bull may stop running and gore and tramp a man who is helpless with a broken leg or other injury. The bull behaves very badly in July, far more so than at any other time.

The Indian used to fight and run buffalo bareback, often with nothing on his horse but a lariat around the lower jaw trailing behind, which made it easier to catch the animal if the rider was thrown. The horse is pointed at the intended victim, and a good buffalo horse will then do everything himself but the shooting and the butchering. As said before, he lays a little abaft the beam, and the rider drives a single arrow in behind the last rib, ranging forward, which skewers many of the interior organs on the arrow. These organs are suspended in the interior by membranes attached to the ribs, which the next jump pulls different ways. The pain is so great that the animal stops where he is. You can continue doing the same thing to others, without fear your previous victims will escape. When you fall behind, you can go back and despatch the wounded one at a time and at your leisure. They won't go away. They will wait for you and will sometimes bleed to death through the lungs. There have been many cases when the arrow, meeting with no bone, has been put clear through the body of a buffalo, to fall on the ground on the other side.

When the pony hears the discharge of bullet or arrow, he sheers away from the animal, which is liable to plant his forefeet and swing his head under the pony if too far forward. The pony may sheer so quickly as to jump out from under one, throwing one to the ground at the mercy of the bull, who is not apt to stop and gore one, unless in July, though this is possible at all times.

A sure-footed pony will usually take you in safety through a prairie dog village full of dog and badger holes. The thing to do as you are running behind the herd is to steer him at the fattest cow you see, judging by the width of her hump, a barren cow if possible, and then trust all to the pony. I rode many of the cream of that herd of fourteen thousand head afterward, and, although I had many falls, horse and all, was never injured, although two Crows were killed among the buffalo while we were with them.

A few guns were used, but most men used a bow and arrow as better suited to the purpose. Ammunition was sold by the traders for exorbitant sums six hundred miles from the railroad. The Indian wanted his cartridges to fight his enemy and never had enough, whereas an arrow could be used many times, or, if lost, could be replaced on the next creek where there was timber. Although I had all the ammunition I wanted, I frequently used the bow and arrow, with which I became very skillful as a boy.

Our cavalry horses were very much afraid of the buffalo, and most of them could not be urged any closer than thirty yards, too far to shoot a bow. We would often shoot a buffalo through with a gun six or eight times without hitting a vital part and have him get away, dying next week at a distant spot. I have known a buffalo to carry fifteen balls without being knocked down.

While we were a couple of miles ahead of the troop, with Jack Baronett, who has a peak in the Yellowstone Park named for him, a discharged blacksmith of the Second Cavalry, Colonel Allen, and some Crows, we dismounted on a high elevation to rest and began to look all around, as was wise to do in those days. Allen took a small pair of glasses out of his waistcoat pocket and looked at the buffalo that covered the country below and beyond us out of sight. Suddenly he exclaimed that he saw a white buffalo. All then took a look through the glasses, and, sure enough, there was something white moving among the buffalo far below us. This threw us into great excitement, for the white buffalo is a rare animal. Possibly one may be found among a hundred thousand black ones.

We adjusted our saddles for a great run, marking the place and our course to it so as to be out of sight and yet have the wind. We lined up on the opposite side of a hill from the white one. When I gave the word, we all came up over the ridge abreast on a fast gallop. I was riding a horse that had won many races in the Seventh Cavalry before I got him and went far ahead of the others. We saw at once then that there were five horses running with the buffalo, one of them white. Nearing a blue roan, I very foolishly put my rope down on him and choked him to a standstill. Having the swiftest horse, I ought to have left the slow one for those that came after and gone for a better horse myself, but, when I thought of this, it was too late. The blue roan had shoes that had not been changed for six or eight months, and the hoofs had grown around them. His heels were so contracted that they were badly split in the cleft.

Forty-nine years afterward in 1926, Mrs. Scott and I were at a convention of Montana pioneers at Fort Benton, and an old fellow came up and asked if I knew him.[2] He was greatly disappointed when I did not. When he told me

2. In 1925 and 1926, Scott actively participated in two great railroad excursions sponsored by the Great Northern Railway. Both times he spoke—in sign language as well as in English—before Indian congresses held at the site of old Fort Union, North Dakota. On July 18, 1926, he met with the Society of Montana Pioneers at Fort Benton. Buck, "Upper Missouri Historical Expedition," 388; Krausnick, "Columbia

his name was Allen, I asked if he still carried that opera glass in his waistcoat pocket to look for white buffalo, which showed that I really knew him. We spent a very pleasant time together until our train left. When I got back east, I found that he had sent me the opera glass in memory of old times. I have it still, nearly fifty years after I had first looked through it on the Musselshell at a white buffalo that was not there.

River Historical Expedition," 244–45. A website—*Streamliner Memories*—has gathered these and other sources relating to these "historical expeditions"; http://streamlinermemories.info/.

11

On the March Again

By the time we had finished reshoeing and refitting at Ellis [1877], orders came for us to go to Fort Benton, the head of navigation on the Missouri, to act as escort to General Terry, going up to interview Sitting Bull in Canada.

We reached Helena, out of food, money, and clothing, and I went to the paymaster, a brother of President Arthur, to get some money as I had not been paid for six months.[1] He told me he had no money. Congress had got into a snarl over the use of the army as a posse comitatus in the South and had failed to appropriate money for us. He took me around to the bank and made arrangements to cash my pay voucher for $125, giving me $100, charging me one-fifth of my pay as discount. We were all ragged, and the Helena paper, commenting on our appearance riding through the town, said our horses were so bony that a hat thrown at one would catch anywhere.

The army would have suffered greatly for lack of money had it not been for that patriotic citizen, Mr. J. P[ierpont] Morgan of New York, who said that, if the government would not pay its officers, he would not see them suffer. He arranged to have their pay vouchers cashed without profit for just what the transaction cost, 1 or 2 percent, until the next meeting of

1. Major William Arthur, brother of President Chester A. Arthur, served in the U.S. Army as a paymaster. Heitman, *Historical Register*, 1:172. This was an invaluable source for identifying the many officers mentioned by Scott.

Congress, for which we older officers have always held Mr. Morgan in grateful remembrance.

Soon after reporting to General Terry at Fort Benton, a courier came from General Miles, asking to have supplies sent to him at once. Benton was a small town, but the quartermaster scraped up fifty two-horse teams. Some of the animals had never worn harness before, and many of the drivers were clerks or town men without knowledge of driving. There were six fine, six-mule teams sent to take General Terry over the Canadian border, but their drivers were infantrymen, picked without experience, who knew nothing about handling a six-mule team with a jerk line. The train was handed over to me to take out, and DeRudio, with E Troop, went as escort. We started from Benton at two o'clock with most of the teams balky and the drivers drunk. I must have lost ten years' growth that day getting the train along. The trail was new to me. We had twelve crossings of the Marias and Teton to make, some of them after dark, so that I did not get into camp and to dinner until one o'clock in the morning. The wagons would stick in every mudhole. As I was the only man in the command who could really drive a six-mule team with a jerk line, I had to stop at every crossing, take out a six-mule team, and, mounting the saddle mule myself, jerk every wagon across. We made a slow and painful progress around the Bear[s] Paw Mountains to Milk River, where we met a squadron of the Second Cavalry to whom I turned over the train. I was never so glad to get rid of anything in my life.

We went down to Milk River in search of the Seventh Cavalry. I was allowed to go as far ahead as I wanted. Far in advance of the command, somewhere above old Fort Belknap, a wooden stockade then used as an Indian agency and trading post, near the present town of Chinook, where the main line of the Great Northern Railway now runs, I ran across a naked Indian lying dead among the sagebrush without a scalp.[2] I searched about on the ground for a clue and soon found four more scalped Indians. Thinking it the work of one of Sitting Bull's war parties from north of the line, I looked about to see if there were any of them still around to treat me in the same way and concluded to leave the neighborhood.

2. The original Fort Belknap served as the Indian agency for members of the Assiniboine and Gros Ventre of the Prairie, or Atsina, tribes living in the area. Lincoln, "Reports of Agents in Montana," 98–100.

I went on down to the camp of a large number of Upper Assiniboines and asked them about it. They said that the five men and two others were Nez Percé scouts who had come to them, asking them to turn out and help them fight the whites. "What did you do about it?" I asked. They said, "We held a council and determined to tell them we had no cause to fight the whites, by whom we were well treated, and advised them to go over and see the Gros Ventres, who might want to fight. We said to each other, 'Give them a good dinner—give them the best you have got—for it is the last dinner they are ever going to eat.'"

After the dinner, I was told, they started toward the Gros Ventre village and were allowed to get some miles away, when the young Assiniboine braves saddled up and went out and killed them all. There scalps were there hanging on a pole to dry in the wind.[3]

Leaving the Assiniboine village, I soon encountered Lieutenant [Marion P.] Maus with ten men of the infantry, mounted, who said he was hunting for Nez Percé fugitives from Miles's fight and thought there might be a lot of them in the village of the Red River half-breeds living on Milk River. I told him that, if there was to be any shooting, I would go with him. We went over and persuaded forty-five Nez Percé Indians to surrender without a fight.[4] Hiring some Red River carts, we loaded them with women and children and started for Miles's camp on the Missouri near the mouth of the Musselshell. I sent a message to DeRudio, saying that I would meet him at the Three Peoples Buttes [Three Buttes in present Blaine County, Montana?], three prominent landmarks halfway between the Bear[s] Paw Mountains and the Little Rockies. We went down through the battlefield, where I killed a fine young bull.

The weather had become quite cold by that time, especially at night, and I had left camp only with my rifle and ammunition. Maus had one moth-eaten robe. We had besides our two wet saddle blankets to sleep on and about a quart of cracker crumbs to eat. I would brush the frost out of my hair on getting up in the morning, stiff with the cold. The children would cry all night until we killed some buffalo and wrapped them up in the green hides and fed them and our men with meat without salt, cooked without utensils.

3. Greene, *Nez Perce Summer*, 318, 492n163.

4. The fight at Bear Paw commenced on September 30, 1877; the surrender occurred on October 5. More than a hundred fugitives escaped initial capture. Greene devotes the majority of two chapters to the dramatic conclusion of the Nez Percé war. Ibid., 313, 318.

Neither of us had intended to be away from our commands overnight when we had started, but we were actually away more than ten days, living on berries, buffalo (straight) [minimally cooked], mule, and anything we could find, watched doubtless by hostile Indians every minute.[5]

While riding along, a Nez Percé named Tippit attached himself to me, and we rode together every day. The horse he rode was branded with a big rooster. Nobody branded stock in the Northwest in those days, and I concluded that it was a Spanish brand and that the horse must have been stolen in Mexico. Tippit started to teach me Chinook, the jargon used intertribally on the Columbia [River] and up the Pacific coast. He would ride silent for a long time, trying to think up the English equivalent. Then he would give me questions and English interpretation:

> "*Cumtox Chinook wawa?*" "You understan' Chinook talkin'?"
>
> "*Tenas cumtox.*" "Me little understan.' "
>
> "*Nuyu cumtox.*" "Me heap understan.' "
>
> "*Wake cumtox.*" "Me no understan.' "
>
> "*Cumtox Boston wawa.*" "You understan' white man talkin'?"

Then to my complete astonishment he began to sing, "Where, oh, where are the Hebrew children?" in Chinook—"*Ika—nika clatawa Siah*"—which he had learned from some missionary on the Columbia when a child. Tippit proved an amusing companion, and we encouraged him to talk as we marched along.

We reached the camp of the Seventh Cavalry on the north side of the Missouri, opposite the mouth of the Musselshell, where I rejoined my troop and returned the bedding roll I had been using. General Miles had started for Fort Keogh across country with the Cheyenne scouts, Fifth Infantry, and the Nez Percé prisoners. All the wounded had been sent to Fort Lincoln by boat. Sitting Bull had sent word that he was coming down out of Canada to wipe us all out, and General Miles held us here to let him try, but he never came, though some of his scouting parties were operating in the country.

5. Contributing a testimonial letter that Scott inserted here in the original text, Maus considered the task of retrieving and transporting the Nez Percé prisoners "an especially dangerous duty . . . considering our small force." He expressed his appreciation for Scott's "gallant and valuable service, voluntarily offered." Marion P. Maus, Washington, D.C., to H. L. Scott, Washington, D.C., June 26, 1902, reprinted in Scott, *Some Memories*, 77–78.

I asked Nez Percé John if he would like to go up and help fight Sitting Bull. He broke out with fervor, "Oh, by God!—that too much—too much fight—eat squash now." He had been fighting all summer and was fed up on it and wanted to turn farmer. A saying originated from this which was long current in the Seventh Cavalry: When a stranger asked about some officer absent from a campaign, he would be told, "He's eating squash now."

Another Seventh Cavalry saying was "to lead the pelican." This came from the plains of Kansas. Custer had a light spring wagon, which he kept right behind the troops while on the march, to carry water, lunch, footsore dogs, or what not. They carried a wounded pelican in it for some time, right behind the last troop. The army regulations used to require that an officer in arrest should march in the rear of the troops, and it would be said of an officer in arrest that "he is leading the pelican."[6]

We were camped on a silted-up channel of the Missouri, which made a beautiful sward, without brush or rosebushes, the edges dotted here and there with giant cottonwood, five or six feet in diameter, reminding one of an English park. The weather was quite cold. At night we would all gather around a huge fire and listen to stories from the scouts, mainly from Liver Eating [John] Johnson, who was said to have eaten a piece of an Indian's liver in a fit of bravado. His language was very quaint, and we would often listen to him until one o'clock in the morning. He was a tall, powerful man with a hairy torso like that of a bull. He carried a sixteen-pound buffalo Sharp's rifle, which, with its belt full of ammunition, was a load for an ordinary man. He would leave camp on foot and soon kill and dress an antelope, cutting off its head and tying all four feet together. This he would swing over his shoulder like a sack, the body under his left arm, and go on and kill another, to be swung under the right arm.

Billy [William] Jackson was a Blackfoot who had been a scout for the Seventh Cavalry the year before and had been cut off in the timber with DeRudio, Gerard, and Sergeant [Thomas] O'Neill, left behind by Reno. Jackson had wintered at Lincoln, Rice, and Standing Rock. I had thought in those days that he was a Sioux half-breed. He had come up the Missouri with us as far as Fort Keogh, where I had missed him until meeting him here. His [older] brother Bob [Robert] Jackson was with him but was not nearly so good a man. When Bob Jackson and Liver Eating Johnson left our camp, it

6. An 1868 photograph that indeed showed Custer and his pelican can be seen in Utley, *Custer*, 59.

may have been a mere coincidence that a bunch of our horses left the same night.[7]

The antelope here were more numerous than the buffalo. They went north into Canada in the spring to drop their young and came back in the autumn to winter in the sagebrush, which rises above the snow south of the Missouri. One of their main crossings was at the mouth of the Musselshell, and their number was incredible. One could see a bunch of five thousand in one place and go on a few miles and see another bunch just like it. Moving camp one day five miles to change the grass, the men shot thirty-five out of the column while marching along. No one knew how many they wounded, for they carry lead like a grizzly bear or a Sulu Moro. I have known an antelope, though unable to run, to walk off with seven .45-caliber carbine bullets through his body, none of which had struck a vital spot. I have known one to run a mile with the lower portion of its heart torn off by an explosive bullet. It is always best to leave a wounded animal alone, to allow him to lie down and bleed, when he will soon stiffen and become unable to rise. Chasing seems to give him a nervous strength that may carry him far away from you.

A dressed antelope would weigh anywhere from fifty to seventy-five pounds. Everybody hunted that cared to during the day, and all the antelope brought in would be thrown on the pile in the center of camp, about eight feet high, and be issued out as meat to the troops by the commissary. When we moved, every wagon would be festooned outside with dead antelope carried along for food. The meat is greatly improved by hanging for a week or ten days in that climate. People said that there must have been millions of antelope in the region. Of late years, I have several times gone three hundred miles a day in an automobile in the same region without seeing an antelope.

General Miles, losing faith in Sitting Bull's threats, started us down the river for home in November [1877]. We passed through Fort Peck, Wolf Point, and Poplar Creek agencies of the Assiniboine and Yanktonai Sioux, great villages of three hundred lodges, newly made white skin lodges of buffalo hide, where everything was full of joy and laughter, with plenty of buffalo meat hanging up to dry everywhere, and dances, horseraces, ring and spear games going on on every side. Here I met old Red Stone [Redstone], head

7. Billy Jackson was a mixed-blood Blackfoot Indian. His brothers Robert and Johnson served as scouts for Miles in 1876–77. Greene, *Yellowstone Command*, 72, 157–59.

chief of the Assiniboines, who came to our camp, made me a great speech in the sign language before the assembled officers at my tent, and threw down a beautiful buffalo robe at my feet as a gift "on the prairie," or a free gift. Nevertheless, I felt that I had to make it up to him with hard bread, sugar, and coffee.

At Fort Buford, I was invited to dinner by Mrs. Robinson, the wife of the post chaplain [George P. Robinson], who was from Princeton, a niece of Joseph Henry of the Smithsonian, and a connection by marriage whom I had known from my childhood. She also invited General Miles, who was going to the railroad with the Nez Percé prisoners of war. Mrs. Robinson set me to freezing the ice cream. When General Miles entered the front door, he looked down the passageway and saw me grinding for dear life at the handle of the freezer.

In 1923, I inspected the Nez Percé Agency at Lapwai, Idaho, where the agent [Oscar H. Lipps] said to me, "You must not leave here without seeing Jesse Paul."[8] I asked why I should see Jesse Paul particularly. He said it was because Jesse Paul had been a little boy among those Nez Percé prisoners of war I conducted to Bismarck in 1877 to the railway on the way to prison at Fort Leavenworth, a ragged little Indian prisoner with no future whatever. When Jesse Paul came in, he took me two hundred miles in his own high-powered touring car and showed me his house far from the agency, with electricity and hot and cold water. He had raised a fine family of boys on his two-hundred-acre farm. The agent said Jesse owned mortgages on the farms of white people and could go into any bank in the neighborhood and borrow what money he wanted without security. He was one on the most respected citizens of Idaho. Where is that man that said, "There is no good Indian but a dead Indian"?

We passed the site of old Fort Union at the mouth of the Yellowstone, built by Kenneth McKenzie for the American Fur Company in 1829—the emporium of the Northwest, now destroyed—and we refitted at Fort Buford a few miles away. Here Joseph and the Nez Percé prisoners of war joined us from Fort Keogh, with some Sioux and Northern Cheyennes on the way to

8. Scott visited this agency in his capacity as a member of the Board of Indian Commissioners, on which he served without pay. He described his work: "We divide the Indian country among us and make annual tours of inspection of the various agencies. Frequently we are able to stop abuses and work benefits for the Indian and also for the Indian agents. I was the enemy of most Indian agents in my youth, but now they are of an entirely different class of men." Scott, *Some Memories*, 625.

General Scott addressing members of thirteen Indian tribes in sign language at old Fort Union, Montana, 1925. From Scott, *Some Memories of a Soldier*, between pages 616 and 617. Editor's collection.

Chicago to see General Sheridan. These Cheyennes were the old friends of the preceding spring. My Troop I, Seventh Cavalry, and a company of the First Infantry were started down the river as escort for the Nez Percés to travel 225 miles to Bismarck, the end of the railway, whence the prisoners were to be shipped eastward by rail. I rode in the wagon with Joseph a part of every day, together with the Nez Percé interpreter, a man from Idaho named [Arthur] Chapman. I rode part of every day in the wagons with the Cheyennes and Sioux, carrying on my study of Sioux and the sign language of which I never missed an opportunity to learn more.

That night we camped at old Fort Berthold, the agency of the Arikaras, Mandans, and Gros Ventres of the Village, many individuals of those tribes came out to see the Nez Percés, whom they had heard of as fighting all summer but had never seen before.[9] At a big council held at our camp, Joseph stood up in the middle of a great circle, containing about fifteen hundred Indians, whom he addressed in the sign language. There were

9. Greene, *Nez Perce Summer*, 335. By "Gros Ventres of the Village," Scott referred to the Gros Ventres of the Missouri, otherwise known as the Hidatsa tribe.

representatives there from eight languages, including mine: Nez Percé, Sioux, Cheyenne, Crow, Arikara, Mandan, Gros Ventre of the Village, and English. Joseph related his trials and tribulations entirely by gestures, without opening his mouth, and he was completely understood by all that vast concourse. I have twice addressed a similar concourse in the sign language, comprising members of thirteen different tribes, brought by the Great Northern Railway in 1925 and 1926 to the mouth of the Yellowstone to celebrate events at the site of old Fort Union, but I never saw a more interesting exhibition of the sign language than was given by Joseph that day.

Joseph was then a tall, stalwart, active, fine looking young man of great force and dignity. His life in Kansas and the Indian Territory, where many of his people died, did much to break his body and spirit. This was quite patent at the times I saw him in Washington in after years. He and his people were among the finest Indians America produced, but they were treated most unjustly by the government, first as to their lands and secondly in their deportation to Oklahoma, where they could not live. These Nez Percés received [Meriwether] Lewis and [William] Clark, [Benjamin L. E.] Bonneville, and many other white men with great hospitality and kindness, but their treatment by the white man is a black page in our history.

12

A Winter's Program

Arriving at Fort Lincoln in the first part of December [1877], we began to get ourselves ready to settle down for the winter. Several snowstorms occurred, presaging a cold season. Suddenly orders came for our squadron to go to the Black Hills, 225 miles southwest. About three hundred lodges of Sioux had run away from the Nebraska agencies.[1] They passed north along the east side of the Black Hills on their way to join Sitting Bull in Canada and were trying to slip through the country unnoticed, but thirty of their young men chased the treasure coach from Deadwood, riddling it with bullets. The driver pulled off the road toward a high rocky hill. Coming near, the Indians succeeded in killing a wheeler, which stopped the coach at the bottom of the hill and enabled the driver and messenger to get away among the rocks. They watched the proceedings from their hiding place and saw the Indians for half an hour unsuccessfully pound with an ax the treasure box, which contained thirty thousand dollars in gold bullion from the mines. Then they all went away, leaving it behind but taking the mailbags with them.

News of this was carried by wagon two hundred miles to Bismarck. Our squadron was ordered out to the Black Hills and had to march two hundred miles to get there. We passed C Troop going in, which had been in garrison all summer. We could not understand why it should be going back. Some of

1. Bray, "'We Belong to the North,'" 30, 41, 45n65.

us were much enraged over this, but I was as happy out there as anywhere else. We went into camp on Cherry Creek, but, during the time news of the trouble was coming in and we were marching, several snowstorms occurred to cover the trail completely. The Indians had been gone a month, and there was nothing we could do but hunt for the place where the mail had been opened. Our captain had been searching in different directions without result when one day I went with him. I suggested that we follow a straight line, from their point of departure to a gap in the hills, which they must have gone through to get out of the valley. About halfway to the gap a small piece of paper was seen blowing about over the snow. We dug in the snow thereabout and found many torn checks on a Deadwood bank. We pieced many of these together and sent them to the bank.

The old people of the Sioux village deprecated the attack of some of their young men on the treasure coach, especially as they had wished to slip through that country without molestation. To mark their peaceful intentions, they drew a picture on a piece of paper of a white man and an Indian shaking hands and put it in a cleft stick standing up in the middle of the road. The white man was drawn with a beard and a plug hat, which differentiated him completely from the Indian, who was drawn with long braids.

As there were no more Indians creating trouble, we were drawn into Fort Lincoln the latter part of January [1878] and spent the rest of the winter in the post. I had traveled with troops more than forty-five hundred miles on horseback since spring and had traveled as much again without troops, exploring and hunting, yet had brought my two horses back in good condition. Some I knew that did no hunting used up three horses.

My spare time for the rest of the winter was occupied in driving Miss Mary Merrill, daughter of General Lewis Merrill, major of the Seventh Cavalry, who has since become Mrs. Scott, all over the country and in visiting the Cheyenne prison village that Benteen had brought down with his squadron from Buford in January to winter at the post. I visited their village every day, subsidizing White Bear, principally with sugar, coffee, and other rations, to teach me the sign language. We both worked hard at it.

I went down for my lesson one day when the snow had melted off in the spring and was surprised to have White Bear tell me that they were all going to run off that night, leaving their lodges standing, and go back to the buffalo country, where they could get something to eat. At the post they drew rations for each member of the family for ten days. He complained that in three days these rations were all eaten up, and so they were always hungry. I could not believe he was telling the truth until I looked about the lodge and saw all their property tied up ready for packing.

I took the news very casually, going around among the other lodges as usual and noticing that all movable property was ready. I hurried to the commanding officer to report. He would not believe it possible at first. Then he sent a guard down to bring up the principal chiefs, using me as the only interpreter at the post. These chiefs all said, "Yes, we are going back to the buffalo country, where we will not starve to death." They became very emphatic and so insulting to the general that I was reluctant to tell him all they said, but I gave him enough to make him very angry in his turn. One of them, Ridge Bear [Bear Who Walks on a Ridge], told him he was a liar when he said they had enough food; he, better than the colonel, knew when he had enough to eat; he had been accustomed to do as he pleased when a little boy, and now a grown man he was not going to let anybody tell him he could not go where he pleased.

General Sturgis could not believe that I knew enough to interpret correctly. So he sent for the Arikara interpreter, F. F. Girard [Gerard], who had left the service and settled near the present site of the town of Mandan, and also for a Cheyenne man married to an Arikara woman. Then the colonel went through the interview again. Starting with English, it went through the Arikara woman to her Cheyenne husband and back again through the same channels, all verifying what I had already said.

The colonel then sent a squadron of cavalry to camp at their village to prevent them from running away at night. Had they succeeded in escaping, they would have had a long start, for the Heart River was up and there would have been plenty of time to put the river between them and us before we learned of their leaving. Moreover, it would have been a long, hard chase costing many lives, and the colonel would have been dealt with severely for permitting the conditions of which they complained and for not preventing their departure.

The general complimented me on stopping their getaway and directed me to have the quartermaster present a voucher for a hundred dollars as compensation for extra service as an interpreter, but I told him I could not do that. He might have done far better for me if he had reported the service, putting it on my record, but this he was afraid to do lest it bring an inspector to investigate his management of the Indians. It did not get on my records for many years afterwards, when it was put on by the inspector general [Ernest A. Garlington], who was at that time the adjutant of the Seventh Cavalry.[2]

The Northern Cheyennes, forced to go to the Indian Territory by the secretary of the Interior [Carl Schurz], ran away the same spring from Fort Reno, Indian Territory, a quarter of the army following them. They killed all the white men they could, coming across Kansas and Nebraska. These Northern Cheyennes were on their way with their women and children, horses and dogs, to the Indian Territory under charge of the celebrated frontiersman and Cheyenne interpreter Ben[jamin H.] Clark, who had been chief of scouts for Custer at the battle of the Washita in 1868. This was part of the harsh policy of the secretary of the Interior, to assemble all Indians in the Indian Territory, no matter where their habitat, even if it killed them, as it did very many. These Cheyennes were escorted to the Black Hills of Dakota and thence to Sidney, Nebraska, by the Seventh Cavalry, from where they were taken on to Fort Reno in the Indian Territory by Captain [Clarence] Mauck's troop of the Fourth Cavalry. A long stay was made in our camp to recuperate their stock, and I used this period to learn much from them and from Ben Clark, with whom I contracted a friendship that lasted during the remainder of his life.[3]

Our camp was immediately under and north of Bear Butte, a single peak some miles east of the Black Hills range, which was regarded by the Cheyennes as their principal medicine place. Many of them climbed to the summit, where they left presents to the medicine that inhabited the mountain. Some would go to the top, about twelve hundred feet above our camp, and stay there three days and nights, without eating, drinking, or sleeping, believing that the medicine would help them get horses or perhaps to strike their enemy.

While the Cheyennes were still in that camp, an eclipse of the sun took place that was announced by the public press. I told the Cheyennes to expect

2. Garlington described Scott's "adroitness" during this "delicate" situation, going so far as to conclude that his "prompt action" even "prevented an outbreak, and possibly a long Indian war." E. A. Garlington, Washington, D.C. to the Adjutant General, Washington, D.C. June 19, 1902, reprinted in Scott, *Some Memories*, 88–89.

3. Biographical information on Ben Clark can be found in Greene, *Washita*, 93–94; and Hardorff, *Washita Memories*, 202–204. The epic trek of the Cheyennes is told in Leiker and Powers, *Northern Cheyenne Exodus*.

it several days beforehand, but they did not believe me. They became very much excited when the eclipse began, shooting off guns and making every sort of noise they could to frighten away the evil medicine, which they thought was destroying the sun. Their treatment was highly successful—the sun recovered.

13

A Packtrain for the Regiment

After the Cheyennes went south, General Sheridan arrived [in 1878] for the purpose of selecting a site for the new post of Fort Meade. He took [Captain Henry] Jackson's Troop C and went over to Spearfish, the best stream in the Black Hills, where we all thought he would locate the post. Something over there displeased him, however, and he would have none of it. When he came back to our camp, he sent Hare and myself to where Fort Meade now is at Sturgis City to make a map of that region. We put our two maps together upon return, and upon this he located the post.[1]

The Seventh Cavalry officers all made an official call on him in a body in our colonel's tent. It was a large hospital tent, but it was so full and my rank so low I could not get entirely inside. General Sheridan expatiated upon the value such a post would have when Indians broke away from the Nebraska agencies and went north toward the camp of Sitting Bull. A telegram to Fort Meade, he said, would enable a cavalry force to head them off here. I took my courage in hand and asked if he thought the post would be any good here without a packtrain. Instead of having me thrown out, it seemed to strike him just right, for he turned to our colonel [Sturgis], saying: "Sam, do you want a packtrain? I'll give you one."

1. The post's founding is detailed in Lee, *Fort Meade*, 18–52.

The Seventh Cavalry had never had a real packtrain before because General Terry thought you could catch Indians with a six-mule team, though he never did it himself. Whenever we encountered cavalry from General [George] Crook's Department of the Platte, away from our wagons, the difference was painfully evident, for General Crook was the father of the modern aparejo train [packtrain]. The sound of the packtrain bell means food, shelter, and ammunition to me. Without these, an officer, even on the verge of victory, must let go and retire to save his men from capture. I fear that the sound of that bell has little meaning nowadays for the men of this age, who listen for the honk of an automobile, which cannot climb mountains where there is no road as can our old long-eared comrade of the Plains, the mule.

Packtrains are expensive to maintain, and the quartermaster general is always breaking them up to save money. It takes time to make a packtrain, and it is not everybody who can make one, even with the money. Custer's train was a disgrace, improvised from the mules taken from the wagon train, and his packers were without experience. His train was scattered for miles and could easily have been captured had the Indians known about it.

Notwithstanding frugal quartermaster generals, the Fort Meade packtrain given us by General Sheridan in 1878 survived even the penurious General [Richard N.] Batchel[d]er, who stripped the army of mules, and this train even survived the retrenchment after the Spanish War. It was sent to the Mexican border in 1912, where the chief packer called on me at San Antonio, and that train serves the cavalry on the border to this day. I used to love every mule in it long ago.

Several times during the summer of 1878 our Troop I would be sent out eastward after Indians with A Troop, Captain [Myles] Moylan in command. Returning from one of these expeditions, we wanted to camp at Washté Springs, but no one knew where it was. Nearing the Belle Fourche River, we saw some men riding off to one side of it to avoid meeting us. I started over to ask them where Washté Springs was when they began to gallop away. I cut them off and asked them why they were running away. They disclaimed running away, saying they belonged to a bull train and were trying to catch up with it. I noticed that their horses were too good for bullwhackers, but there was nothing to be done about it. I got the directions for the springs and let them go. We made camp at the springs and were sitting down to dinner some hours afterward when along came Seth Bullock, marshal of the hills, with a posse in pursuit of the men I had stopped. They had had a battle with the messengers of the Sidney treasure coach, had killed a telegraph operator on the box, and were going east with thirty thousand dollars' worth of gold bricks from the mines. There was five thousand dollars reward offered for each one of them. I had had them in my hand with two troops of cavalry to help hold them, but they were ahead of the news. We knew nothing about it until Seth Bullock arrived.

Bullock followed them with his posse toward the Missouri River, where they were seen camping at a water hole. Seth wanted to take them right away, but his posse refused, well knowing they were desperate, having already killed one man. They agreed to go on past as if they knew nothing about them and return to surround them in the darkness and tackle them at daylight. This they proceeded to do, but, when daylight came, there was nobody there. One [Thomas Jefferson Goodale] was captured trying to sell a gold brick in Iowa and was being taken west of Omaha when he jumped out of the car window. The train was stopped, and a great search made for the fugitive until the conductor had to go on, leaving the search party still hunting for the prisoner. It was found later that he had never left the car but had climbed up and was lying flat on top and was carried swiftly away from his pursuers. He was captured further west however, and was sent to the penitentiary.[2]

In 1920 I was inspecting the Sioux Agency at Standing Rock [as a member of the Board of Indian Commissioners] when the governor of North Dakota [Lynn J. Frazier] invited me to Bismarck. A dinner was given to me and other old-timers. Alexander [J.] McKenzie, who had been sheriff there in my youth, was one of the guests. He had become very wealthy and was the political power of that region. We got to talking about old times, and he asked me, "Do you know who those robbers were you had in your hand?" I told him that I did not and that we were continually on the march for months afterward without sleeping in a house or seeing a paper. He said, "Those were Frank and Jesse James who did that job, and you had them both."

◆ ◆ ◆

While moving along the trail of the Bismarck stage, we noticed that the passing stages were overladen with passengers. We asked what the excitement

2. Bullock's posse was one of many combing the area. The story of this celebrated stagecoach robbery and the capture and escape of Goodale is told at length in Spring, *Cheyenne and Black Hills*, 265–74; and Wolff, *Seth Bullock*, 50–52.

was and were told that "color" had been found in the Bear[s] Paw Mountains of the Upper Missouri and that there was a stampede for the Bear Paw. Everybody was leaving from the Hills. We even saw men riding that 225 miles to Bismarck on the break-blocks [brake blocks?] because the stage was too full to hold them—all to no purpose, it developed, for there was never pay dirt in the Bear[s] Paw Mountains.

We were sent east again to Pinau [Pino] Springs, about seventy-five miles out on the Sioux Reservation, because the Sioux were reported as bothering the stages. On the return we passed through a gap in the outer rampart of the Black Hills and saw a battalion of infantry going south. Encountering their wagon train, we asked where they were going. It was then we heard that Red Cloud, chief of the Ogalalas [Oglalas], had broken out on the Missouri River after killing his agent and had gone back into the hinterland, nobody knew where. The Northern Cheyennes, taken down to the Indian Territory in 1876 by Captain [Henry W.] Lawton, Fourth Cavalry, had broken away from Fort Reno and were coming north, killing everybody in their path through Kansas and Nebraska, to join the Ogalalas with whom they were intermarried. I made passing reference to this before, but it was in the foregoing manner that we learned of the danger.

The orders were for us to draw thirty days' rations, catch up with the infantry battalion and other troops of the Seventh Cavalry, and prevent the Cheyennes from forming a junction with Red Cloud. We stopped right there, fortunately near some water, unloaded our wagons, throwing everything on the ground, and Hare took the empty wagons to where they were building Fort Meade for the thirty days' rations. On his return we took up the trail down into the badlands of Bad and White Rivers, across the Cheyenne [River], making night and day marches, camping at times without water, in a frantic effort to overtake the others. After a toilsome night march, we reached their camp on White River at the mouth of the Wounded Knee [Creek] (Chankpé opi wakpala) at seven o'clock in the morning, just as they were leaving camp. We were told to get breakfast there and join the infantry right away, although our men and animals were nearly done for.

We caught them up near the Porcupine Tail Butte in the forenoon. When we stopped for lunch, the officers all congregated on a high place from which we could overlook the country, when someone exclaimed, "There are Red Cloud's horses now!" I carried a small telescope, through which we all took a look. We could see color and movement about six miles away, and everybody was convinced that they were Red Cloud's horses. It was all settled to everybody's satisfaction when I declared that they were not horses but Texas cattle. That brought out a roar of derision. The buffalo were hardly out of the country, and there were no cattle ranches yet established. How did I, a four-eyed man, have the impertinence to maintain my views against those of men who could really see?[3]

Nevertheless, I stuck to my opinion, and, sure enough, when we got near, we found that it was a beef herd under contract for the agency, being driven up on the cattle trail from Texas. Then they wanted to know how I had come to the conclusion they were not horses, too far away to distinguish the shape. I told them I had spent some time the previous summer with the Crows, who had more than fourteen thousand head of horses. Each lodge would have from two to five hundred head, many of them bred in that bunch. A little Indian boy could round them up, drive them to water right through the other bunches. If one got separated from his own bunch, he would howl until he was answered and go back among his own. After watering they would be driven out to the hillside and left where there was room to graze in bunches, each belonging to a different lodge. The animals we saw on the Wounded Knee were not bunched—we could see movement and color—but they were scattered irregularly over the hillside. I knew that they were cattle because they were not in lodge bunches as cattle have no such affinity for each other as horses.

There were old captains there who had served on the northern and southern Plains and had been in every fight the Seventh Cavalry ever had who did not know that. Many were first-rate garrison soldiers, who knew their drill, took good care of their men, and never made a mistake in their muster rolls, but who were blind on the prairie.

3. Here Scott mentioned the wearing of spectacles to help correct his nearsightedness, striking a masculine figure rarely depicted in western art and literature. In fact, one of the names the Kiowas attached to Scott was "Glasses Man." Harrington, "American Indian Sign Language," 28.

14

Trouble with Red Cloud

Going up to Red Cloud's village on White Clay Creek [in 1878], I noticed ugly signs. Red Cloud was said to have five thousand young men, many recently from the hostile village. I could see that they were in a very ugly mood. When passing one on the trail, he would draw off to one side, cover his face with his blanket, and refuse to answer a question. When riding near, they were seen to be carrying two belts of ammunition, one around the waist and the other over the shoulder. I could feel trouble in the air.

There was no interpreter with the command when one was needed most, nor any Indian scouts. When the head of the column stopped at Red Cloud's lodge, they sent back in the column for me, and I was told I was wanted as interpreter.

Red Cloud was in a most surly mood. There he stood in the presence of eleven troops of cavalry and boldly asked: "What do you come looking for here? My young men don't want you here. If you come here looking for a fight, my young men will fight you. If you don't want to fight, you go home."

It was a good deal of responsibility to throw on a young man only two years out of West Point. I not only had to act as interpreter and extricate the commanding officer from the tense situation but must preserve his dignity. Fortunately I succeeded.

It was found that Red Cloud had not killed his agent [James Irwin] as reported but had left the Missouri, where the Ogalala [Sioux] with Red Cloud and the Brulé Sioux with Spotted Tail had been taken the year before to save the two-hundred-mile haul of their supplies. Red Cloud had broken away, taking the agency beef herd without permission. They were evidently very cross, and I warned the commanding officer to look out for trouble.

We went a day's march away to camp. I was sent back to live in Red Cloud's lodge for a few days to keep tab on what he was doing. Indians are always hospitality itself, and he made me welcome in his lodge. I stayed there three nights watching. I could not see that anything overt was under way, but felt that I had no friends there and that hostilities might be brewing without my knowledge.

Red Cloud was an excellent sign talker, but he made his gestures differently from anyone I had ever seen before or since. While each was perfectly distinct, they were all made within the compass of a circle a foot in diameter, whereas they are usually made in the compass of a circle two and a half feet in diameter.[1] We talked about everything under the sun, but he would not give me any clue to what made him so ill-humored and to what was actuating his young men. I never did learn until I made a visit to Pine Ridge in 1920, when the half-breed Sioux interpreter Billy [William] Garnett told me that Red Cloud saw troops coming from [Fort] Laramie and from every direction to rendezvous near him.[2] He would not believe that it was on account of the Northern Cheyennes coming north from the Indian Territory but thought we were all brought there to arrest him for making off with the agency beef herd without permission, until one of the Cheyennes left Dull Knife (Mila Pésni) and Little Wolf somewhere south of the Niobrara [River] and came in with one lodge to tell Red Cloud that it was true—the Cheyennes were at war—after which Red Cloud softened and matters returned to their normal condition.

When the Cheyennes neared the Red Cloud country, for which they headed, they slowed down, intending to work their way a few at a time unnoticed among the Sioux. Little Wolf separated from Dull Knife south of the Niobrara and went far east among the sandhills of Nebraska. Dull Knife worked his way slowly and cautiously north of the Niobrara and, encountering

1. Red Cloud's skill in the Plains Indian Sign Language was reflected in his autobiography, which tells of his easily conversing on separate occasions with members of the Arapaho, Cheyenne, and Crow tribes under less-than-ideal conditions. Paul, *Autobiography of Red Cloud*, 103, 117, 139, 181–82.

2. This August 1920 visit and the conversation with William Garnett resulted in an extremely valuable historical document that shed light on the Plains Indian wars and specifically on Crazy Horse's 1877 death. Powers, *Killing of Crazy Horse*, 526n13.

a squadron of Third Cavalry suddenly in a fog to the surprise of both parties, surrendered without a fight.[3] The prisoners were brought into Fort Robinson [Nebraska].

Their principal men, Dull Knife, Wild Hog, and Old Crow, got permission to come down to my tent under guard. They were the scareheads in the eastern dailies at that time. We all wanted to know why they had run away from Fort Reno. The officers of the seven troops of the Seventh Cavalry present gathered at my tent to learn. They told us the whole story in the sign language. I would interpret the technical signs, but many others were made that were such natural imitations that everybody there who did not understand signs comprehended what was said with little assistance. They told also of a visit to Washington in 1873, where they attended a circus and saw a white man jump off a springboard over five horses. They made everybody understand that they had seen an elephant, although the language contains no sign for an elephant.[4] They told us with great earnestness that they had run away from Fort Reno on account of the many deaths from fever, determined to die quickly in battle rather than at a slower rate by fever. They said they would die in the North rather than be sent back. I reported to Colonel [Caleb H.] Carlton, commanding the post, that they would never go back alive.

Moylan gave me an order to search the country for Little Wolf with ten men within eighty miles to the eastward between the Niobrara and White Rivers and to bring him in without a fight. A large proportion of the army had been chasing Little Wolf for months, and how Moylan conceived the idea that I could bring him with ten men I never learned. We had no scouts, and I wanted one of the Cheyenne prisoners to go with me. The matter was broached among the prisoners in the barracks where they were confined. After a discussion among themselves, they announced that Old Crow would go with me. I told them that was all very well so far as it went, but would he come back with me? He promised that he would. The commanding officer, however, refused to let me take him, saying that he had him safe as a prisoner and I might lose him. I sent Captain Moylan to try to induce him to let

3. Buecker, *Fort Robinson*, 134.

4. Seeing the sights of a circus seems quite plausible. The members of the 1873 Cheyenne delegation, along with those from the Crow and Ute tribes, found themselves embroiled in an accounting scandal after their host hotel in Washington flagrantly overcharged the government for their expenses. Notable expenditures on behalf of the Indian delegations included tickets to the opera, an excursion to Mount Vernon, countless cigars, and possibly the services of prostitutes. Viola, *Diplomats in Buckskins*, 64–68, 123–24.

me have Old Crow, giving many solid reasons, but he was adamant. Meeting Old Bill [William] Rowland, who had been with the Cheyennes for forty years, I asked him whether he thought Old Crow would really come back with me. He replied, "He certainly would if he said he would." I took Bill Rowland with me to Colonel Carlton, who knew him, and at his request the colonel let me take the Indian.

We got about ten miles from Fort Robinson when Old Crow wanted to leave the column to go up on a high butte to look around. Coming back, he said he had seen a troop of cavalry from Fort Laramie going in to Fort Robinson with eleven pack mules and three Sioux scouts, which I verified when I got back and found to be just as he said. I gave him a rifle to go off and kill an antelope. He shot the antelope in some peculiar way so that it could only walk, and, instead of killing it and carrying the meat, he herded it down to the trail on which I was about to pass. He made it furnish its own transportation and killed it right in front of me.

About forty miles east of Camp Sheridan he announced that he could see Little Wolf's band in the east. We traveled low in the ravines, out of sight, and came up suddenly over a ridge to find the Indians to be [George F.] Chase and [George K.] Hunter of the Third Cavalry with a fine packtrain. I could get no packtrain at Robinson and had to borrow three wagons from the quartermaster, with sawbuck packsaddles, and had to pack the bedding, food, and ammunition myself, for there was no one else to do it until I had taught one man to pack on one side. Chase and Hunter, however, who were in General Crook's department, had a packtrain with every comfort.

I returned to Fort Robinson without Old Crow's seeing even a track, convinced that Little Wolf had never been in that region. This was confirmed afterward by Little Wolf himself in Montana. If my orders had told me to find Little Wolf instead of directing me to search a certain country, where he had never been, I would have kept on until I found him. I went back to Robinson without him and returned Old Crow to the commanding officer with thanks.

We all started north for Fort Meade. Nearing the post, [Herbert J.] Slocum went ahead and bought up all the canned oysters, intending to give a party in a few days.[5] He had a hole dug in the floor of his tent in which to

5. Landlocked residents of the American West were wild about this seafood. Hedren, "The West Loved Oysters Too," 3–15.

keep them. Suddenly the trumpets sounded the signal to pack up, and we started for Fort Lincoln, 225 miles to the northeast. Slocum came away, forgetting the oysters, which may be in that hole yet. He resents even to this day my asking him how his oyster bed is thriving.

I admired a horse of Benteen's troop that was being ridden temporarily by the lieutenant colonel. At every halt I would go up to take in his points. The orderly holding him would say, "Look out, lieutenant. He don't like fur and will strike you with his forefeet if you get too near." I noticed the lieutenant colonel was not wearing his fur coat, although it was quite cold. I asked Benteen to let me buy the horse from the government, and he said I might if his lieutenant, [Albert J.] Russell, did not object. Russell said to take him with his blessing as he wanted a driving horse. They had put a harness on this beast last winter at Fort Rice. It had taken all H Troop to get it off, and I was more than welcome to him.

15

In Station at Fort Totten

I bought the horse at Fort Lincoln. The troops received their winter assignment here, and we were ordered to Fort Totten, two hundred miles further east, to take station. My captain ordered me to go to Jamestown by rail, taking a batch of recruits just received. My new horse was shipped also by rail, the troop marching along the railroad.

The day after arrival I got an order to carry a despatch in a hurry to Fort Totten, eighty-two miles north. The trails were all covered with eight inches of snow, and a black cloud in the north promised more storm. It was quite cold, and it was necessary to wear a buffalo coat and other furs. The new horse and I had a battle in the streets of Jamestown, but I soon got on him, furs and all, and trotted him twenty-five miles without dismounting. This was quite contrary to my habit of riding horses, but I was afraid that, if I got off him alone far out on the prairie, I might not be able to mount again. There was a string of road stations twenty-five miles apart all the way to Totten, but they were hard to find since the trail was completely covered. If I should miss Fort Totten in that great white expanse, I could go a thousand miles north without ever seeing a human being. But I reached Fort Totten safely and delivered my despatch within twenty-four hours on Thanksgiving Day, 1878. The horse was fresh enough to have gone back next day, had it been necessary.

The troop arrived in about ten days, and the men settled down for the winter. Fort Totten was one hundred miles east of the Missouri River on

Lake Miniwakan, the Medicine Lake of the Sioux, foolishly called Devil's [Devils] Lake by the whites, fifty miles long and, opposite the post, nine miles wide.[1] The water was not too brackish for animals to drink, and it contained many large pickerel or pike weighing from three to twenty pounds. This was the agency mainly of the Eastern Sioux from Minnesota, who had lived east of the sign-talking area. When I tried to use signs with them, they thought I was crazy to make those foolish gestures.

The ice on the lake would sometimes freeze five feet thick. The Sioux would cut a hole through the ice, put some rushes on the windward side, then put down the head of their robes on the rushes on which they sat, bringing the robe up over their backs. Then, putting a hook and line down through the hole, baited with a chunk of meat, and the other end of the line tied to the middle of a stick, three feet long, for a pole, they would jiggle the line up and down for an hour and would usually catch three or four big pike.

The wood for the post was hauled nine miles across the lake. This hauling packed down the snow. The roadbed was raised higher and higher, often six feet above the ice. This track was the only one easily traveled as the snow was too deep to go elsewhere. I usually rode across and back on horseback for exercise, then drove a sleigh over, the weather often 20° or 40° below zero. I wore a buffalo overcoat, leggings of buffalo calfskin, over heavy clothes, a fur cap, gloves, and mask. I wore Blackfoot winter moccasins of buffalo hide, with hair inside and with a felt insole an inch thick, silk or cotton socks next to my feet and over these heavy Dutch socks. It was necessary to wear hide clothing, for no woven material would keep out that piercing wind.

My [former West Point] classmate Slocum and I occupied the same quarters, and our main task was to keep the stoves well stoked, for that was the coldest part of the United States, the coteau of the Missouri, where blizzards come straight from the Arctic Circle. The snow would bank up in front of the windows so that no one could see through them and remain that way until it melted in the spring. Often we would not get our mail for one or two months. Sometimes it would be brought in by dogs.

The lake broke up on May 5 [1879]. There was something uncanny about the disappearance of the ice. It would melt and freeze for days, melt all around the edge, thirty to fifty feet from the shore, this space getting continually

1. For a brief survey of the military history of Fort Totten, Dakota Territory, see McCormack, "Soldiers and Sioux," 3–23.

wider until there could be movement of vast ice fields. Then some night it would disappear completely, leaving no trace. The Indians and Red River [of the North] half-breeds believed that it sank. I have seen an explanation of the disappearance somewhere in print. The surface does not melt, for what melts in the daytime refreezes at night. It is the undersurface that melts—because water is warmer than ice—and the water eats it way up into the underside of the ice, leaving long spiculae [needlelike structures] in the space between. Thus the ice gets very thin without showing on top. One night the force of the wind moves the ice field, and it begins to break up. The spiculae are rubbed together. Being rotten, the ice ground up by the waves vanishes entirely.

When the ice would melt for thirty feet out from the shore, we would walk along the edge with a carbine to shoot the big pike coming out from under the ice to the open water to spawn. They would thresh about, merely stunned by the shot, and you have to get hold of them quickly, or they would escape under the ice.

Lieutenant [William W.] Robinson shot one and jumped into the water up to his armpits and threw the fish up on the ice. We helped him to climb out. Then instead of taking the fish by putting the points of his thumb and forefinger in the eyes to get a leverage against the skull, he put his fingers in its mouth. The teeth were long and sharp, and the fish closed down on his fingers and would not let go until I pried his mouth open with the muzzle of a carbine.

Slocum and I could be seen a large part of the day chopping pine boxes into kindling wood and hauling it down to the shore. We had a small flatboat, rigged with an open iron basket held high above the bow to burn this kindling wood, making a light by which we could see a big pike at a distance. We would then pole up on him quietly and strike him with a fish spear. We got seventy-five one night, more than four hundred pounds, most of which went to feed the troops.

At the opening of spring the prairies were covered with upland plover running about in pairs. Many sicklebill curlew would hover over one. The prairie chickens would begin to dance, as did the sandhill cranes. The shores of the lake would harbor quantities of bay birds, yellowlegs, willet or stone curlew, just as is seen on Barnegat Bay in New Jersey. Then the innumerable varieties of colored wild flowers began their changing season, showing great splashes of color, varying as the seasons came and went.

The soil about Fort Totten was a dark brown loam, immensely rich, and the land was rolling and diversified, holding many small freshwater lakes hidden among the hills, usually with little oak groves somewhere on their shores. The buffalo had left this part of the country after a fire that burned over the whole region in 1867. They fled across the Missouri, never returning. There were still a few elk and deer. The last black bear was killed by a soldier in the winter of 1878.

We had a small schooner and a sloop, built by the post quartermaster and handled by a soldier brought up in Finland with a knowledge of small boats. I put myself under his charge to teach me what he knew. My spare time was occupied in this way after the warm weather began until the prairie chickens were large enough to shoot. I applied myself very diligently and believe I could navigate a small schooner now from New York to Cuba if I wanted to.

When the chicken season began, I was in high spirits. The pointer brought out from the East had too close a range, and I bought two others, father and son, splendid dogs. The father was self-taught and had no fine points in his education, but he was the greatest chicken dog I have ever known. He seemed to perform miracles when he wanted to, but he never wanted to in the heat of the day. He was old. I bought him to use for one season and used him three. Everybody used him for years. He had probably seen the death of more than ten thousand chickens. We had trouble getting his son from a French half-breed who had sold him to us. When Slocum and I went to get him, he refused to part with the dog because of his wife. Slocum asked him if he were not master in his own house and could not do as he pleased with his own property. He said, "Lieutenant, it is easy to see that you are not married." But we got the dog finally, and for four years I had wonderful chicken shooting. The bay birds and curlew were in countless numbers there, but, about the time they raised their young, the chickens which could be hunted with a dog were ready to shoot, and I never bothered about the others. All sorts of ducks nested in that country except the black mallard, and the season began about August 28.

The officers told me they would show me how to get ducks and would drive out to the mallard slough. If the birds were flying there that evening, we would have some sport. Otherwise they would announce that there were no birds flying, and we would have to go home empty-handed. I wondered about this all season. There were millions of ducks seen in the air and on the small lakes and ponds. Why would they fly in the mallard slough one day and not the next? When not shooting, I was driving about seeking an answer to the question. All the birds and animals have laws of nature that compel each kind to do the same thing under the same circumstances. These laws are very simple and, when once deduced, make the finished sportsman and deliver the game into his hand with little effort.

I learned the laws of the rabbit when a boy at home. The rabbit, followed by a slow hound, will return to where he is started from. One has only to wait until he comes back to shoot him. I learned of the black bear from the Caddo Indians by watching their movements when hunting. They cannot give one their reasons for doing certain things. The only means of learning lies in close observation. I learned the laws governing the mountain sheep from the Crows, the black-tailed deer from the Sioux and Cheyennes. I never did master any law for the white-tailed or Virginia deer, perhaps because none prevailed.

The ducks at Fort Totten rafted in immense bodies far out on the lake during the heat of the day and would go inland toward evening to feed and spend the night, flying over water if possible. I soon discovered that the law governing this flight was their desire to fly from the big lake against the wind. If the wind were from the south, they went out on the south side, and vice versa. I soon had twenty-five duck passes and, applying the law, never again missed a flight. Why does a duck want to fly against the wind? Because his feathers are then smoothed down rather than ruffled. When they are ruffled, the sharp points of the quills hurt him. Whenever you see a robin perched on a tree or fence, his face will always be toward the wind, if there is any, to keep his feathers smooth. These observations are not to be found in books.

The quartermaster asked Saint Paul for a steam engine for our schooner. When it came, it was too large for the boat and would have sunk her if used. Then we began the construction of a good-sized tug, cutting and hauling the oak logs and sawing them at the agency sawmill. We built a fine dock of crib wood filled with boulders far out into the lake, giving eight feet of water off the end of the pier, into which we could dive. Many a large pike was caught off that pier, although we were told by the former garrison that it was of no use to fish in the lake, for the pike would never bite.

This time, not being very expert marine engineers, we made the boat too large for the engine, though it was excellent in every other way. The boat went very slowly, not more than seven miles an hour. General Sherman came to the post for an inspection, bringing his daughter and an aide,

Captain [John M.] Bacon.[2] I invited them, as post quartermaster, to go out on the lake in our homemade steamboat. After we got out a short distance, the general asked, "What makes this boat go so slowly?" I told him of our trials and tribulations, and he turned to Bacon and told him to see that we got a proper engine for our boat. This time we got what we wanted. Our boat plowed those seas for years, a credit to a real shipyard.

Those were the days before vegetables were issued to the soldier. We raised wonderful crops of potatoes, cabbages, tomatoes, carrots, beets, and onions. My troop had one thousand bushels of potatoes and splendid heavy heads of cabbages and root vegetables such as I had never seen before. These we stored in a root house and issued to the troop all winter. The half-breeds would bring in a train of Red River carts, loaded with frozen pike from springs that never froze on the Mouse or James River, where the pike would congregate in the warm springwater in winter, so thick they could be thrown out with a pitchfork. The trader bought these, threw them in a great pile on the floor of an empty storeroom, where one could pick out the fish that pleased him, thaw it out, and thus have fresh fish for dinner. During the summer the Sioux women would bring in wild raspberries and give us half an oilcanful for twenty-five cents. All this enabled us to live better and cheaper that we have ever lived anywhere since. We felt abused when the price of beef went up to seven cents a pound. We killed our own game and fish and raised our own vegetables. When the frost threatened the tomatoes, we picked them green and ripened them in cornmeal.

◆ ◆ ◆

I went on a leave of absence for four months in January 1879. My mother was then living in Princeton with her sister at Morven, the old Stockton place. My grandfather had died. When I turned a corner and met my grandmother, she put her arms around my neck and cried as if her heart would break. My aunt's children got scarlet fever soon after my arrival, and, fearing to be put in quarantine, I spent my time going back and forth between New York and Philadelphia until the fever was over.

Just before leaving Totten, news came that what I had predicted about the Cheyenne prisoners at Fort Robinson had happened. Ordered sent back

2. Sherman crisscrossed the country on various inspection trips during his tenure as general of the army. For one example in 1883, see Kime, *Sherman Tour Journals*.

to the Indian Territory by the secretary of the Interior, they had broken out in the dead of winter at Fort Robinson and, without food or clothing, had been nearly all killed refusing to surrender to the troops which tried to recapture them. Dull Knife himself escaped and reached asylum among the Sioux. Wild Hog, who had been the most earnest in his determination to die in the North rather than go back to die of sickness in the Indian Territory, was captured at the beginning and tried to stab himself with a fork. This treatment of a fine, virile tribe, one of the most moral on the Plains, marks another black page in our history. I had warned Colonel Carlton, commanding at Fort Robinson, months before the affair took place, but he had been sent to take station at Sidney, Nebraska, and there was a new commander at the time.[3]

Returning from leave through Chicago, I stopped at the Palmer House, then the army hostelry, where General Sheridan and his brother Mike were living. General Sheridan saw me sitting in an armchair against the wall in the lobby, came and sat down by me, tipped his chair back against the wall, and talked to me for an hour about conditions in the Northwest. I had all the Indian gossip of the Plains—what Sitting Bull was thinking about—which the general could get from nobody else except Ben Clark. When he called me "Scott," placing me on a conversational level with himself, I swelled up with pride so that Chicago could scarcely hold me. Both Sheridan and his brother always asked me to dinner whenever I passed through Chicago. I never appealed to either of them for help in vain. The general left me to go to the barber shop, and a scion of a prominent Philadelphia family, whom I had known when he was in college at Princeton, came up and asked me who had been talking to me. I replied, "General Sheridan." When he asked where he had gone, I said, "To the barber shop." About an hour afterward I met him again, and he told me he had bought the razor with which the general had been shaved.

I had seen Miss Merrill a number of times while she was at school at Philadelphia. Now that she was back at Fort Yates at Standing Rock, Dakota, I got a month's leave from Fort Totten to go there. I went back over that road in June to be married at Standing Rock. It was on a still, clear night, with the moon at its fullest, that Mrs. Scott and I started out on our honeymoon

3. The new commander at the time of the January 9, 1879, "Cheyenne Outbreak" was Henry W. Wessells. This tragedy is detailed in Buecker, *Fort Robinson*, 125–48.

that has lasted until now. We drove back those eighty-two miles from the railroad in an ambulance covered with wire netting to shut out the flies and mosquitoes that were unendurable. The greensward was dotted with bluebells and other flowers, with now and then a tiger lily sticking up through the grass. We started our life together at Totten and spent there three happy years, sailing, fishing, and shooting. Our eldest son, David Hunter, was born here.[4]

I used frequently to swim my old horse a mile into the lake, forcing him against his will, then allowing him to turn back. He would stretch every effort to go straight back in a hurry, towing me by his tail. The art of controlling a horse in the water and making him go where you want him to, whether it is according to his will or not, was taught me by Hare when camped on the Belle Fourche River in 1878. It was taught to my two boys at Fort Sill when they were little, and I have never seen anyone else able to do it. Many horses will swim a river willingly when they can see the other side, but to be able to turn them up or down the river and back and forth at your pleasure or straight out into a lake where they cannot see the other side is a difficult art.

In the fall of 1882 Mrs. Scott took our son and went to visit her father, General Merrill, who commanded all the troops escorting the contractors of the Northern Pacific Railway from Bismarck to the Rocky Mountains, with his headquarters at Billings, Montana. I was going to go after her but was put to building the telegraph line from Fort Totten, seventy-eight miles east to Larimore [Dakota Territory], to meet the Great Northern Railway that had stopped there for a while. It was time for Mrs. Scott to come back when the line was finished. Department headquarters had notified us that there would be no change of station that year. We were settling for the winter when an order came sending us on a four hundred march to Fort Meade in the Black Hills. I gathered up my six dogs and started with the troop. Mrs. Scott was picked up with our boy at Bismarck, and we marched across the Sioux Reservation for the Black Hills without any sort of comfort. We lost one man, a recruit who had started out on foot in the snow to kill a buffalo. I rode fifty miles next day in search of him. Many parties looked for him far and wide, but no trace of him was ever found.

4. The Scotts were married in June 1880; David was born in 1882. Harper, "Hugh Lenox Scott," 11n17, 12.

We encountered plenty of buffalo, and Mrs. Scott shot her buffalo on the Moreau or Owl River. After a long march in great cold, wet, and discomfort, we arrived at Fort Meade. We had left comfortable, brick, two-story barracks, the best in the Northwest, to march four hundred miles through inclement weather to a post where there were no quarters for us. We had to start building our own of logs in winter. There was apparently no emergency to cause this change of station. It seemed nothing but a wanton disregard of the comfort of troops.

Shortly after our arrival in January 1883, Mrs. Scott took our boy and went east with Mrs. [Augusta Virginia Hancock] Hare and her little girl on the stage to visit her family in Philadelphia. The ground was frozen hard, and the stage carried them right through to Fort Pierre on schedule time. The stage line now ran from Deadwood 230 miles to Pierre instead of to Bismarck as formerly. They [presumably with the Hares] started back in the spring, and Mrs. Scott had one of the hardest trips anyone ever had. It was really a wonder she lived through it. One night on the stage is enough to play out a strong man, but they were seven days and nights on that stage on account of the condition of the gumbo soil, which rolls up on the wheels like glue when at all wet. I have known a stage on that line to be eight days going twenty miles.

About halfway the boy was taken with convulsions because of his teeth. Mrs. Scott expected every minute to lose him. She borrowed a pocketknife, carried by a passenger for cutting tobacco, and lanced her son's gums, relieving the pressure on his brain. There was little chance of getting food for anyone, let alone a sick child. The four big horses would pull about five hundred yards and stop, out of breath, the wheels glued up with gumbo. Then the messenger would call for the gumbo paddle and pry great chunks of clay from the wheels, matted with grass. Those same chunks were lying on that trail ten years after, baked hard as a brick. Mrs. Scott expected me to meet her seventy-five miles from Fort Meade with a light wagon and four horses to hurry her in with Mrs. Hare, but instead of that they met a lawyer from Deadwood going out on horseback, and, upon asking if he knew me, were told that he did and that he had lately seen me going out the other way with a large command and a packtrain after Indians. That was almost the last straw. They [again, presumably in a party that included the Hares] reached Fort Meade finally, exhausted completely, and the boy barely alive.

16

A Mission of Pacification

A telegram had come to Fort Meade, directing a large force to be sent after some Indians reported to be depredating west of the Black Hills. I told the adjutant that there was no use for a large force. He could take a few men and packs. I would go as his interpreter, and we two would take care of it. This pleased him and the commanding officer until the telegram was reread, which called for a "large force." It was seen that a squadron, at least, must be sent. I was told that I could go as interpreter, for there never was an interpreter or any Indian scouts kept at Fort Meade. I demurred at this. The commanding officer said I would have to go anyhow since there was no other interpreter. I told him I was not employed as an interpreter and declined to put my reputation in the hands of an officer who was going in command, who would be sure to saddle any disaster which might come from his inefficiency on me as an interpreter. The commanding officer told me to get out, and I got out before he changed his mind again.

He ordered out a squadron of the Seventh Cavalry with the full train of fifty cargo animals, but the troops were slow in getting ready, furbishing up their private wagons, which, if they had been taken, would have been stuck in the gumbo yet. It was so bad that some of our pack mules, newly shod, pulled off their shoes. Two pulled their shoulders out of joint. The commanding officer lost his patience with them. I was awakened at night by the adjutant, saying the order had been changed. The commanding officer had directed that I take what amounted to a squadron, composed of large details from every troop, two other officers, and the packtrain. We got away next morning, leaving everybody mad behind us, because, though the officers of the squadron had been grumbling about going, they did not want to be superseded by a lieutenant. All the lieutenants of higher rank were angry at being passed over for such a command, which was equivalent to that of a major. All the troop commanders were disgruntled at having such a large proportion of their troops taken from them.[1]

Though the Indians were said to be depredating west of the Black Hills, we got word at Spearfish that they were now north on the Little Missouri [River]. We crossed the Belle Fourche and camped on Iron Creek just as a blizzard started. We had only our shelter tents since it was April and the season for snowstorms was over. The train carried some grain, and we sheltered men and animals on the lee side of a bluff on Iron Creek in an oak grove, giving us plenty of firewood. The snow was blowing horizontally and fell two feet deep, keeping us here three days, hardly able to see a yard. Then it began to rain. This was the time Deadwood washed out [May 16, 1883], and every river in the Northwest was more than bank-full.

We heard at the Little Missouri that the Indians had moved down sixty miles to the Short Pine Hills. We started down after them, through wind and snow, none of us dry for a week. Every night I had to put my boots under the pillow to keep them from freezing stiff. We met a buffalo hunter at the Short Pine Hills who said the Indians had crossed there before the river rose and were somewhere on the other side beyond the river. The snow was standing in patches then, and the Little Missouri was bank-full, a hundred and fifty yards wide and twenty feet deep, with a roaring current. The question was how to get the command across the river without any facilities.

The matter was discussed with the other officers, and they said: "You can never get across here with this outfit. You came out with fifteen days' rations, and nine of them are gone already. You are more than a hundred miles from the post. You can't wait for the river to go down. You will have to start back right away for there are rivers up between us and the post to be crossed."

This looked very black. I went off by myself to reread my orders. They said, "find those Indians" but nothing about giving up the effort. So, "Find

1. The Seventh Cavalry detachment, under command of Lieutenant Scott, left Fort Meade on April 29, 1883, with orders to find "a camp of Crow Indians on Powder River to warn them to return to their reservation." Terry, "Report," 1:113. See also Hoxie, *Parading through History*, 112–16.

them we must," I argued, and ordered all the sling and hash ropes to be brought from the train and joined together by bowlines and all the lariats without picket pins. I could see a cabin on the other side, made of ties left by tie cutters for the Northern Pacific. Out of these a good raft could be made by our carpenter if I could get him over there, for he could not swim.

I found an old extension top for a farm wagon, rotting in the grass, which someone had thrown away long before. I wrapped this frame with canvas mantas [blankets] from the packtrain until it would float and carry a man and called for a volunteer to swim across with the rope and drag this canvas boat across, carrying the carpenter. The buffalo hunter said he would do it for a plug of tobacco. I promised him three plugs and to have a hot blanket thrown around him when he got back and a drink of whisky to warm him up. He undressed to take the rope, but one of those dancing sawyers came around the bend, made when a cottonwood tree is undermined. It comes down with the current, root first, until it strikes a bank. Then, top first, the branches broken and sharp, it dances up and down with the waves like a chevaux-de-frise ready to rip up anyone who gets in front of it.[2] The buffalo hunter, not liking the looks of this, changed his mind and concluded that he did not want the tobacco enough to earn it.

A call was then sent out through the squadron, and one of the men volunteered, undressed, put his foot in the flow, and drew it back, pronouncing the water too muddy and cold. The call was then sent up to the packtrain, but no one there cared to try it. Seeing that we were getting nowhere, I threw off my clothes, tied the rope around my waist, and jumped out into ice water that made me gasp loud enough to be heard a mile. I pulled the carpenter and one other man over and put the rope around a tree in an endless loop. They hauled me back in the boat, then sent several men over. In two hours we had a raft ready on the opposite shore.

Hauling it across, the water boiled over it so as to wash away the property if any had been on it. The raft was taken off the main rope and put on a short one, tied to the main line in such a way as to give more buoyancy and lift the raft when the strain came rather than submerge it. The boat was put on a crib built with ties on the raft, so that, when the current submerged the raft, it boiled across under the boat, in which men and property were loaded.

2. A chevaux-de-frise, a classic anti-cavalry obstacle consisting of a log with protruding spikes, was used as late as the Civil War.

We crossed everything except the horses before sundown, swimming the mules across in a body after the bell.

We attempted to swim the horses across in the way laid down in the drill regulations. I attached one of my horses to the rope and had him pulled across as a guide for the others. They waded in to their bellies, but, disliking the cold, began to mill around in the water and turn back. We were all around them and attempted to drive them ahead after the guide, but they broke through the cordon of men and started for home. I caught my other horse as he went past, hung on and stopped him, put a man named [John H.?] Barron of E Troop on him bareback, and told him to head the bunch, lead them around in a circle, and bring them back.[3] We felt pretty sad out there afoot, more than a hundred miles from home. The pessimists gave up getting the horses back at all, but I directed a number of fires to be built to guide Barron to the camp, for it would soon be dark. After it had grown really dark, we could hear them coming. Barron rode in, followed by every one of the horses, a little blown by their run. The men went up quietly, caught them, and tied them up for the night, without losing a horse. The next morning we tied their halter shanks to the endless rope, six at a time, and hauled them over, ate breakfast, packed up, and were on the Indian trail by ten o'clock.

We camped that night on the Box Elder [Creek] near the Hole in the Rock (Inyan Okeloka). Here was a roaring stream to be crossed, of a different kind in a different way. The stream was usually dry and its bed fifty feet below the plain with perpendicular clay banks, with places for entrance and exit only on the buffalo trails that crossed it at times. The water was now thirty feet deep with a roaring current. A good-sized cottonwood tree was growing there, much bent, which we cut down. A detachment was sent ten miles up the river with axes to cut and float down any other cottonwoods over six inches in diameter that they could find, from which resulted the trunks of three green cottonwoods.

We set about to build a floating bridge. All the ropes were gathered again, and the trees were lashed in such a way as to reach in a great convex curve. On the upper side this was eased off by the ropes, the butt end of the cottonwood wedged into the near bank, the other end pushed by the current into the far bank. Then some long lodgepoles, left by the Indians, were

3. White, *Index to Indian Wars Pension Files*, 83.

gathered up and pushed into the mud, to which ropes were tied so as to make a handrail. A man holding to this rail, feeling under the water with his foot for the cottonwoods, and looking away from the current could get across and carry property. The horses and mules were both hauled across six at a time by the endless rope so as to prevent them from being washed downstream past the landing place. By ten o'clock all the property was across except one aparejo cinch that fell off into the water and was carried away by the current. The ropes were soon recoiled, and we were on the road again.

Coming into a valley, the trail scattered so as to make it impossible to follow. I was asked, "What are you going to do now that the trail has disappeared?"

I said, "I am not going to try to puzzle out this trail. We are going to go straight for that gap at a trot, twenty miles ahead, where we will find all these trails coming together again."

Nearing the gap, we found a lost dog. Then all the trails swung into a large beaten trail that could be followed with the eyes shut. We began to double up on the camps until we found that the ashes were warm. Next we came to a camp with the fires still burning. I proposed to take an officer and a man and go ahead into their camp before they saw the troops coming and stampeded away from us. At first no one wanted to leave the command, but a little gentle ridicule changed this. I started out with my [former West Point] classmate, Lieutenant [Horatio G.] Sickel [Jr.], and one man.

We had not gone far on the trail when the man said he could hear a mountain lion. We looked all around but could not see a lion, but looking farther we could see two women riding at a distance against the background of a high, pine-covered bluff, which made them difficult to see. They were traveling slowly on horseback as if they had not discovered us. It was necessary to cut them off before they could stampede the camp. Desirous of not frightening them, we kept on our course until they had crossed out of sight over the ridge, then gave a little time for them to look back to see what we were doing, whereupon we started straight for them at a sharp gallop to catch up with them. Instead of keeping on slowly, they had begun to gallop just as soon as they had got out of our sight but away from the direction of the [Crow] village, probably with the intention of drawing us away from it. We let them go, however, and, turning back to the lodgepole trail, we soon went over a ridge close to the village and got into it before we were noticed.

The first lodge was entered and the head chief sent for, but he was not in camp. The next chief came. He was told of the approach of troops and that he was to prevent his people from stampeding. The troops were not going to hurt anybody if they behaved themselves. A crier was sent out to make the announcement. By the time a good defensive camp site was selected, at a little distance that would command the village, the troops came along and went into camp where I told them.

We kept our horses tied up tight under a strong guard. Everything passed quietly during the night. Finding the Indians reassured, I told them that they would have to come with me. We conducted them to their reservation and let them go. It was not long after, however, that I read that the head chief was in jail in Fort Snelling, Minnesota, near Saint Paul.[4]

There we were, seventy-five miles south of Fort Keogh, the nearest place we could get a supply of food, two and a half good marches and only one day's rations left. We issued half rations and made the seventy-five miles into Keogh in two days. Several deep, cold rivers were crossed. Our mission ended.

While superintending the reshoeing of the animals at Fort Keogh, I received a telegraph order from Saint Paul to find another band of hostile Indians and put them on their reservation. No one knew where they were to be found. All sections of the country were eliminated by telegraphic inquiries, except the Powder River valley, which could not be reached by telegraph. We struck the Powder about twenty miles above its mouth. I was lying on top of the highest peak available at dawn the next morning, searching the valley with a glass, hoping to see a number of parallel columns of smoke rising in the still air from the different lodge fires kindled at that time to cook breakfast and to warm the lodges, but none were seen. Fearing to stampede the village if we were seen approaching it, we left the valley, marched up the river thirty miles, and came back to the valley. At dawn the next morning we searched for smoke without result. We were rewarded on the fourth day by finding what we were looking for. Hiding the troop on the bluffs, I got into the village before being seen and calmed the chiefs, who reassured the people, so that no attempt was made to run away. We put them on their reservation and started back to Fort Meade. We had to devise means to cross all the rivers except the Powder, which we crossed on a deep ford above the boots of the aparejos, wetting the cargoes but slightly.

4. This may have been the Crow leader Crazy Head, incarcerated at Fort Snelling in 1887 for his involvement in the Sword Bearer Incident. Hoxie, *Parading through History*, 164–65.

When I became superintendent of West Point, I determined that no cadet should graduate in my time without a knowledge of the various means of crossing rivers with few facilities. I had the professor of military engineering [Gustav J. Fieberger?] set up a course in addition to that of building pontoon bridges. I had him make a canvas imitation of a bull's hide to simulate the bullboats made by the Indians of the Upper Missouri, round in shape like a coracle, with a framework of willows, by which I have seen an old Arikara woman transport two men with their horse equipment, leading their horses swimming behind, across the Missouri at its worst. I allowed such facilities as are always carried in a packtrain—an ax, rope, canvas mantas, and even some soft wire from a bale of hay. We crossed thirty-five cadets over the Hudson River and back in an hour and a half. I do not know whether this is still kept up or not. If it is not, the graduates are losing something they can ill afford to miss.[5]

Upon my return I found that I was still very unpopular. All sorts of dire predictions had been made that I would be hung up on some river and would not be back for months. About my only friend was Hare, who said he would give me five days to return, successful in my mission, which faith I justified by getting back in two. I felt very bad that my old friends should abandon me for nothing, looked about for some employment with the idea of leaving the service, and picked out a most valuable place to start a horse ranch at the head of the Little Missouri, but, losing my resentment, decided to remain in the service—most fortunately for me, for they were canning horses in that country within seven years. I would have gone broke. The horse industry revived during the Boer War. The Earl of Portsmouth [Oliver Henry Wallop] was said to have made a good deal of money at his ranch in the foothills of the Big Horn, furnishing horses in South Africa to the British Army, but that market did not last long. One can get a good saddle horse out there now for five dollars.

We found that a large part of Deadwood had been washed out during our absence. Large logs, three feet in diameter, deposited by the high water at the stable doors, were still stranded there.

5. Here Scott inserted a testimonial by Horatio G. Sickel, Jr., who detailed the 1883 scouting foray to find the Crow village, adding, in particular, descriptions of the difficult river crossings. H. G. Sickel, Columbia Barracks, Cuba, to the Adjutant General, Washington, D.C., Mar. 20, 1900, reprinted in Scott, *Some Memories*, 119–21.

We went east to see our people on four months' leave of absence early in 1884. The Cheyenne River was very high and floating large cakes of ice when we arrived there in the stage. The mail and passengers were transferred to stages on the other side in a cranky skiff. I tied our trunk handles to the thwarts to have the boat as a buoy for the trunk if it tipped over as it seemed likely to do. I took our boy on my lap to swim out with him, trusting to Mrs. Scott to save herself, with a little help, as she was a good swimmer. The risk was great from the large ice cakes and character of the boat, but we crossed without mishap. When we reached the Missouri, the ice was pronounced too rotten for the stage to cross and liable to break up at any minute. What to do no one knew. There was no place to stay there. We did not want to go back on the stage, so I hired a boy's sled and a man to haul it by a long rope. Mrs. Scott sat on her trunk with the boy. She carried a long dry pole to support her if the sled should break through the ice. We others carried similar poles, marched at some distance from her sled, and all got across in safety. An officer's wife was drowned there the following spring. That season no more stages crossed on the ice, which broke up with a loud crash that night.

While visiting my [older] brother [Charles] in Pittsburgh, our daughter Anna [Merrill] was born [on March 13, 1884], after which we went on to Philadelphia and Princeton. My [younger] brother, who is professor of geology and paleontology at Princeton [William Berryman Scott], was getting up an expedition of college students to hunt for fossils in the Big Horn Basin. I concluded that I wanted to go with him and went to Washington to see General Sheridan, who had just moved from Chicago to command the army.[6] I asked him for permission to go as my brother's escort and to take a small packtrain and dozen men of the Seventh Cavalry. Those were the days before electricity, and the general smashed down his hand on his desk bell to call his brother Mike, who was his military secretary. He said, "Mike, fix this fellow up." I soon got an order giving me what I wanted.

After assembling my party at Fort Meade, there were three hundred miles to go across country to Fort Custer on the Big Horn to meet my brother. There was no trail, but I guided our party across and was chief packer, interpreter, commanding officer, guide, and hunter for the party all summer for fifteen hundred miles, through the Big Horn Basin, Yellowstone Park, and

6. Sheridan received this promotion on November 1, 1883. Hutton, *Phil Sheridan*, 347.

back to Fort Custer down the Yellowstone River. Many were the vicissitudes of flood and field. Our camp was washed out by a cloudburst on the Gray Bull [Greybull River].[7]

I killed my last wild buffalo nearby, the last I ever saw, in August 1884. Another was killed among the horses by the horse guard on the Gray Bull also—just scabby old bulls, for the spring of 1883 saw the last of the buffalo. I was on the range for a month at the Short Pine Hills, killing meat for my troop, which was accumulating a fund to buy vegetables by selling its salt meat in the mines above Deadwood. I replaced this with buffalo meat. I had no trouble in January 1883 to keep a six-mule team going into the post all the time. There were about three thousand men on the range killing buffalo for their hides when the railroad got near. Whenever a dollar can be made on the hide of an animal, that animal is doomed. The hunters would sometimes get a stand on a herd of buffalo and kill one hundred or more. The weather was intensely cold, 40 degrees below zero for days and never above 20 degrees below at noon for weeks at a time. After taking the tongue and skinning one animal, the hides would freeze on the others and would be left untouched by the knife. The waste was terrific. Major James McLaughlin, the Sioux agent at Standing Rock, took a large contingent of Sioux out on the range to make meat and hides.[8] They killed five thousand head and dried the meat to take back. That was the end of the buffalo.

I traveled with Hare five hundred miles in search of buffalo in September 1883. They had been plentiful the year before, but now we did not see even a recent track. We met an old Sioux Indian who had been searching all summer and had killed one old, scabby bull. Many thought they had gone north into Canada. The Indians thought they had gone underground to rest and would come again as they were told in their ancient legends had happened before.

But the buffalo never returned. Many Indians starved to death in consequence, starved to death under the American flag, wards of our government, because our government was too weak and too careless to protect their food from wanton destruction by white men.

7. The 1884 fossil collecting expedition took up more space in his brother's autobiography than in Scott's. William Berryman Scott, *Some Memories*, 161–64.

8. Scott knew McLaughlin previously to this incident, having met him earlier at Fort Totten in the latter's capacity as Indian agent there. McCormack, "Soldiers and Sioux," 18–19.

The army regulations in those days encouraged an officer to take hunting leaves, provided he would turn in a map of the country traversed. I turned in maps of the country for two hundred miles about Fort Meade in every direction. I got the urge every now and then. If it were not the hunting season, I would just travel with some congenial friend exploring the Black Hills and beyond, far and wide, with a couple of packers, a couple of orderlies, and a cook.

One day we were on top of the Slim Buttes (Paha Zipzipela), where Anson Mills had his fight with American Horse. It was raining hard, and all the dry washes were full of running water. I came along behind in a heavy overcoat, riding bareback. My horse attempted a greasy clay bank and slipped backward, sitting down in a dry wash two feet deep. I fell backward off his wet slippery back. He sat on my chest, clawing the bank with his front feet, his hind feet far in front of him where he was unable to get them on the ground under him. The swift current was carrying gravel down the neck of my overcoat. I could look up and see light through the muddy water and reflected that it would be a curious fate for a man who had swum the Hudson River to be drowned in a dry wash two feet deep.

The horse was making violent struggles to regain his feet. I feared he would put his hind hoofs in my face. He stood up just before I would have had to give up holding my breath and got off my chest, allowing me get my head out of water in the nick of time. He ran on to catch up with the others, giving them their first knowledge of a mishap. They hurried back to find what had happened and found me sitting in the wash, too weak to stand up, the water up to my armpits. I soon recovered, however, and went on again. The clay washed into the fabric of that coat was still in it when I gave it to an Indian years afterward in the Indian Territory. I really believe that I came nearer to drowning in that two feet of water than I ever did in my life before or since. The others decided that any man who could make an escape as narrow as that must be reserved for a hanging, though I hope they were mistaken.

17

Recruiting Service

In August of '86 I was given the two years' cavalry recruiting detail for the Seventh Cavalry, with station in Philadelphia. My horses, cow, and other property were put up for sale at auction at Fort Meade, preparatory to moving east. When my old buffalo horse was bid up higher than his cost, he seemed to look at me with reproach and say, "After all our times together among the buffalo, are you really going to sell me?" I withdrew him hastily from sale, although I needed the money.

His first trip with the Seventh Cavalry had been with Custer to the Black Hills in 1874. He had been shot in the foot on the Little Big Horn with Reno. He died at Fort Sill at about thirty years of age, after having drunk in every important stream from the British line far down into Texas. He was very nervous and quick to act. Once when I put my hand on him at Fort Totten, while his head was down in the manger, he kicked me in the ribs with both feet, clear across the stable passageway, from which my ribs did not recover for twenty years, but it was done in fright and not in malice. When I proposed to break him to drive, Slocum said it would have to be done with one of those ironbound treasure coaches from the Black Hills, for no wagon could stand it. Nevertheless, he was driven for years. At first no one but Mrs. Scott would drive with me. I was often remonstrated with for trying to kill her, but she is still alive, I am thankful to say, while the prophets of evil are not. Whatever distrust Mrs. Scott may have about me in other ways, she has always accorded me her full confidence with a horse or dog, in the water, or in an Indian tanglement. Her confidence has never been misplaced in those particulars.

Leaving Fort Meade, we drove twenty-five miles to Rapid City, which the railroad had just reached. We soon established ourselves in Philadelphia, where our daughter [Mary] Blanchard was born [on July 3, 1887]. We both had many relatives in Philadelphia and Princeton, forty miles away. We were able to have my mother stay with us from time to time. We saw much of Mrs. Scott's relatives also. I examined, enlisted, and shipped recruits every day but Sunday and besides became acquainted with large libraries.

I felt that my two years in the city were wasted, away from troops and away from the peculiar service for which I had trained myself in the Indian country, but I did not have enough money to take myself and family at any one time back to the Plains until, at the expiration of my tour of duty, I was ordered to Fort Sill, Indian Territory, the station of my Troop M, Seventh Cavalry.[1] I rather pitied myself for going to a post where the Indians were too tame, but I need not have done so for I found the Kiowa, Comanche, and Kiowa Apache Indians still as wild as the Sioux and Cheyennes I had left in the North. They were all blanket Indians still and were capable of kicking up a serious bobbery if not carefully handled. They were quite primitive in every way.

1. Scott joined his troop in February 1889. Post Return, Fort Sill, Okla. Terr., Feb. 1889, *Returns from U.S. Military Posts, 1800–1916*, Records of the Adjutant General's Office, 1780s–1917, Record Group (RG) 94, National Archives and Records Administration (NARA), Washington, D.C.

18

Into the Southwest

I got off at Henrietta [in Clay County], Texas, the railroad point for Fort Sill at that time, and drove sixty-seven miles north in the mail wagon in a piercing wind that kept me chilled to the bone. I was received at Fort Sill by my old friend, Lieutenant [Theodore A.] Baldwin of the Seventh Cavalry, and by Thomas Clancy, my new orderly, who stuck to me for many years clear to Cuba and Porto [Puerto] Rico. He fell out of a window in Manila and was killed, much to the sorrow of my whole family, for we all loved him for his fidelity. The only fault Mrs. Scott ever found with him was that he would purloin her kitchen utensils for our camp cooking when we were going into the field. He loved the horses, the dogs, and the children, who looked on him as their protector and friend. He stayed with us for nine years at Fort Sill. I had only to tell him that I would have so many in my party, wanted so many horses and dogs, would be away so many days, and wanted to find him camped, say, at the spring "where the Osage cut the heads off the Kiowas" in 1834, and that was enough. We would wait for the mail next day, then, trotting forty-five miles to the hill looking down on the spring, would find Clancy there with the tents up, the dinner cooked, and the beds made.

A party of Kiowa and Comanche scouts, the principal Indians of that region, were sometimes camped nearby waiting for a conference. After hearing the news and the troubles of the region, I would ask who knew where there were any "foolish" turkeys in that country. In their parlance a "foolish" turkey was a tame one that would allow himself to be killed. A "wise" turkey was a wild one that would get away quickly and escape. The Indian of the buffalo country never ate birds or fish in those days. The quail and turkeys might be everywhere under his feet without notice. He had nothing to do with them. They are glad enough to get them now, but then, so long as they had beef or buffalo meat, they did not really need anything else, though they liked bread and sugar and coffee well enough but did not feel deprived if they went without.

I was presented with two dogs the day of my arrival, one of which became a most excellent quail dog and the best turkey dog in the Southwest. Wild turkeys were plentiful then as were quail. The whole country was soon mine, from Kansas to Texas, and a wonderful primeval country it was. The streams were bordered with elm, cottonwood, oak, hackberry, pecan, and walnut. Fort Sill could not afford to haul coal sixty-seven miles from the railway and contracted for many cords of hardwood as fuel every year. When I became quartermaster of the post, I induced the higher-ups to erase pecan and walnut from the list of hardwoods in the wood contracts and, when receiving the wood under the contracts, would throw out pecan and walnut, refusing to take them. This soon stopped the burning of those valuable woods. There are many alive down there now that otherwise would have been burned many years ago. I also stopped the Indian women's custom of cutting down trees to secure the nuts, a wasteful habit which had arisen from their migratory lives with the buffalo. Here today and gone tomorrow, possibly never to see that part of the country again, the women knew no reason for conservation, which comes later in the history of peoples. We are only coming to it now ourselves.

Wherever I live near mountains, they call until I go to them. The Wichita Mountains were within plain sight and twelve miles from Fort Sill. They began to call to me the first day. It was not long before I started with a visiting cousin, accompanied by I-see-o and five of the Kiowa and Comanche scouts, a cook, a packer, and two pack mules, to answer their summons and to learn about the country.[1] We rode all around the Wichita group and through the middle before we got back, the Indians pointing out the sites of historical occurrences and relating their legends in the sign language.

1. I-see-o and Scott enjoyed a long, close relationship, one that extended past the Fort Sill years. The Kiowa scout became one of Scott's best teachers and probably his greatest Indian friend. Swett, "Sergeant I-See-O," 341–54. Scott once referred to I-see-o as "my right hand man on the southern Plains." McCoy and McCoy, *Tim McCoy Remembers the West*, 142.

Having learned the sign language on the northern Plains, the Indians of the southern Plains were surprised to see me, a new man from the East, come there with a good knowledge of it, something never seen before. The Comanche called me at once "Molay tay-quop," "he talks with his hands" or "sign talker." It enabled me to get into the good graces of all the Indians of that district almost at once, giving me their confidence and goodwill within a radius of two hundred miles from Fort Sill.

My first journey away from the post on duty was to go after fifty thousand dollars of "grass money" back at Henrietta, Texas. A large part of the reservation of the Kiowa and Comanche Indians was leased to cattlemen in large pastures, and the rent was called "grass money" to indicate to the Indians that they were leasing only the grass on the land and not the land itself. The grass money in those days was paid directly to the Indian per capita, the payment supervised by the agent and witnessed by some officer of the army. Nowadays it is paid directly to the Treasury, and an act of Congress is required to get it out. The Indian cannot get it when he wants it.

I took with me a sergeant and three mounted men as guard for the money, for it had been noised abroad that the money was coming. It was freely predicted that I was going to be held up and have it taken away from me. I started back, carrying it loose in the ambulance, without a safe, and sat on the box with the driver with a six-loading shotgun filled with buckshot across my lap, ready to shoot as soon as anybody made an attempt. The mounted men went ahead and searched every ravine before I would go near it.

We camped at Elm Springs the second day, one of those hot days they call a "weather breeder" in that country, a forerunner of a "norther." A number of cattlemen came up and camped with me, without any tentage or cooking facilities. I had to take them in with me. We were all in a perspiration putting up the tents when—bang!—the wind changed like a flash. A norther was on, nearly freezing the perspiration on our faces, our teeth chattering with cold, inside of five minutes. I have known Mrs. Scott to be playing tennis in light summer garments, wet with perspiration, and hardly be able to get into the house when struck by a norther. These northers go down as far as Vera Cruz, and how much farther I never learned.

The cattlemen had with them an old man from Chicago to whom I had to give my bed or he would have died that night with the cold. I had a sick dog to take care of and fifty thousand dollars and did not sleep much. With the cattlemen there were two deputy U.S. marshals whom I did not trust a great deal for no one trusted a marshal in those days. They would start out as marshals, and many would graduate as bank and train robbers. Fifty thousand dollars was a good deal of money. They had no bedding, and, as a great kindness to them, I rolled them both together in the canvas cover of my bedding roll and strapped them in tight so that they could not wander around at night. Their subsequent history showed that I had made no mistake.

Those cattlemen have since all come to great fame in Texas, some of them having become multimillionaires from their oil wells, especially Burke [Samuel Burk] Burnett, after whom the great Texas oil field was named, but they are all dead now, with the possible exception of [William T.] Waggoner. They were an interesting lot, prone to shoot quickly and often. They were the product of their time, growing up in the Southwest in the period after the Civil War when there were no school facilities and no restraint. I am glad to have known and to have been on friendly terms with them. We do not see people out there like them anymore. They were real cattle barons, each running from thirty-five to a hundred thousand head of cattle in a pasture, leased from the Indians besides other ranches they owned in Texas.

The word "pasture" is sometimes deceiving. Lieutenant Baldwin, Seventh Cavalry, was taking a wagon train from Fort Sill to San Antonio. When he arrived at Elm Springs to camp after dark, he was advised to turn his mules into the pasture for safekeeping. He did so and found to his dismay next morning that the pasture was thirty miles square. He did not get his mules rounded up for a week.

I turned the money into the agency at Anadarko next day, glad to get rid of it, and got a receipt for it. I found Colonel Carlton there with a squadron of the Seventh Cavalry to overawe the Kiowa into giving up their sun dance. They gave it up very reluctantly, believing that the well-being and health of their tribe depended on it. They held much resentment for a long time. They were doing no harm to anybody and should have been led away, not forced away, from it. Soon they all gathered into Anadarko for the payment, surrounded by white gamblers, fast women, and bootleggers, with every device to cheat the Indian out of his money. Those payments, military as well as Indian, attracted the vultures of society and were a crime against humanity. We could never get a law that would permit us to take proper care of our men and protect them from such vultures until Secretary [Newton D.] Baker got us one for the World War. Congress would not extend it further, and the officer is without the necessary power now. Congress is willing to protect the volunteer but cares nothing for the health of the Regular Army.

The two troops of the Fifth Cavalry were ordered over to the Canadian River to take part in the opening [to a land rush] of the original Oklahoma, April 22, 1889. I asked to go with them but was refused permission. It was only a few days, however, before our squadron got their orders, and we all started east to take our position on the line under Colonel [James F.] Wade, Fifth Cavalry, who assigned us our places and directed us to synchronize our watches.[2] Our station was at Purcell [in present McClain County] on the main Canadian. We marched through the site where Oklahoma City now is, without seeing a vestige of life, although there were doubtless "sooners" hidden in the timber, ready to pop out at twelve o'clock noon and beat some honest man to a claim, but we did not see them. By sundown the next day ten thousand people were camped on that site.

We lined up about five thousand people on the line at Purcell, as motley a land-hungry crew as ever gathered in America. When the signal was given at noon, they surged forward on foot and on horseback, with every sort of vehicle, some drawn by horses, a mule, a cow, or a woman. For years afterward I would be accosted by someone I did not know, who expected me to know him because he had ridden past me on April 22 and thought I ought to be able to swear to the fact of his identity and presence on the claim he had chosen.

That method of opening the land gave rise to innumerable lawsuits over title. Many honest men were cheated out of farms by bullies and crooks of high degree. Law seemed conspicuous by its absence. I have been told that there were a few United States marshals about, but I did not see them and would not have known they were marshals if I had. Of course, there could have been no municipal officers until matters had settled down long enough to elect them. In the meantime the crook and the bully had free swing. Two or three armed crooks would see some inoffensive claimant located on a farm they fancied, probably for speculation, would flash a gun on the man, and tell him to leave. He would have to go and, being without witnesses, could never establish his superior claim in the courts. While often the first on the ground, the only thing he would get out of it would be a lost lawsuit. Many piteous cases were laid before us, but, having no civil jurisdiction, we were equally helpless.

2. Merritt, "Report" (1889), 1:163–66.

I did, however, drive out a band of thugs from the week-old town of Norman, where the University of Oklahoma now is, without breaking the law. A man came into our camp soon after the opening, announcing that he was mayor of Norman and stating that the town was terrorized by an armed band of thugs engaged in jumping the best lots in town, driving out their holders. He wanted protection from the gang. I was told to take ten men and go up and drive them out, an order for which there was no legal basis. If I had been foolish enough to do anything overt, I could have been proceeded against in the courts, but I was then old enough in the service to know better. I asked the mayor if he had a policeman in the town. He said no. "Then you hurry on ahead and appoint one and have him ready by the time I get there," I advised him.

Reaching Norman, it was found that the news of my approach had acted to give some touch of legal formality to proceedings. Ruffians had before boldly taken a lot, warning off the owner, and had built a board shanty on it. Now they hired a woman of the town with a hired baby to occupy it, thinking that no one would dare to disturb a woman with a baby for fear of public opinion. I told the mayor and policeman to conduct me to the lot and dismounted my men all round it, telling the policeman to get a team and haul that shanty out into the middle of the public street without disturbing the woman and the baby.

The gang was afraid to interfere, not knowing my legal limitations. The house was hauled off the lot by municipal authority. My wagon came up by that time. They saw us go into camp as if we were going to stay there indefinitely. I told the mayor to issue a municipal ordinance to get that house out of the public street. The gang, seeing no prospect of making a haul and desirous of not losing the value in the house, returned their hired baby, tore down the house, disposed of the lumber, and left town for greener pastures, without my having violated any law and without my speaking a word to anyone in Norman but the mayor and the policeman. Although we remained at Purcell for some months, I never heard of a recurrence of the trouble anywhere in that neighborhood.

When I first went on the Plains, there was no semblance of law or justice. Wherever the railroad ended or any settlement was made, criminals of every kind were present. The criminal was master until things became so intolerable that a vigilant society would be formed to put down lawlessness by lawlessness and force. These conditions could all have been avoided by giving the higher commanders of troops civil jurisdiction in the Indian country, just as the Northwest Mounted Police of Canada had civil jurisdiction. When the latter arrived in Alberta in 1873, the crooks and criminals disappeared at once. The mere presence of the police acted to drive the undesirables over to our side of the line, where they could operate with impunity.

There were numerous military posts all over the Plains, the commanding officers of which represented the power of the United States. They comprised the only force capable of maintaining law and order. If they had been given legal power, they would have cleared the Plains of the criminals and avoided the orgies of crime that disgraced our frontiers for more than a hundred years. They would have enforced our treaties, keeping faith with the Indians, and so avoided our shameful Indian wars. They would have been able to enforce the law and protect life and property over all the Plains. But our Congress read accounts of the most horrible crimes year after year on the Plains and never made an effort to use the remedy that lay at hand.

Shortly after the opening of Oklahoma, while we were still kept at Purcell, a deputy U.S. marshal named Carr came into camp and asked for a posse comitatus of troops to assist him in arresting the McDonald brothers, a gang of seven men, who were camped about five miles away.[3] There had been many gangs of outlaw brothers in those days: the Dalton brothers, who tried to rob a band at Coffeeville [Coffeyville], Kansas, and came to grief; the Cook brothers; the Marlow brothers; the James and Younger brothers; and now the McDonald brothers.

The commander explained that he could not furnish the posse under the law, which forbade him to do so under penalty of losing his commission. This made the marshal sorrowful at the loss of a gang he thought he had held in the hollow of his hand. I thought there might be some adventure in this and asked for a seven-day leave to go with the marshal in a civil capacity, which was granted me, although a moment's consideration would show that I could not divest myself of my military status in that way. When I sent for my horse, it became known where I was going. One of our sergeants asked for a furlough to go also. We three started off together on horseback, three civilians.

3. This may have been William H. Carr, listed in "Robert King's Oklahoma and Indian Territory U.S. Marshals and Deputy U.S. Marshals," available online on the website of the Oklahoma Outlaws and Lawmen History Association (www.okolha.net).

Arriving at a place where we could reconnoiter the camp with a glass, the seven men were seen to be engaged around the fire, busy cooking dinner, all their rifles standing against a blackjack oak tree in a bunch. The camp was on a blackjack knoll, with a ravine coming down on each side of it and a wood to the left of one ravine. I laid out the plan, which was for me to ride up the left ravine, putting myself between the men and the woods in the event they should attempt to break that way. I would appear suddenly as if coming up out of the ground, drawing their attention, while the sergeant and marshal would ride up the other ravine behind their backs and dismount. The marshal would gather up their rifles and put them out of reach. The sergeant was to hold them under his gun when they found out what was going on behind them.

It turned out exactly as planned. They were greatly surprised to see me sitting quietly on my horse between them and the woods. While they were engrossed in me, the marshal carried their rifles out of reach before they knew he was there. When they saw the sergeant standing with carbine in hand, their rifles gone, and me between them and the woods, they allowed the marshal to come up and handcuff every one of them without a word. I sat on my horse without saying anything and could not be breaking any law by just sitting there. The marshal put them in a wagon and took them off to Fort Smith, Arkansas, for trial by the celebrated Judge [Isaac C.] Parker, who was a terror to evildoers, after having eleven men hung in one batch.

Running out of clothes in this camp, I got permission to go to Fort Sill and started off with Clancy. The first day out we jumped a spotted fawn, which I ran down and caught. Clancy took a gunnysack from under his saddle and cut four holes in it. Through these we put the legs of the fawn, which was tied in the sack. We carried it into Fort Sill, where it grew up in our yard, the last deer I will ever raise or have about.

From Purcell we were all sent up to Chilocco to take part in the first real maneuvers the army ever had conducted, under General Wesley Merritt [commander of the Department of the Missouri] on the Kansas border near Arkansas City. These maneuvers were long known as "the bloody war of 1889." They had the salutary effect of awakening a good many of us to the fact that the day of Indian wars was over and that we must fit ourselves for war with civilized peoples. After these were over [in September], we all returned to our posts. All the way home to Fort Sill, we had wonderful quail shooting.

The influenza that was prevailing all over the United States reached Fort Sill. I had a case that kept me in bed for two weeks, after which I began to make arrangements to receive Mrs. Scott and the children from Philadelphia. I met them at Henrietta with a four-mule ambulance and took them off the railway. The weather was gentle and warm. Everybody complained of the four buffalo robes in the ambulance, but, when we were struck by a norther, the complaints changed to commendation.

The children were all young then. One of their strongest recollections of that time is of a prairie fire that came down on us swiftly from the north on both sides of the road. One might try to force a pair of mules through it but not four, for the leaders would certainly whirl around, jackknifing the team and upset the ambulance, probably breaking the pole and setting the ambulance on fire. We set fire to the grass and followed it into the smoking prairie and let the fire go on without harm to ourselves.

Those were the days of the presidency of Grover Cleveland, whom we had met at Philadelphia with his bride, where she had charmed all hearts. The president was desirous of opening the Cherokee Strip along the south border of Kansas to settlement. Each time he made preparation, the western senators would represent the hardships this opening would work on the men whose cattle were running on the strip and who were continually putting in new cattle to prevent the opening, until the president got tired and ordered everybody out of the strip, forbidding the introduction of more cattle. I was sent with F Troop, Seventh Cavalry, to take the cattle that came up from Texas on the cattle trail and escort them to the Washita River, where Captain Jake [Jacob A.] Augur, Fifth Cavalry, would convoy them through the strip into Kansas. They were not allowed to run loose anywhere along the way. The job was turned over to the army because the president knew it would be faithfully performed.

I had Lieutenant A[ndrew] G. C. Quay, Fifth Cavalry, son of the senior senator from Philadelphia [Matthew S. Quay], and one of Mrs. Scott's cousins with me, as well as some Kiowa and Comanche scouts. The cattle began to strike the trail in bands of two to five thousand head, all intending to turn loose on the Indian reservations and drift later into the Cherokee Strip in violation of the president's proclamation. The trail came up through Vernon [in Wilbarger County], Texas, and crossed the North Fork of Red River, which was then the boundary line between Texas and the Indian Territory. The foremen were up to every device to cross above or below me and turn loose, without my knowledge, in the Kiowa and Comanche country, which I had been directed to prevent.

A Kiowa or Comanche scout was stationed on the flanks of the mountain in the rear of the camp with a field glass. He signaled down whenever he saw the dust of a herd trying to cross twelve or fifteen miles above or below. Another scout would be sent with a polite note to the foreman of the herd, asking him to come to see me. He would usually arrive in a great rage, declaring that he got his orders only from his boss and was not going to be told by any soldier what to do. It would then be politely explained that he would be acting against the proclamation of the president if he crossed into the Indian reservation, rather than on the cattle trail. As I was aware that no legal penalty was attached to the violation of the president's proclamation, I would not oppose his crossing but would allow him to proceed five miles into the reservation if he wanted to, against my advice. He would then, however, be a trespasser, and I had one hundred mounted men here who would be used to chase his cattle back into Texas. Driving off their fat and causing many, doubtless, to get their legs broken and others to be mired down in quicksands of the North Fork, this would cost real money, which his boss might be rich enough to afford but which would get him nowhere, for the same would be repeated at every subsequent attempt.

Soon thirty thousand head of cattle, their owners unwilling to have them go on through into Kansas, banked up at our crossing on the North Fork. The owners began to appear, saying that they were losing big money and asking if I could not help them in some way. Some produced a permit from the agent of the Kiowa and Comanche [W. D. Myers?] to turn loose on that reservation but were told that I did not take my orders from the agent but from the commanding officer at Fort Sill [Carlton], who had sent me here. Their cries for help were piteous. I told them that the only way I might be able to help them would be to send an Indian seventy-five miles to Fort Sill, asking the commanding officer whether I should honor the agent's permit. This was done. The commanding officer called on the agent to explain, and the agent became frightened and repudiated his own signature. The cattlemen had been paying him to give them permits illegally. The commanding officer sent me word that there would be no change in my orders. This and the daily loss convinced the owners it was no use to wait there longer. A few elected to drive onto Dakota and Montana. Others turned back into Texas and disappeared. But none turned loose on the reservations or on the Cherokee Strip, which was soon prepared for the opening.[4]

4. Dealing with cattlemen and their trespassing cattle took up considerable time and effort by the Regular Army. Merritt, "Report" (1890), 1:196, 197.

A Kiowa Indian came in and told us of the location of the nest of a war (golden) eagle, high up on a cliff on a mountainside five miles from camp. My cousin and I went over to see it with Arose, a Comanche scout.[5] We could see it plainly up against the face of a cliff and concluded that the best way was to go above it and climb down. Looking around for Arose, we found that he had disappeared. We climbed down and made our way with some difficulty along the edge of the cliff and found there was only one young bird in the nest, surrounded by the remains of a jackrabbit and several prairie dogs. We put our captive in a gunnysack and climbed down with him to the horses, where we found Arose, who had been watching our progress with great fear.

We staked the young bird out in camp. The old ones came hovering over next day, answered by the shrill pipe of the fledgling. The Indians told us that we ought not to have taken the only bird in the nest lest misfortune come to us. This bird grew large and strong. When leaving Fort Sill, I shipped him to Fairmount Park, Philadelphia, where he is probably alive yet as they are said to live a hundred years. An account of his capture may be seen in Richard Harding Davis's *West from a Car-Window*.[6]

The golden eagle has twelve feathers in the tail, from which the Plains warbonnets are made. We plucked this bird's tail five times to make a Kiowa warbonnet of sixty feathers. It was beautifully made by I-see-o, Elk Tongue, and Chaka. One war eagle used to be equal in value to a good horse before the days of automobiles, when horses cost money.

I fell sick in this camp with malarial fever and had to be carried seventy-five miles to Fort Sill in an ambulance. The morning after I left, one of the men drowned while swimming in the North Fork. The Indians attributed all these misfortunes to our taking that single eagle out of the nest. "No one can go against the wisdom of the elders without suffering for it," they said.

5. This probably refers to the Comanche leader Isa-Rose or White Wolf. Haley, "Red River War."

6. Davis, *West from a Car-Window*, 171–72.

19

Problems of Fort Sill

After recovering from the fever, I was appointed adjutant quartermaster and commissary of Fort Sill. It was not long before the post was put on the list for abandonment. The reasons were several. One was that Fort Reno, only seventy-five miles away, had been the station of General Merritt, who considered that two posts were not needed in that country so close together.[1] He preferred Fort Reno. I told them that they would never be able to get any good drinking water at Reno because the red gypsum beds sloped right under the region. They would always get bad water. They had hauled their drinking water five miles from the Caddo Springs for thirty years and now sank a well twelve hundred feet deep, costing fifteen thousand dollars, only to get water that would curl your teeth, whereas Fort Sill had good, clear limestone water and plenty of it.

General Merritt objected to Sill also because the stone gables were falling outward. Nothing could be done to keep the plaster on the rooms from crumbling. Captain [George E.] Pond, then at the height of his fame building Fort Riley, was sent down to inspect the post. He reported that nothing could be done for it. For one thing, the stone was too soft. The post ought to

1. Wesley Merritt advised Nelson Miles, his immediate superior, "The garrison at Fort Sill should be reduced as soon as practicable." Merritt, "Report" (1890), 1:198.

be torn down completely and a new post of brick constructed, at an estimated cost of three hundred thousand dollars.

I felt that the post ought to be saved for many reasons. It was in a far more agreeable country than Fort Reno, with clear streams and a view of the mountains within twelve miles. It had a history not be lightly tossed away. More than all, troops were needed there. If they could not live in the post, they would have to live in tents. So I set out to save Fort Sill in spite of everybody. I made a close examination and found the stone quite hard, bearing the quarry marks as sharp as the day it was quarried. I soon found also that the gable ends were falling outward because originally the grass had been merely scraped to lay the foundations. In fact, there were no foundations. This was the cause of all the trouble. I saved three hundred dollars in the erection of a water tank and proposed to the chief quartermaster to expend this money on the worst set of quarters—which had the gable ends propped up by large logs—mainly for the purpose of buying lifting jacks. This he promptly refused, saying that the gable ends would fall in on me just as soon as we began to excavate under them.

We fenced with each other at long range over this for six months when he finally allowed the saving to be used. When the lifting jacks arrived, an excavation was made under the wall, four feet wide and four feet deep, the wall being held up in the meantime by jacks. The work was done by a stonemason brought down from Kansas City. The limestone quarry a mile away furnished stone for the foundation, and we burned our own lime right there. Great slabs of stone were put in the excavations and a real foundation built. But how to get the weight off the jacks without allowing the wall to sag a little, and perhaps fall out, no one knew. I was passing down the front of the quarters soon afterward, looking at the ladies' flower beds, many of which were contained inside a circle composed of old tires taken from six-mule wagons. I gathered up all the old wagon tires to be found everywhere, had the blacksmith cut them into wedges, eight inches long and half an inch thick, wedged the walls so as to lift them off, freeing the jacks. My work was accomplished. The ends of those wedges may be seen yet in the old post. The chief quartermaster came down to see what had been done with his three hundred dollars on the worst set of quarters, pronounced himself satisfied, gave me eight thousand dollars, and promised twenty-five thousand the next year.

No money had been spent on the post for a long time in anticipation of its abandonment. The original floors were rotting so that I could stand on the ground in the middle of the drawing room, my feet through holes in the floor, while every time it rained, Mrs. Scott would place milk pans all over the floor to save her carpets. The cook would have to hold an umbrella over the range. I roofed the post with the eight thousand dollars, put in new floors where needed and new foundations, ran two chimneys up in each house instead of one, which smoked so that the open fireplaces could not be used, and built an extra room on many of the houses. Colonel Peter [D.] Vroom inspected the post and said, "Well, you have been fighting to save this post for three years, and now you can stop. The post is saved, and Reno is to go."[2] The twenty-five thousand never materialized because the chief quartermaster was retired. The headquarters were transferred from St. Louis to Chicago, where they had other uses for the money.

Fort Sill was then in the Indian Territory, neither in Texas nor Kansas. It had no congressional delegation to fight for it in Washington. In fact, it had nobody but me, a first lieutenant of cavalry, who did not count for much in the halls of Congress, where it was not known that I was even alive.

Our ice machine had been put in an old building, 1,020 feet from the pump. Our boiler was a little upright contrivance that would not allow the flues to be cleaned. These flues, covered with scale from the limestone water, were eternally leaking, putting the fire out, and in need of repairs. It was plain when I first became quartermaster that the boiler would soon be useless. An auxiliary boiler was asked for and refused.

One Sunday night the engineer came in and reported that the flues could be repaired no longer. They had leaked so that the fire was put out and could not be lighted. I hurried down and tried to heat the flues with a fire outside the firebox, but this failed. From the post trader I got an old hand fire engine that had been condemned and sold years before, gave each family a water barrel, filled by an abandoned water wagon, which in turn was filled by pumping water through the fire hose out of the spring.[3] They had drinking water but no ice. We dug up the two-inch pipe carrying water to the stables and watered the horses in the creek. The two-inch pipe was coupled up and laid between the ice machine and the pump to carry steam, but it lacked two hundred feet of reaching the pump. The hiatus had to be filled with

2. William Sturtevant Nye, a fellow officer from a later generation, agreed with Scott's assessment of the two forts. Nye, *Carbine and Lance*, 290.

3. Later in his book Scott referred to the post trader as William H. Quinette, "my old friend for many years."

inch pipe. When we tried the pump, it gave a couple of chugs and stopped. The steam cooled down so as not to do the work. Going past the corral, I saw one of the old iron telegraph poles, two inches in diameter, that used to be on the line running into Kansas. The abandoned poles were used for closing corrals. We soon gathered all we could find, cut threads on them, coupled them up, put them in the line, built fires under them to dry off the steam, and began to make ice for the hospital first and later for the post until we got our new forty horsepower, horizontal boiler from Chicago and hauled it down the sixty-seven miles from Minco [in Grady County, Oklahoma], which had now become our railroad point.

A Plains quartermaster used to live by his wits in those days, for almost nothing was given him. If he ever saw a real twelve-inch pine board, he would have put it in his safe, if there had been room, for often he would have to make his coffins out of packing boxes. It was a fine school for a young man, however. The modern quartermaster must have everything to his hand called for by the books or he cannot turn a wheel.

That ice machine makes me think of an incident which occurred a long time after. I was dining at Yale with Dr. [Arthur T.] Hadley and a party of gentlemen and asked my neighbor what was the most remarkable thing he had ever seen. He could not answer. Soon the discussion became general. Finally they said to me, "You started this. You tell us the most remarkable thing you have ever seen!" I told them that I had seen Pharaoh—the one who "would not let my people go." I had had my face within two feet of his and could see his own teeth, his own face, and knew what he looked like in the museum at Boulak, just on the outskirts of Cairo. It had given me a thrill I had never felt before. Then I told of my putting the same question to a crowd of Comanches, who went out to agree upon the answer. Coming back, they announced that the most remarkable thing they had ever seen was the ice machine at Fort Sill, where a white man made ice every day out of hot water in the summertime.

Formerly most all my studies had gone toward warfare with the Indian, which I used to think at one time would last during my lifetime, but conditions on the Plains were rapidly changing. Instead of protecting the white man from the Indian, it was now for the soldier to protect the Indian from the white man. My military ideas had been changed by the maneuvers at Chilocco in 1889. I began to study civilized warfare intensively, perceiving that the day of the Indian on the Plains was over. While I was always too busy with something important to go to the school at Fort Leavenworth,

I studied its textbooks and began to fit myself for war with a foreign country, although no sign of such war could yet be seen.

The same question was soon taken up in our post schools and continually discussed in our clubs. My [former West Point] classmate Arthur [L.] Wagner put out his work on "Strategy and Information," and a new era dawned for our army—a new epoch ushered in—that was to progress until it found us, at the outbreak of the World War, with our officers the best instructed of any army in the world.[4]

4. Scott is referring to Wagner's *Service of Security and Information*, which indeed served as an influential text for the American army as it approached the twentieth century. Coffman, *Regulars*, 177–78.

20

A Messiah on the Plains

In the summer of 1890 those who were in communication with the Indians began to hear rumors of the coming of a Messiah. Vague stories were heard at first that there was a white man out on the Staked Plains of Texas, with long, fair hair and beard, who might show you your dead relatives and who bore on his hands the scars of the crucifixion. Small attention was paid to these stories for some time, but they became more and more insistent, attracted more and more attention, until by the beginning of winter they were causing the whole of the Plains, north and south, to rock with what Mulvaney called "invidjus apprehension."[1]

The story was now that Jesus had come back to this earth, which was worn out since the buffalo and wild horses were all gone, the white man had cut off all the wood, and the rivers were dry. Jesus was on top of a new earth somewhere in the Northwest, coming with a slow movement like that of a glacier, covering the old earth. On it were the spirits of the buffalo, the wild horses, and all our dead relatives. Jesus had come once to the white man, who had killed him, and now he was coming to the Indian, bringing with him all the conditions of the golden age before the white man. This slowly moving new earth was going to push the white man off into the sea, forcing him to go back whence he came or to drown. All that was necessary for the

1. This term comes from Rudyard Kipling's poem "My Lord the Elephant."

Indian to do was to believe and to cultivate the dance. Otherwise, he would be pushed off with the white man into the sea.

Colonel Caleb Carlton, Seventh Cavalry, commanding at Fort Sill, placed this matter, pertaining to eight tribes, in my hands.[2] I spent the winter wherever the excitement was greatest, going about with an orderly, cook, driver, and light wagon, a saddle mule, and a pair of quail and turkey dogs, often accompanied by my cousin and my son Hunter, then a young lad, besides some Kiowa scouts, notably Sergeants I-see-o and Clancy, and Chambers, driver and packer.[3] It was recognized that something dangerous might be hatched up underneath the surface, of which I might be kept in ignorance until it broke. So I-see-o was told that a very serious situation was developing, which bade fair to bring about a clash with troops that would probably wipe out those eight tribes if they persisted in acting under this delusion. But, if he would do as I told him, whether his tribe disapproved or not, we would save them all, and he would be thereafter, like a man standing on a high peak, looked up to by everybody. I-see-o was a very simple, honest Indian, brought up in the old times with the buffalo, having spent a large part of his life on the warpath on the Arkansas, in Texas, and in Mexico. He had little or no influence in his tribe and was too simple to initiate any policy or to put one over alone but was faithful to the last degree and would do exactly as I told him. After considering the matter for a week, he agreed to my request, and we went about together everywhere. He kept me informed of everything going on underneath the surface. Nothing could start without my knowledge.

The excitement became as great among the white communities as among the Indians, the former expecting an uprising, a feeling that was greatly intensified by news of the battle of Wounded Knee [on December 29, 1890] in South Dakota with the Sioux, [and] when Sitting Bull was killed near the Missouri River [on December 15]. The press called for the disarming of the Indians all over the Plains. Some of the agents, notably the agent in charge of the Kiowas and Comanches at Anadarko [Charles E. Adams], were insistent

2. Carlton later praised Scott lavishly for "his courage, skill and successful management of these affairs by which he undoubtedly saved many lives." Brig. Gen. C. H. Carlton, Fortress Monroe, Va., to the Adjutant General, Washington, D.C., Jan. 15, 1909, reprinted in Scott, *Some Memories*, 210–14.

3. An "I. Chambers" is listed as a contractor for packers and teamsters at Fort Sill, 1885–86. Holabird, "Report of the Quartermaster-General," 1:407. John Chambers, a civilian, died in 1902 and is buried in the Fort Sill post cemetery.

upon the use of troops to bring about disarmament and the stopping of the dance, a policy I resisted with all my force. Meanwhile, the Indians still looked for the coming of the Messiah, who was fully expected to arrive in the spring.[4]

I was awakened one night far up on the Canadian, eighty miles from Fort Sill, by a Kiowa Indian scout who brought out a telegram from General Merritt, commanding the Department of the Missouri, directing me to get ready to disarm the Indians. The rest of the night was spent with a candle, the stub of a pencil, and a piece of manila paper, giving reasons why this should not be attempted. I took the view that I had control of the situation. Ample warning would be given of anything overt. The Indians were going to dance anyhow. If not allowed to dance openly where I could keep my fingers on their pulse, they would dance somewhere in the mountains secretly, where they could hatch up anything they pleased without our knowledge. Moreover, it would not be possible to disarm them, for they could ride one horse and lead another into any of those little towns in Texas and Oklahoma and exchange a horse for a rifle and ammunition, which would then be hidden somewhere in the brush away from their villages until needed for use. Many were already without rifles who would go and get them in case of such a movement. A spirit of animosity would be wakened that would not be ended for ten years, which was altogether unnecessary. The doctrine taught did not call for any action by the Indian. Jesus was going to do it. If Jesus were to come in the spring and shove us all into the sea, he could not be prevented by mortal means. If he did not come, the whole fabric would fall of its own weight. The best way to treat the situation was to stand by quietly and let it fall without interference. In the meanwhile I would see that nothing untoward was being hatched up secretly.

General Merritt approved of this policy, and the eight tribes were carried through the excitement without the firing of a shot or the shedding of a drop of blood, although the news of the battle of Wounded Knee in the North, where many were killed on both sides, caused the excitement in the South to be greatly intensified.

General Merritt was rather put out by the sending of troops from his department to General Miles in the Sioux country, where a large part of the

4. Jensen, Paul, and Carter, *Eyewitness at Wounded Knee*, 94, 99. Adams, "Report of Kiowa, Comanche, and Wichita Agency," 186–89.

army was congregated, as he had the same trouble in his own department and did not want his troops taken away.[5] The last time I saw him in the Metropolitan Club in Washington, he said, "I will never forget you. You kept me out of trouble when I didn't know enough to keep myself out."

When news of the Messiah first began to circulate in Oklahoma, a Kiowa Indian by the name of Ahpiatom [or Apiatan], or Wooden Lance, was deeply affected. He pondered some time over it and concluded to go north and see that Jesus with his own eyes. He went north to the Sioux Agency at Pine Ridge and was told that he could go back and tell his people that the story was true. Jesus was not actually there—he was over in the Shoshone and Arapaho country. All Ahpiatom need do was to go home and "push hard on that dance." He said, "No, I am going to see that Jesus with my own eyes."

He went back south to the Union Pacific Railroad and made his way to the Shoshone and Arapaho Agency, a hundred miles north of the railway [near present Riverton, Wyoming]. Here they told him the same thing: "Jesus is not actually here. He is over at Fort Hall, Idaho. It is all right. You go back and tell your people it is true."

He said, "No, I am going back until I see that Jesus with my own eyes."

Then he made his way back to the railway a hundred miles, footsore and hungry, having to stop to work at times to get something to eat, and thence in the same manner to Fort Hall to hear the same story. This time Jesus was over on Pyramid Lake in Nevada, which he reached after a long journey. He was told that Jesus was there in a lodge not far away. He put on his best clothes and approached the lodge with the most reverential feeling. It appeared to him that if that was the real Jesus, the latter would recognize him at once and would speak to him in his own language, saying, "You are Ahpiatom, that Kiowa man who has been worshiping me for three years." He would show Ahpiatom his son who was dead and his other dead relatives and show him likewise the scars of the crucifixion on his hands.

Ahpiatom was taken on arrival into a lodge where there was a P[a]iute Indian by the name of Jack Wilson [or Wovoka] lying in a bed on the ground with a blanket over his face, singing. After a long time Wilson took the blanket off his face and asked him who he was in the Piute language. "Why," he

5. The troops sent by Merritt to Sioux country turned out to be those of the Seventh Cavalry, the soldier combatants at Wounded Knee. Jensen, Paul, and Carter, *Eyewitness at Wounded Knee*, 28.

said, "I am Ahpiatom. Don't you know me? I am that Kiowa man who has been worshipping you for three years."

Wilson said, "What did you come looking for here?"

Ahpiatom said, "I have been traveling for a long time, going from tribe to tribe looking for Jesus."

"Well," Wilson said, "you don't have to travel any more for I am the only Jesus there is. What do you want?"

"I want to see my son who is dead."

Wilson said, "I haven't got any dead people here," and began to excuse himself for the killing of the Sioux at Wounded Knee. It was not his fault that the Sioux people should go wrong and have so many killed in one day.

During the conversation Ahpiatom was watching him carefully, and, seeing that the scars of the crucifixion were not there, he came to the conclusion that he was being spoofed. He returned to his people at Anadarko to whom he announced that was a false Jesus and his religion false, too. This was a tremendous disappointment to his people, who were expecting the coming of the Messiah. It made Ahpiatom very unpopular. They said that Wilson might be a false Jesus, but Ahpiatom had not gone to the right place. Ahpiatom had seen an Arapaho who had gone only as far as Pine Ridge and had accepted the dictum of the Sioux that the doctrine was true. He was enriched on his return by gifts from his people. I have seen Sitting Bull, the Arapaho John the Baptist, drive off forty horses and a dozen beeves at one time, presented to him by the different tribes, together with rifles, saddles, blankets, buckskin, and other Indian property. Ahpiatom was told that his people would make him rich if he would take the same message, but he said, "No, that is not for the good of my people."[6]

I represented this to the president [Benjamin Harrison], who presented him with a silver medal. Indian Commissioner [Thomas J.] Morgan promised to build him a house—a promise that was never fulfilled.

Commissioner Morgan promised to give a house also to Quanah Parker, chief of the Comanches, but withdrew his promise when he heard that Quanah (Odor or Smell [or Fragrance]) had seven wives. He had no sort of knowledge of the people over whose lives and fortunes he had control and thought he could change the manners and customs overnight as so many

6. The journey of Ahpiatom/Apiatan and the report he made after his return to the Kiowa reservation appeared in Mooney, "Ghost-Dance Religion," 165–75.

good narrow-minded people have thought before him as well as since. He ordered Quanah to get rid of all but one of his wives at once. Quanah remarked on hearing this that a man with seven wives needed a house much more than a man with only one.

It was not for any commissioner to enact ex post facto laws, to break up and scatter families of young children and throw them out on the world. It was for him to go at the matter gradually and forbid any new plural marriages. Time would soon attend to the old ones without disturbance. The status quo should not be altered violently.

Quanah went to Washington to interview the commissioner on this wholesale divorcement and said to him:

"A long time ago I lived free among the buffalo on the Staked Plains and had as many wives as I wanted, according to the laws of my people. I used to go to war in Texas and Mexico. You wanted me to stop fighting and sent messages all the time: 'You stop, Quanah. You come here. You sit down, Quanah.' You did not say anything then. 'How many wives you got, Quanah.' Now I come and sit down as you want. You talk about wives. Which one I throw away? You pick him? You little girl, you go 'way. You got no papa—you pick him? You little fellow, you go 'way. You got no papa—you pick him?"

But the commissioner could not "pick him." Quanah died long after, still holding his seven wives.[7]

The next time that Sitting Bull (Arapaho) came down to Anadarko, Ahpiatom challenged him to a public debate and denounced him before a great crowd for deceiving the people for the sake of gain.[8] Sitting Bull said that he had never asked for any gifts; they had been presented to him without request. He stood ready to return them if it was so desired. Ahpiatom replied: "No, that is not the Kiowa road"—custom. "Whatever has been given you should be kept. But you are deceiving my people. I want you to cease."

7. At his death Quanah Parker "maintained a twenty-two-room house for his seven wives and numerous children." Hosmer, "Parker, Quanah." Parker has been the subject of many biographies, often the centerpiece of several cultural and historical studies of the Comanche tribe.

8. Ethnologist James Mooney described Sitting Bull as "the great apostle of the Ghost dance among the southern tribes." He continued, "He is a full-blooded Arapaho, although rather light in complexion and color of eyes, and speaks only his native language, but converses with ease in the universal sign language of the Plains. It was chiefly by means of this sign language that he instructed his disciples among the Caddo, Wichita, and Kiowa." Mooney, "Ghost-Dance Religion," 150.

Notwithstanding Ahpiatom's efforts, the Kiowas did not give up their beliefs in the coming of the Messiah for some time. The excitement among the Caddo, Wichita, Delaware, Southern Cheyenne, and Arapaho [tribes] continued unabated. The Comanches, being a skeptical people, never did have the craze as badly as the others. The Caddos danced continuously day and night for twenty days. When some dropped out to eat or rest, others would take their places, although it snowed at one time eight inches deep.

While this was going on, I would be sitting by the fire discussing such important matters with the old people as they propounded from time to time. Old Caddo Jake [otherwise known as White House] would begin to flatter me, and I would know at once that he was going to try to lead me into a trap to get the laugh on me before the others. But, being warned, I was usually able to turn the tables on him, though I would never have suspected him if it had not been for the flattery, which an Indian always uses to lay a trap. All these Indians received me into their camps with freedom, confident that I had no ulterior purpose and was not seeking evidence against them or going to try to stop their dance.

I traveled far up into the Cheyenne and Arapaho country where the Washita could be stepped across and killed wild turkeys in the tributary gulches. We spent three days hunting for stone on the site of Custer's battle of the Washita with Black Kettle's band of Southern Cheyennes. Clancy had been a stonemason at one time and engraved "7th Cavalry, Nov. 27, 1868" on a large, flat stone, which he placed on a pile of rock with some of the bones of horses Custer had killed to keep the Cheyennes from recapturing them. He killed seven hundred in all. Many of the bones had been carried away and sold.

When the Cheyenne country was about to open for settlement, I sent a photograph of this monument to the *Minco Minstrel* [Minco, Grady County, Oklahoma] with an appeal to the new settlers not to disturb this monument or Black Kettle's tree, under which he was killed. The tree was a cottonwood that had been blazed by the Cheyennes shortly after the fight. The last I heard, the monument had been torn down, but the slab and tree were still there.[9]

9. Greene, *Washita*, 195–96.

I had great curiosity to see Sitting Bull, who had taught the Messiah dance up and down the Plains. I would always arrive when he had just left, until I heard that he was expected on Sugar Creek in the country of the Caddo, Wichita, and Delaware Indians. I put four fine mules on a light buckboard, drove fifty miles in a day, and found him.

He was remarkable in that he had light eyes. He was an excellent and graceful sign talker, most affable and obliging. I greatly enjoyed talking to him. I put my camp near his lodge and spent a great deal of time with him, watching him and his proceedings. I saw there all the scenes depicted in the Bible about Jesus. The Wichita and Caddo women would surround him weeping and touching him "to get some of the virtue out of him."[10] Presents of every kind were heaped on him. It was said that he had six thousand dollars deposited with a trader at Fort Reno.

Some time previously I had wished to photograph the dance on the Canadian River and could easily have done it without their permission for none of them knew at first what the camera was.[11] I told them I wanted to show a picture of the dance to General Merritt at St. Louis so that he could see the men, women, and children dancing together without guns or war costumes and would not believe the lies told him about their going on the warpath, but they were terribly disturbed lest I should "break their medicine." I gave it up. Some talked afterward about breaking the camera. I-see-o told me that there had been talk of killing me rather than have the medicine broken. I could even then have taken the photograph without their knowledge, but I never treated them that way, never played tricks on them.

At this visit I asked Sitting Bull, who had control of everything, about it. He gave his permission with alacrity and even stopped the dance when I raised my hand. This photograph was on my last film and was the only genuine photograph ever taken of a Messiah dance, either on the northern or southern Plains, for no one else was allowed near them with a camera.[12]

10. "And Jesus said, 'Somebody hath touched me: for I perceive that virtue is gone out of me.'" From Luke 8:46.

11. Scott's camera must have been a recently introduced Kodak, whose relatively small size and widespread popularity made it a logical alternate for amateurs versus the bulky, box camera and its glass plates with which professionals were saddled. See Southwell and Lowett, *Life at the Kiowa, Comanche, and Wichita Agency*, 10–11, 49–50.

12. This statement is disputed, although Scott's key word is "near" since a couple of northern Plains photographers succeeded in capturing rare photographs of the Lakota Ghost Dance—both taken from some safe distance. Jensen, Paul, and Carter, *Eyewitness at Wounded Knee*, 7, 8.

The Sioux ran away into the badlands to dance in spite of the agent's prohibition, and they killed Lieutenant [Edward W.] Casey for intruding.

In this picture will be seen a number of people lying on the ground in a hypnotic trance, where they would be surrounded by their women to prevent their being touched. Their spirits were thought to have left their bodies and to have gone above in conference with Jesus. If a dog should even touch them with the point of the nose, their spirit would be jerked rudely away from the presence of Jesus.

While constantly watching them, I could see a new religion growing up around me, which, if they were not dominated by the white man and the times were suitable, might have grown into something like the religion of Mohammed [Muhammed]. But the times were unfavorable, and it soon died. The Indian was then most susceptible to conversion to Christianity. The name of Jesus was on every tongue. Had I been a missionary I could have led every Indian on the Plains into the church, but the missionaries were not awake to their opportunity.

Many preposterous and impossible statements were made by Sitting Bull, which he evidently expected to have believed but which no white man would consider for a moment. The Indian, however, could and did believe them and was willing to stake his life on their truth, without a particle of proof. I am convinced that, impossible as they were from the standpoint of our superior knowledge, Sitting Bull himself believed the whole thing implicitly.

The mind of the Indian was prepared to believe the impossible as our forefathers of the Middle Ages believed in dreams, apparitions, and miracles. Something seen by them in a dream was "confirmation strong as proofs of holy writ."[13] We others must not judge the Indian as we judge the actions of the people of our time for the older ones are still living in a more backward age, the age of barbarism, when we too had much the same beliefs and had not acquired the mass of knowledge that we now enjoy. The attitude of mind of the Indian, brought up on primitive legends without the correction due to modern thought and information, was altogether different from ours. He was prepared to believe anything presented to him from a source in which he had confidence.

13. In act 3, scene 3 of Shakespeare's *The Tragedy of Othello, the Moor of Venice,* Iago declared, "Trifles light as air are to the jealous confirmations strong as proofs of holy writ."

I saw Sitting Bull last at the cantonment on the North Fork of Red River in 1920 and asked him, "How about that Messiah dance?"[14]

He said: "My father's brother, I hope you won't talk about those things now. I have put them all away behind me. I pray now only to the Spirit above and go to the white man's church."

14. A sub-post of Fort Sill, this cantonment was the site of Fort Elliott, Texas, near Mobeetie in present Wheeler County. Frazer, *Forts of the West*, 149–50.

21

Lo! The Poor Indian

The credulity with which the Indian accepts what he is told, with no backing of proof, seems amazing in our eyes. It is this credulity that makes him so dangerous. Some ignorant or designing person may take advantage of it to arouse him against the law or against the troops. It required but one shot at Wounded Knee to produce a bloody clash, unforeseen and undesired by both sides, at a moment when the troops and Indians were in close proximity with no time for consideration and reflection.

Besides apprehension of this credulity, there is an inborn racial fear of the Indian in our minds, due to our ignorance of his thought, enhanced by the tales of scalping and bloodshed we were fed on in our youth. We cannot get over this since it has become instinctive in many who cannot perceive that the times have changed and that the Indians have changed with them. Many have still a fantastic and untruthful view of the character of the Indian. I have taken, through my Indian camp at Fort Sill, visitors who have exclaimed in surprise at seeing an Indian woman kiss her child as if the Indians had not the same human nature that they had themselves. This ignorance on both sides brings about a mutual racial mistrust, which I have never felt toward the Indian. But I could recognize its existence in myself at Canton, China, among the teeming millions of foreigners of different race and language from whose minds and intentions I was completely shut out.[1]

1. This observation probably occurred in 1903, when Scott accompanied Leonard Wood on a west-to-east, intercontinental journey from Washington to the Philippines. The party's members passed through several Asian cities before reaching their new duty station. Hagedorn, *Leonard Wood*, 1:409–15.

Someone who understands both parties is always needed in times of stress to prevent a clash with disastrous consequences and to keep them far enough apart so that the nervousness of one man may not bring it on, perhaps by a single gesture. For placing such unstable forces as armed Indians and troops together is like putting an open powder keg in front of an open fire, needing but one spark to explode it all. The troops should be kept from the immediate presence of the Indians in a strong defensive position, yet near enough to answer a summons promptly. If the Indians are then treated with sympathy, kindness, patience, and tact, no body of red men that ever lived can stand out against you, no matter how ugly their mood or how outraged their feelings, provided always you can reach them so as to talk without being fired on.

Some time afterward while talking to the Kiowas in the camp of the families of my Indians at Fort Sill, I stated that the Kiowa chief, Lone Wolf, had sold out his people to the Cherokee Commission.[2] The next day about four hundred Kiowas came up to the post with Lone Wolf. Their spokesman said it was a matter of hearsay that I had made certain statements about Lone Wolf. They did not know whether I had actually made them or not. They only heard that I had, but, if I would make them again before that crowd, they would know exactly what had been said. They were told to bring a chair and to put it down in front of the one I was sitting in and for Lone Wolf to sit in it, right in front of me. In the sign language, understood by all of them, I replied that last night I had said that Lone Wolf had sold out his people. "Lone Wolf, did you sell out your people?" I then asked.

His only reply was to hang his head in silence. The attention of the crowd was then invited to him. "Look at that," I said, "a man that calls himself chief of the Kiowa people. Just look at him—afraid to look at me! Lone Wolf, you look me in the eye. You are walking today down your chief's road. You are going to hear something coming after you like a hound after a deer. I am going after you, and I am going to overtake you. I am going to break your chief's road and throw you away. That is all. You can go."

Whenever, for months after that, I would meet parties of Kiowas on the prairie, at the agency, or elsewhere, this dialogue would take place:

2. This was Lone Wolf the Younger. Anderson, "Lone Wolf." The Cherokee Commission with its so-called Jerome Agreement, occurred in 1892. Corwin, "Delos K. Lonewolf," 434–35.

Q: How do you like to have a chief that sells you out?
A: We don't like it.
Q: What kind of chief do you like?
A: We like an honest man.
Q: Who is the most honest Kiowa you know?
A: Ahpiatom.
Q: Why don't you get him for a chief?
A: I think we will.

Later the feeling coalesced and resulted in the first regular election the tribe ever had for a chief. They chose Ahpiatom. That was about 1894. He is still their chief today.[3] The hound had overtaken the deer.

◆ ◆ ◆

About ten days after the battle of Wounded Knee between Big Foot's band of Sioux and the Seventh Cavalry in South Dakota, Colonel Carlton, who commanded Fort Sill, asked my advice regarding a telegram he had just received from the Indian agency at Anadarko, thirty-three miles away, in which it was stated that a little Kiowa Indian boy had been whipped in the Kiowa school, after which he had run away secretly and taken two other boys with him. All three had been caught in a blizzard on their way to their village and found frozen to death. The Indians were very much excited over this, and the agent [Adams] desired a squadron of cavalry sent there immediately to save the agency.

I reminded the colonel that this was no kind of weather in which to send troops out in the field. There had been a heavy fall of rain, filling up the streams, after which two feet of snow had fallen. Now it was raining and sleeting again. If troops were compelled to march all night in such weather, they would arrive in Anadarko in a very ugly frame of mind. The Indians were coming there, armed, from every direction, much excited over the loss of the children. A very serious clash was probable and would cause a great deal of bloodshed. If he would let me go up there, I would settle it without any troops.

The colonel replied: "You are asking me something very difficult. Suppose you go up there and are not able to handle the situation, and the agency

3. Ahpiatom/Apiatan died on August 8, 1931. Methvin, "Ahpeahtone," 335.

is destroyed. What kind of a defense could I put up before a court-martial when asked by the judge advocate, 'Did you get that call for a squadron of cavalry from the agent?' I would have to say, 'Yes.' The next question would be, 'What did you do?' I could only answer, 'I sent one man.' What sort of a defense would that be, do you think?"

I had to reply that, no doubt, that was possible, but he was commanding officer, and it was his duty to take such responsibilities and of two evils to choose the lesser. If he believed that I would not be able to handle the situation, he had better send troops. But the probability of bloodshed was very great, and he would have to take his choice.

Our old interpreter, Horace P. Jones, was there. The colonel asked if I wanted to take him with me. I had no need for him, but the last thing I wanted to do was to hurt his feelings, so I said, "Yes." The colonel asked him when he would be ready. He said next morning at nine o'clock. The colonel asked when I would be ready. I said, "I am ready now. The weather is too bad to take Mr. Jones on horseback, so we will have to have a covered wagon. If you will order one, I will be ready by the time it gets up."

We started out, with I-see-o going ahead on horseback, carrying a lantern to enable our driver to keep the road, and arrived at Anadarko about four o'clock in the morning.

The agent was so frightened that nothing could be got out of him. I- see-o was sent out to round up the Kiowa chiefs after breakfast. We settled the whole matter satisfactorily that morning. The teacher who had whipped the boy had been hidden the day before over the rafters in one of the stores until after dark, when he was taken out of the country and has never gone back.[4] The Indians were feeling greatly outraged over the loss of their children and really acted in a very commendable manner.

We were invited that evening to dinner at the house of one of the traders and strolled over to the store after dinner. One could feel vibrations of great excitement the moment we entered the store. Inquiry developed the fact that the uncle of one of the boys had just come in and heard of their death and, coming around the corner suddenly on the principal of the school, had hit him over the head with a quirt.[5]

4. This person was Bart Wherrett (or Barton Wherritt), listed on the rolls as "Teacher and disciplinarian," who left government service on January 26, 1891. U.S. Congress, *Report of the Secretary of the Interior* (1892), 2:729.

5. The school principal was G. P. Gregory. Ibid.

The Kiowa village was camped right behind the school about three quarters of a mile away. Taking I-see-o and my cousin, who had come with us from Fort Sill, we ran down to the school as fast as we could and found the women teachers in great distress. They abused me roundly for not bringing troops in and for "allowing innocent women and children to be butchered in their beds." I offered to go down into the Kiowa camp and see if there was anything wrong down there, but they seized me by both arms and said I would not be allowed to leave the house. I was the only thing that stood between them and death and would have to stay there all night. So I-see-o was sent down into camp and directed to go around all parts of it and listen to the conversations, bring back word to me if anything overt was contemplated, and summon the chiefs to the agent's office the next morning at nine o'clock to meet me there.

Nothing happened during the night. At the meeting in the agent's office the agent and the principal were present, with the Indians sitting on the floor around the wall, wrapped in their blankets, some of them crying about the children. The principal insisted upon the arrest of the uncle of the dead boy. I represented that the excitement was very intense over the Messiah question, and the news of the recent battle of the Sioux had greatly intensified this. If that man were arrested at this time, it would probably be all that was needed to push the Kiowas into war. The principal, however, insisted upon it. He and the agent had no more respect for the feelings of those Indians, sorrowing for their children, than they had for the feelings of the chairs. Finally, however, they agreed to forgive the Indian, whom I scolded for using his quirt. I then told the Indians to go out of town and stay out until the excitement was over.

A short time after this I was told by a friend that, notwithstanding the forgiveness by the agent and the principal, the principal had gone to the deputy marshal and requested him to make the arrest, and he was going to make it. In response to a protest the marshal replied that it was his duty to arrest the Indian, and his duty was always paramount. After some pleasant argument, which failed to move him, he was told that my duty was always paramount also. I could see it very plainly. He said, "What is your duty, lieutenant?"

"I see very plainly that it is my duty to go down to the telegraph office and get your commission as a deputy marshal revoked by telegraph as unfit to hold it."

He said, "If you feel that way, lieutenant, I won't do it."

I said, "That is just the way I feel." He dropped the matter.

A telegram was sent down to the commanding officer at Fort Sill saying that no troops were needed as the trouble was all over.[6] It can be seen from the attitude of the agent in this matter, as well as the insistence on disarming and the stopping of the dance, how many of our Indian outbreaks have been brought about, without real intention on either side, and for the lack of some person with authority who understands both sides.

◆ ◆ ◆

The following summer [1891] a Kiowa Indian was killed by a cowboy sixty-seven miles west from Fort Sill at the mouth of Elk Creek, a tributary of the North Fork of the Red River, which then formed a boundary between Texas and the Indian Territory. The killing happened at the headquarters of a cattle company on the Texas side. News of the occurrence was brought in to Fort Sill. The colonel asked me what I would need to go out and settle it. I told him I needed an orderly, a cook, a packer, and a couple of pack animals. He said, "No, I am going to send out some troops and let those people out there see that they cannot kill an Indian with impunity. You take a troop of cavalry and start."

I took my own troop as escort, commanded by its second lieutenant, as I was detailed away from the troop as adjutant, quartermaster, and commissary of the post and did not take command. The road was very heavy, the wagons heavily loaded. It was extremely hot. We got a late start, went into camp after making seventeen miles and were eating dinner when an Indian came in and said there was a large band of armed white men on one side of the North Fork and Kiowas on the opposite, scouting for each other, the Kiowas outraged by the killing of one of their kind. A battle was imminent if it had not already taken place after he left. He was asked to have some dinner. He said he could not wait. He had to go back. Feed his pony? He said, no, he hadn't time to eat. I realized that things must be in a very dangerous condition indeed. The troops were established in camp for the night. It would be impossible to take the wagons across country in the darkness without a road. Six Kiowa scouts were made ready, and we started to make the fifty miles

6. The tragedy of the boys who froze to death, which remains a bitter memory to the Kiowa people, became the subject of a play, *The Indolent Boys*, by the renowned Kiowa writer N. Scott Momaday. Momaday, *Three Plays*, 1–71.

that night, leaving the troops to come on next day. Being very thirsty along in the middle of the night, I asked for water but was told, "You can't have any water here. These are the No Water Mountains we are going through."

Shortly before dawn the Indians said, "Dismount. Keep quiet." We listened for about five minutes when we heard a dog bark. They said, "All right. Come along." They had been afraid that their camp had been attacked and perhaps taken after the Kiowa had left, but there was something peaceful in that dog's bark that reassured them.

Since these Kiowas considered that they were at war with the white men, the kind of reception I would get in their camp was somewhat doubtful, but I felt that, if I could get into the lodge of old Big Bow, the head soldier of the Kiowas, he would protect me, certainly as long as I was in his lodge.[7] If necessary I would stay there until the troops arrived.

I got into his lodge before dawn without being discovered. After sunrise the headmen were all invited in so that their views might be ascertained. It seemed that there were about a hundred white men on the other side of the river, all gathered with their arms at the cow ranch. The two parties had been scouting for each other till dark the night before. The white men had sent their women and children out of the country far down in Texas, away from harm. It was represented to the Kiowas that, if a delegation would come down with me into Texas, I would cause the arrest of the man who had shot the Kiowa and leave the matter to the civil authorities. I would see what reparation I could get and would disperse the white men. They agreed to this, and Big Bow took me in his wagon. I caused the arrest of the cowboy by the civil authorities. The Indians said they wanted him to be hanged right there, where they could all see him. The white men were advised to go home and bring back their women and children. The war was over.

The ranch owner was asked if he intended to live there and expected to do business after that Indian was killed on his ranch. He said he would like to. I then told him that he would not do it unless he made a settlement according to Indian ways. Otherwise, he would be going about some day on horseback, and a bullet would come out of the brush and kill him. But all the soreness could be wiped out by a present. He asked what sort of present would be acceptable and was told that, if he would give them half a dozen beeves, I had no doubt the matter could be settled amicably. He gave the

7. For more on Big Bow, see Anderson, "Big Bow."

Indians the beeves. The matter was settled and has remained settled to this day.

The cowboy contended that the killing had been done in self-defense, which was probably true, for the Indian was a mean one as the Kiowas themselves acknowledged. The cowboy was at once released by the civil authorities after getting away from our proximity.

We went back to the Indian camp and on the way recovered a lost government mule from a man who did not want to give it up. I went to bed for a rest in Big Bow's lodge, having been on the go for several days and nights. The troop came in next day, but everything had been arranged. There was nothing to do but go home, which we did, going south of the Wichita Mountains, where there was no trail and where no one had ever attempted to take wagons in all the history of Fort Sill because of the roughness of the country. I would not care to go that way again.

While driving into Texas with Big Bow, I noticed his fine buckskin costume. His leggings each had twenty parallel, rectangular marks, three-eighths of an inch wide and three inches long, down the outside. Putting my finger on one, I asked what it meant. Big Bow counted it several times very carefully from the top to make sure of its identity. Then he announced that it represented an Osage he had killed. Each of the forty marks represented a member of some tribe he had killed—Pawnee, Cheyenne, Utah [Ute], and many others. If he had told the whole truth, I have no doubt that some of those marks represented white people he had killed when at war.

I asked if he wanted to sell those leggings. All our conversation was carried on in the sign language. He replied, "My uncle"—a term of great respect—"I don't want to pick up money for these leggings. I am getting old, and soon my die day will arrive. Then my women will plait my hair, paint my face red, and put these clothes on me. My spirit will go out of my mouth up to the Wolf's Road"—Milky Way. "When I get there, they will look me all over and will say, 'Big Bow, you are well dressed.'" As I did not wish to interfere with such laudable proceedings, I told him we would drop further consideration of purchase.

He had one of the two oldest and most historic buffalo shields among the Kiowa, and I asked if he wanted to sell that. He said that shield had protected him all his life by its medicine or magic power. "My life is in that shield, and I don't want to part with my life," he said, so we talked no more about it. Six months afterward his son brought the shield to me as a present from Big Bow. It seemed that, although the medicine in it had always protected him heretofore, it had now allowed him to lose control of his face—facial paralysis. Since it no longer protected him, he wanted me to have it.

Dr. [and Captain] J[ames] D. Glennan, my next-door neighbor, was making a collection of Indian curios and was eager to get a good shield. Good ones were extremely scarce. I already had the best shield in the Southwest, which used to belong to the celebrated Kiowa chief Satanta, more than a hundred years old. Satanta had it on when he was roped by a Mexican just outside of the town of Durango, Mexico, before the Civil War. He was dragged some distance behind a horse until Frizzlehead [Frizzle Head] and some others rescued him after both sides had been skinned from his head to his heels. When Satanta's son died, he [Saloso] left the shield to me in his will, which was probated by the Indian court while I was in Washington. The shield was sent me by the agent.[8]

I told Big Bow's son to take the shield to Dr. Glennan and charge him fifty dollars for it, which was cheap enough, for he could probably get a thousand dollars for it now.[9]

It will show how ignorant most Indians were of values and the white man's way of bargaining and how easy it was to cheat them to tell how Big Cow [Bow?] brought a horse to sell to me. I told him I already had all the horses I could feed. He seemed quite downcast at that, evidently counting on the sale. He said, "I have come in a long distance to sell him to you."

"What do you want for him?" I asked.

"I want ten dollars or five dollars."

I told him to take the horse to Major [H. C.?] Cook, who wanted a horse for his boy, and to charge him fifty dollars. The horse brought forty-five dollars and later went up to Chicago in a carload of polo ponies. He had genuine polo talent and later was sold on Long Island for a thousand dollars.

The character of the Indian of the gloomy forests of the East partook of the nature of those forests. He was vindictive and cruel beyond limit. He used to burn his enemy at the stake, prolonging his life so as to enjoy his torment the longer. The nature of the Plains Indian reflected the open, sunny character of his habitat, and his rages were soon over.

8. Satanta's shield is part of the collections of the Phoebe A. Hearst Museum of Anthropology, University of California, Berkeley. "Honoring Their Grandfather," 1–3.

9. According to the Smithsonian Institution's online Collections Search Center, the war shield of Big Bow came to the National Museum of Natural History in 1945 as part (no. 385891) of the Glennan collection.

Some strange Comanches from a distance brought whisky into the scouts' camp one night. The officer of the day, responsible for good order, reported that there were drunken Indians down there, firing off their guns and making a disturbance. The commanding officer told him to go down, arrest them, and put them in the guardhouse. He demurred a little at this, asking if he did not think Lieutenant Scott had better go, for nobody likes to deal with a drunken Indian, who is usually a monomaniac in that condition. Mrs. Scott and I were dining out and could not be found for some time, but finally the Indian was lodged in the guardhouse. I went off the next morning to Anadarko, thirty-three miles away, and forgot about the prisoner until nearly there, when I telegraphed to the commanding officer, asking him to release the Indian and give him back his rifle. The Indian loaded his gun, hiding it under his blanket, and walked up and down in front of my quarters for an hour, waiting for me to come out. Some Indian told I-see-o about it, who jumped on his horse bareback, galloped up to the Comanche, and stripped off his blanket with one jerk, disclosing his rifle, loaded and at full cock. I-see-o took it away from him, kicked him, and knocked him about and told him to get out of there at once. If he ever tried anything of that sort again, he would kill him.

I came back in about a week and heard about this. Going into the trader's store ten days after, I saw the Comanche leaning on the counter with his back to the door, his head resting on his hands with elbows on the counter. I walked around behind the counter, leaned on it in the same way, our noses about a foot apart, and asked what was the matter with him. He asked, "Why?" in some surprise.

I said, "A little bird told me that you were walking up and down in front of my house with a loaded gun the other day. What was that for?"

"Oh!" he said, "that was a long time ago—away back there," making the sign for a time tradition tells of. "I have forgotten all about that. That is all over long ago." I told him he had better keep on forgetting it if he wanted to walk around on the ground like other live people.

"Oh!" he said again, "that was all over long ago," and it was. If he had been a timber Indian, he would have been apt to kill me a year afterward if the right opportunity occurred. I was warned in the Choctaw country that if I ever had a quarrel with a Choctaw or Seminole to kill him right away or he would kill me if it were years afterward. But the Plains Indians are entirely different, some being very jolly, others more reserved and stately, but all good-tempered. The Kiowas were more difficult than the Comanches, who were remarkably open and friendly, although our literature makes them appear otherwise.

The first expedition of the First Dragoons in 1834, which my Uncle David Hunter accompanied as captain of Company D, First Dragoons, passed near the site of Fort Sill, which was not built until [1869–]1870. George Catlin, the artist, was with it also and told about it in his [*Manners, Customs, and Condition of the*] *North American Indian*[s], which made a deep impression on the country. They met the Kiowas and Comanches.[10] We have heard the expressions ever since, "He rides like a Comanche," and "He yells like a Comanche." They then acquired an undeserved reputation for fierceness, but, to tell the truth, they yelled and rode no differently than other tribes of the Plains.

◆ ◆ ◆

At the close of the Sioux War in South Dakota in the spring of 1891, the secretary of war [Redfield Proctor] desired to fill some of the skeleton troops of cavalry with Indian soldiers. The Sioux flocked to be enlisted because they had no food, no horses, no blankets, nor clothing and were willing to do anything that would bring them food and shelter. The Kiowas and Comanches, however, were well off, some of them having as many as two hundred horses. Since the tribes were negotiating with the Cherokee Commission concerning their lands, the chiefs held their young men back so as to keep them under their influence. They refused to enlist.

The secretary of war sent Captain Jesse [M.] Lee, Ninth Infantry, who was most successful in enlisting the Sioux, down to Fort Sill to find out why I did not enlist the Kiowas and Comanches. A council of the Indians was called to meet him at which he stated his case. Old Tabananaca [Sound of the Sun or Hears the Sun/Sunrise], a Comanche chief, got up and replied, thanking him for coming so far to talk to them and bringing the word of Washington. He said that Lieutenant Scott had already told them those things. The kindest thing he could do was to go back to Washington and tell them that the Kiowas and Comanches did not want to be soldiers. Whereupon he wrapped his blanket around him and stalked out, followed by his lifelong friend, White Wolf, who had grown up with him from boyhood, side by side.

10. This was the Dodge-Leavenworth expedition, quite an adventure as told and drawn by Catlin, *Manners, Customs, and Condition*, 2:36–80.

Captain Lee went back to Washington and reported that the Kiowas and Comanches could not be enlisted. Although I have seen hundreds of councils, this was one of only two occasions when I had seen a rudeness perpetrated.

A month after that, Poor Buffalo, a Kiowa chief, invited me to his lodge. Talking in the sign language, he said, "Heretofore we have held our young men in a corral from enlisting, and today I am going to tell you something good. We are going to open that corral and drive our young men right at you like a herd of horses." In a short time a troop was enlisted—the only one of the Indian organizations to serve out its appointed time.[11]

None of the Indians could read or write, so Ernest Stecker of my Troop M was appointed first sergeant to take care of the paperwork; Thomas Clancy, quartermaster sergeant to look after the property; and I-see-o as first sergeant, who was, however, a figurehead, unable to deal with white men, never having learned any English. The other noncommissioned officers were all Indians. The troop was above the middle of all the organizations of the army with the rifle, fourth among eighteen troops of cavalry in the Department of the Missouri with the revolver and was considered by the War Department as a success in every way but one. They said it was a success as long as I stayed with it, but its officers could not be changed around as in white troops. Since all the other troops were a disappointment, the experiment of enlisting Indians was regarded as a failure.

It seems a remarkable thing that British officers could make efficient soldiers of Egyptians, who have been slaves for three thousand years, but American officers could not make soldiers out of Indians, who had fought us successfully for a long period and who, when suitably armed and mounted, were the best light horsemen the world has ever seen. The truth was that the army was angry at General [John McAllister] Schofield for mustering out the white men of the two troops in each regiment and did not want the experiment to succeed. Innumerable obstacles were thrown in my way by unthinking officers. Support in Washington was withheld by a change of the secretary of war [Stephen B. Elkins]. The men of that troop nevertheless are men of power and influence now in the Kiowa reservation and dictate its policies. I have been told by a number of agents that the marked difference between this agency and those surrounding it was caused by the discipline, instruction, and general improvement brought about by service in that troop

11. The last members of Scott's troop were discharged on May 31, 1897. Lee, "Warriors in Ranks," 301.

and that it would be of advantage to the government to have a similar troop at every agency. The men were made to save their money. By the time that they were discharged, they received help from troop funds, so that every one of them had a house on his lot to which he retired.

At first the men held off a little from enlistment by the fear of being made to cut their hair. They were told they might cut their hair or let it drag on the ground so far as I was concerned, and they all enlisted. After some months an order came down from the War Department to have every one of them cut his hair. This placed me in a very awkward position, and I felt much dismayed over it. All during the winter I would make a little fun of them, saying that they called themselves soldiers going around with hair like that and telling them to put their braid down under their coat collars so that I wouldn't see it. At the end of the cold weather eleven of them came up and asked to borrow a quarter each. I asked what they wanted it for. They said they wanted to have their hair cut. Then gradually they all followed suit but one man, an Arapaho by the name of Yellow Bull, who declared he would not cut his hair for anybody. He was reported absent from retreat one evening. Inquiry developed that he was inside the barracks, and the reason he did not come out to retreat was that he was ashamed. He had been sleeping on his bunk when some young Kiowa rascals had cut off his hair on one side. He was ashamed to come out. Afterward he had the other side cut to match. The orders of the War Department were complied with, and I was not made out a liar after all.

22

Memories of Buffalo Bill and Other Famous Plainsmen

In the summer of 1893 General Miles ordered me to the World's Fair in Chicago to deliver an article on the sign language of the Plains Indian before a World's Congress of Ethnologists.[1] I knew of this six months beforehand and sent east for books on philology in order to find out the fundamental laws of language, lest, studying alone on the Plains, I should have acquired a one-sided or distorted view of my subject. This study of philology is still one of the great pleasures of my life. Before my lecture, at which General Miles and my mother were present, I asked Buffalo Bill [William F. Cody] for an Indian to use in demonstration on the stage. He replied in his hearty way, "Take the whole show," but I compromised on six Ogalala Sioux. The audience asked that my time be extended. I was told afterward by the management that this was the only time such a request had been made during the life of the Congress.

General Miles detailed me with one of the police detachments at the fair, which duty would give me a room on the grounds with extra pay and access to everything, but it was my misfortune to fall ill again with malarial

1. This was the International Congress of Anthropology. A version of Scott's paper, "The Sign Language of the Plains Indian," can be found in Umiker-Sebeok and Sebeok, *Aboriginal Sign Languages of the Americas*, 2:53–67.

fever. When I asked him to send me back to Fort Sill, he was much surprised and asked my reasons. I told him I had a strong fever every other day. The warm water of the lake got on my nerves and that I wanted to allay the fever in the cold springwater at Fort Sill to get some gooseflesh on myself once more. So I went back without seeing very much of the fair.

The days I felt well enough, however, I would sit with Buffalo Bill in a little sentry box with two chairs at the heel of the arena of his Wild West Show, where we could look out at the performers coming in and going out. I asked him who of all his people were the best performers. He told me that the American cowboys were the best, for, besides doing their own stunts remarkably well, they could do those of all the others, too. Just then a Circassian prince [from the northern Caucasus] came in at a gallop standing on his head. Cody said, "The cowboys can do what that Circassian prince can do as well as he can, but there would be no money in allowing them to do it in the show."

There was one performer, however, who was not an adept. While I was walking around with Cody between the acts, he sent for an Australian he had imported to throw a boomerang as a stunt in the show. It was soon found that the various currents of air about the amphitheater prevented control of the boomerang, which frequently went into the seats of the amphitheater. After trying him for a while and convincing himself that it was dangerous, Cody said, "That act is no good. Take him away, and put him in digging postholes." Imagine importing a man from Australia to dig postholes in Chicago! But the show could stand that after clearing seven hundred thousand dollars during the season.

Buffalo Bill and I both got in the Deadwood coach one day. I sat on the box by the driver, driving six fine, strong mules when the team was made to run away, chased by Indians firing blank cartridges at us. I thought at first that I was being powder burned by the Indians but soon discovered that what had stung my face was not powder but the gravel thrown up by the flying feet of the galloping mules.

That was the most realistic show I have ever seen. Those old Deadwood coaches used to pass our house at Fort Meade twice a day. Mrs. Scott and I had often ridden in them. I knew the Indians were genuine because I had known some of them on the Plains. When I first saw the show in 1884 in Philadelphia, I could hardly believe my eyes when I recognized Shunkamanito Ota [Plenty Wolf], alias Yankton Charley, and Red Shirt, who guided

General [Ranald S.] McKenzie [Mackenzie] into the Cheyenne village on Powder River, both Ogalalas.[2] The West was still a far country in those days, and one seldom met Ogalalas in Philadelphia.

Everything was exactly as represented in that show but one thing. The shields carried by the Indians were not genuine. Instead of being made of indurated [hardened] rawhide from the neck of a buffalo bull, which had then gone from the Plains, they were barrel hoops with canvas painted and decorated with feathers. They resembled shields so well that no one in the audience knew the difference.

Cody was always very generous with his men, in fact, with everybody. One time I was sitting with him in 1884 at Philadelphia on the upstairs veranda of a clubhouse when the show passed by to entrain. A cowboy left the column and called up asking for an advance of a dollar on his pay. Cody told him to hold his hat and threw down a twenty-dollar gold piece into it as a gift. No old-timer ever came to him with a hard-luck story in vain. In fact, he was far too generous for his own good.

Johnny Baker was his nephew and general executive, a sort of aide-de-camp for every sort of confidential use. We loved the colonel as did everybody else, but Cody was Johnny's idol. The first time I ever saw Johnny was at Philadelphia. He was standing on his head, breaking glass balls with a shotgun, alongside of Annie Oakley, who was doing the same thing, although standing well planted on her own feet. The last time I saw him was lately in his museum and teahouse outside of Denver, near which the colonel is buried on the top of Lookout Mountain, where I hope his spirit can look far off over the Plains he used to scout and loved so well.[3]

The colonel came up with Johnny to the office of the chief of staff in the War Department in 1916, bringing a photographer, who took a picture of us both together. He invited me to stay with him for a month at the Hot Springs of Wyoming in the Big Horn Basin and to stay another month at his ranch above Cody [Wyoming]. He said, "You have been sitting in that chair too long. It will build you up—build you up." That was the last time I ever saw

2. Red Shirt was considered a sergeant of Indian scouts; Yankton Charley, a member of his squad. "William Garnett interview, Jan. 10, 1907," in Jensen, *Voices of the American West*, 1:27.

3. Johnny Baker spent the remainder of his life preserving Cody's legacy at the Buffalo Bill Museum and Grave in suburban Denver. Friesen, *Buffalo Bill*, 147–55. An illustration of Baker as the Wild West marksman that Scott remembered appears on p. 47.

him, for he died within a month.[4] It was the last photograph he ever had taken, a copy of which was sent to Mrs. Cody after his death.

He loved the army, with which he had been associated nearly all his life, and never let army officers pay to enter the show if he could help it. He would give them a box or a dozen boxes if they wished. He rather mortified me a little by his kindness in 1908. For several years he invited the whole first class at West Point to the show at Madison Square Garden and told me to bring down all the officers any and every time I wanted to come. But one time he invited Mrs. Scott and myself especially. We took two boys of one of our friends to shake hands with Colonel Cody as I wanted them to remember his personality. He sent us to our place with an usher, and we found ourselves in the most important place in the show, acclaimed by all the Indians when they massed up in front of the box for a demonstration. This was all very well until I looked down to a very inconspicuous position and saw the general commanding the department there, hidden away almost out of sight, which mortified me extremely, lest he should think that I had engineered things. Mrs. Scott and I discussed the question of going down and exchanging with him but concluded that we were guests and would have to stay where we were put. The facts were that the general had come from the coast artillery, and Cody had never heard of him on the Plains.[5]

A number of the officers of West Point, including Chaplain [Edward S.] Travers, asked me to take them to the show at Madison Square, saying that they had never seen the sign language used. When we went together, I told them we would get Cody to take us into the Indian village between the performances. The Indians were a new lot of young men I had never seen before, but I would be able to gain their friendliness by the sign language within ten minutes. Cody was not about and had to be sent for to his hotel. He took us down to Iron Tail's lodge, where the others soon congregated. I was on excellent terms with them all within five minutes, asking about their relatives who were no longer with the show.

When I first saw Cody in Chicago, he had a magnificent head of long, dark hair. With his tall, stalwart frame, I thought he was the handsomest

4. Cody died on January 10, 1917. Ibid., 142.

5. The likely candidate of this slight, someone who had "come from the coast artillery" and who also commanded a department, was Ramsay D. Potts, commander of the Department of the Gulf in 1908. A process of elimination involved comparing the 1908 and 1909 annual reports of the secretary of war and his list of department commanders against their service records in Heitman's *Historical Register*.

man I had ever seen. In later years I several times heard him say that he despised a man with long hair and that his first act after going out of the show business would be to cut his hair. His long hair was part of the Buffalo Bill show as much as the horses and Indians.

Colonel Cody was a most remarkable man. As a boy in Kansas he had started out in a lowly capacity in a bull train, not even with the full title of bullwhacker but as the bullwhacker's assistant, a bull wrangler. From that humble position he raised himself by his own talent and determination until he became a welcome guest of presidents and kings, the idol of every red-blooded boy in America and withal a most genial, kindly gentleman, the success and adulation he everywhere received never for a moment affecting his poise and judgment. He was the foremost plainsman of his day, the exponent of one class of scout as Ben [Benjamin H.] Clark and Horace Jones were of another.

◆ ◆ ◆

Ben Clark had been the trusted chief of scouts for Custer in 1868 on the southern Plains. He was the most accomplished white sign talker I ever met. I have visited him several times at his Fort Reno home, which was scrupulously cared for by his Cheyenne wife, and extracted from him all the knowledge of the sign language I could, which it afforded him much pleasure to impart. Ben spoke very fluent Cheyenne and once wrote a dictionary and grammar of the tongue for General Sheridan, who died before its publication could be arranged for.[6] He had a comprehensive knowledge of the individuals of the different tribes of the Plains—their character, legends, and customs—and knew how they would react under given conditions. His different commanders looked to him for advice as long as the Cheyennes were wild and dangerous. They trusted his opinions implicitly in a crisis, as the Fort Sill commanders did that of Horace P. Jones, interpreter for the Comanches, who had lived long with the Kiowas and Comanches. General McKenzie had him in his house with him so that he would be immediately available in troublous times. Both interpreters were simple, efficient, dependable, honest men, and both died poor, scorning innumerable opportunities to become rich in an unethical way.

6. Clark and his manuscript were described in detail in Mooney, *Cheyenne Indians*, 430–31.

When General Sheridan wanted to know real facts about the southern Cheyennes or Arapahos, he would telegraph Ben Clark directly without regard to the post commanders, who seldom knew about anything off their parade ground and took little interest in the Indian. Ben Clark had letters and telegrams that anybody would be proud to have from General Sheridan, General Miles, and other high commanders. I first saw him when he conducted Little Chief's band of Northern Cheyennes from Fort Lincoln, Dakota, to Fort Reno in the Indian Territory in 1878. He had just returned from a mission given him by General Sheridan in the northwest provinces of Canada, where he had been in Sitting Bull's camp trying to induce White Bird, a Nez Percé chief who had escaped across the line during General Miles's fight with Joseph at the Bear Paw in 1877, to surrender and join his people.

Buffalo Bill was not this type of plainsman. He spoke no Indian tongue and had no particular knowledge of Indians other than that which he had acquired from experiences at different ends of a gun until after contact with them in the show. He was a wonderful shot on foot or on horseback, a superhunter of large game, a splendid guide for troops in the field, and a pony express rider without peer. His endurance was most remarkable, his courage undaunted, and there was no country infested with hostile Indians too dangerous for him to carry through it an important despatch. He was greatly liked and admired by the troops. His service was more with troops against Indians than with the Indians themselves. I am sorry to say that the world will never see another Buffalo Bill, the friend and companion of the army.

There came a transitional period in the history of the Plains, after the Indian wars were over, when Ben Clark and Horace Jones had become old after serving the government many times from their youth up at the risk of their lives. General Sheridan, their greatest friend, was dead. Their other old friends were scattered everywhere. A new race of young officers new to the Plains were coming into responsible positions. A certain quartermaster general [Richard N. Batchelder] was in Washington who did not care what happened to anybody on the Plains so long as he could save a nickel, not for the government but to enhance his own prestige as an economical administrator. By this scheming policy the army was nearly ruined. Most of the mules and spring wagons, even from the posts far from the railway, were sold off, and Ben Clark, Horace Jones, and my packer Chambers were discharged, although Jones and Clark were still needed as interpreters. I went into a campaign along with General Miles, though he was then persona non grata in Washington, and we got them all restored in spite of the quartermaster general.

I was sitting at my desk in the palace in Havana in 1900 [1901] when two letters were handed me, the first from Horace Jones at Fort Sill, saying that he had fled from the railroad for more than forty years but now it was crossing the creek below his house, blowing smoke in his windows. He was bedridden and could not go away any farther and did not expect to last much longer. He had an old fox horn that he had used as master of the hounds when he was a young man, he said. Since there was no one in the world whom he would like to have it as he would me, he was having it sent to me by mail. I have it now.

The other letter was also from Fort Sill from my old first sergeant, Ernest Stecker, then quartermaster sergeant of the post, later a captain of Philippine scouts, and still later agent for our old friends, the Kiowas and Comanches at Anadarko. His letter told me that Colonel Jones had died in the night and that he was sending me the interpreter's fox horn as he had been requested to do.[7] I prize the gift most highly to this day.

Poor old Ben Clark became afflicted with a painful disease and shot himself about 1915 at Fort Reno, leaving a paper behind him saying that he could stand the pain no longer.[8] He had been a trapper and a mountain man with Kit Carson in his youth, had been in the Utah war [1857–58], and like Cody and Will Bill Hickok had served throughout the Civil War. He was my friend for many years, and I mourned him sincerely. It was a great privilege for me to have known intimately all those men. They were the product of a time that is gone forever.

General Miles was once sitting in the office of the chief of staff, talking with me about old times on the Yellowstone. I said, "General, if we could go back to those old days with the buffalo and all those old conditions, I would trade my commission as a major general for that of a second lieutenant of cavalry before you could get out of that door." He said he would do the same.

◆ ◆ ◆

The Wild West Show closed on October 31 [1893], and Colonel Cody was brought down by General Miles to hunt with us in the Indian Territory at

7. Jones died on November 16, 1901. Thoburn, "Horace P. Jones," 390.
8. Ben Clark died on July 24, 1914. Hardorff, *Washita Memories*, 203.

the end of November, in which interval he had spent thirty thousand dollars, throwing it to the birds. I had two troops of cavalry on Cobb Creek as escort to General Miles, who brought with him a number of such celebrated plainsmen as Ben Clark, Jack [Simpson E.] Stillwell, who had carried the despatch that brought succor to Sandy Forsyth beleaguered on the Republican by Southern Cheyennes in 1868, and Pony Bob [Robert Haslam], who was a rider on the Pony Express, and had helped carry the news of the election of Abraham Lincoln from St. Joe [Joseph], Missouri, to San Francisco in seven days. I had Indians of various tribes, making a notable camp. After dinner in my huge tent they told delightful stories every night for two weeks. I had to go out to give the orders for the next day, assigning such and such horses, dogs, and Indians to this and that party, laying out their hunting grounds. I would run back as fast as possible to avoid missing the stories.

Colonel Cody called one day with Mrs. Miles on old Doc [Jacob J.] Sturm, who had lived long with the Caddo lower down on Cobb Creek, taking with them my boy Hunter, who had never been allowed to have a gun on account of his youth but had loved a gun since before he could walk. He would pull away from me walking in Pittsburgh when he was two years old whenever we passed a gun store to look at the guns in the window with delight. Cody began to throw empty cans up in the air and perforate them with the .22-caliber Colt rifle he had used to break glass balls from horseback in the Chicago show. Looking around he saw the hungry look on Hunter's face and said, "Hunter, do you want a shot?" Hunter wanted it terribly and perforated the first can he ever shot at, which pleased Cody so much that he cried out, "Hunter, I give you that gun!" Hunter carried it next day with General Miles at the lower end of Cobb Lake. Colonel [Marion] Maus had wounded a mallard duck, which came over them slowly at the lower end when General Miles called out, "Give it to him, Hunter!" and Hunter killed it on the wing. Hunter's own boy now has that famous gun.[9]

9. Hunter's son was Hugh Lenox Scott II, born in 1909. "Miss Dickensheets Married in Houston; Architect Wed in Garden of Her Parents' Home to Hugh [Lenox] Scott 2d, Grandson of General," *New York Times*, June 3, 1937; Hugh Lenox Scott II, Glenwood Cemetery, Houston, Tex., "Find a Grave Index."

23

Chiricahua Apache Prisoners of War

All during the incumbency of Secretary [Daniel S.] Lamont at the War Department, 1893 to 1897, he had been badgered by the good people of the East about the Chiricahua Apache prisoners of war. This band was credited with the press with twenty-five hundred homicides in Arizona and had held back the state for twenty-five years. They had been chased for years in and out of Arizona and Old Mexico through a fearful country, first by the troops of General Crook, then by those of General Miles. When at last they tired, Lieutenant [Charles B.] Gatewood, Sixth Cavalry, boldly entered their camp and negotiated their surrender.

The band, under Geronimo and Naiche, were sent as prisoners of war to Florida, then to Mount Vernon [Barracks], Alabama, where they failed to thrive.[1] Many of them died of tuberculosis, and the death rate was higher than the birthrate. The secretary was continually being abused in the press for keeping children, born since the surrender, as prisoners of war, which he could not legally help, for Congress had passed a law forbidding the sending of that band west of the Mississippi River. There was nowhere else to put them. The secretary had tried to induce the Cherokees in the mountains of North Carolina to receive them, but their reputation had preceded them. The Cherokees refused.

1. Naiche, Geronimo's colleague, is a prominent figure throughout Geronimo's biography. Utley, *Geronimo*. See also Robinson, *Apache Voices*, 57–59.

After much trouble in reconciling General Miles, a bill was introduced that would permit sending them west of the Mississippi. This bill, sponsored in the [U.S.] Senate by Senator Joe [Joseph C. S.] Blackburn of Kentucky, at that time defender of the policies of President Cleveland in the Senate, was strongly opposed by the delegates from Arizona, New Mexico, and Oklahoma, joined by the representatives of Utah and other states. Dennis [T.] Flynn, then delegate from Oklahoma, made a very impassioned speech in committee against the project, declaring it a crime against humanity to "turn loose four hundred red-handed murderers amid the law-abiding population of Oklahoma." Senator Blackburn asked if his eloquent friend, the delegate from Oklahoma, wished the committee to believe for a moment that the turning loose of four hundred red-handed murderers among the population of Oklahoma would increase the proportion of crime in that state. The bill passed in the laugh that ensued and finally became a law.

The troubles of the secretary did not end here, however, for there was no place west of the Mississippi where the Apaches would be welcome to go, their reputation having preceded them everywhere. The secretary nearly lost his mind over those prisoners. Captain Maus of General Miles's staff wrote me to come up to Chicago to talk with General Miles about the feasibility of locating them in the Kiowa and Comanche country. I answered that I was just going into the field and would telegraph him on my return.

Soon after I had sent Captain Maus notification according to my promise, the [Fort Sill] post commander [Alfred T. Smith] summoned me to tell me that he had telegraphic orders for me to go to Chicago and asked if I were going to hunt with General Miles. I told him I could not afford to hunt with their party. They were going in a private car with [U.S. Senator from Ohio and later] Secretary [of State] John Sherman. My share of the expenses would be more than a month's pay. He then asked, "What are you going to do then?"

I said, "The papers are carrying an item discussing the sending of the Apache prisoners of war to Fort Sill, and maybe that is what the general wants to talk to me about."

The post commander broke into a violent rage against General Miles: "The idea of his sending for a first lieutenant of my garrison to consult him about sending a lot of blankety-blank Indians to my reservation without saying a blankety-blank word to me about it!"

I said, "Colonel, it is possible he wishes to talk to me about something else," but this failed to quiet him.

The article in the paper was noted by the Kiowas and Comanches, who held a council at Anadarko and appointed a delegation to go to Fort Sill and inform me of their knowledge of the article. They had never liked those Apaches who used to kill Comanches whenever they could, but I was not to wait for authority to bring them to the Comanche country, for I had the authority now to do as I saw fit—to bring them or not. Armed with this, I reported to General Miles at his camp at Evanston [Illinois], where he was just clearing up affairs pertaining to the Chicago riots.[2] He directed me to go to Mount Vernon, Alabama, to talk to the Apaches and handed me a vast mass of correspondence connected with them to read on the train.

I asked them how they liked Mount Vernon. They answered that they did not like to live there at all. They were rapidly dying off with tuberculosis. They were harassed by the civil authorities. The reservation they lived on was no larger than your thumbnail on which the trees were so thick that you would have to climb up to the top of a tall pine if you wanted to see the sun. When you climbed down and went somewhere to sit down and rest yourself, there was always something waiting there to bite you. Of course, they all wanted to go back to Arizona. They were told that this was impossible since the white men of that state would kill them all because of their former crimes. If they would promise me to behave themselves, I would take them to where they could see the sun without climbing a tree and would be able to see the mountains in the same view. They all promised.

Eskimazin [Eskiminzin] told me that he and his forty people were in a different category from Naiche, Geronimo, and their people, imprisoned for killing white men, for Eskimazin, he explained, had not been at war for twenty years. Somebody had said that he had seen the notorious Apache Kid the week before. Then, on account of that bit of gossip, he and his forty people had been kept in prison at Fort Wingate, New Mexico, for three years and three years more in Florida and now ought to be allowed to go back to Arizona.[3]

The correspondence given to me to read on the train bore out this statement. Returning to General Miles's camp, I recommended that Geronimo, Naiche, and their people be sent to Fort Sill and that Eskimazin and his

2. The riots mentioned were those associated with the 1894 Pullman Strike. Wooster, *Nelson A. Miles*, 198–201.

3. Chapters that discuss Eskiminzin, his son-in-law the Apache Kid, and their troubled relationship can be found in Robinson, *Apache Voices*, 65–85.

people be sent home to Arizona. General Miles flushed up at hearing the recommendation in the case of Eskimazin and became quite angry. He declared that Eskimazin should never again set foot on the soil of Arizona as long as he, Miles, was alive because Eskimazin had buried a white man up to his neck in an anthill. I reminded the general that this had been wiped out by the lapse of twenty-five years and that he himself had condoned many acts of savagery in the case of other tribes. Why single out Eskimazin who had led an extremely good life for many years? He had located off the reservation in Arizona, had become self-supporting by his own efforts, and had been driven away from his place by designing white men who had stolen and destroyed his property and forced him to give up his place and go back to the reservation. It seemed a little stiff that he should be imprisoned with forty of his people for the crime of speaking to the Apache Kid, of which fact there was no proof, even if it were true. The general was adamant, however. After I told him I thought he was making a mistake, the matter was dropped. I never mentioned it to him again.

Eskimazin had learned his lesson and had not misbehaved for twenty years. There was a vast difference in my mind between him and a criminal who has had the advantage of civilization and example. I thought he had already been punished too much. Since he had not been concerned in the recent crimes for which Geronimo and Naiche were being punished, he should go back to Arizona. Forty of his people were not concerned in the episode of the anthill. Why punish them at all?

Neither Geronimo nor Naiche was being punished in one sense. To be sure, they were not allowed to go back to Arizona because they would have been killed if they had gone. They had duties to perform, but they had the freedom of the place otherwise. They and their children were called "prisoners of war," a sort of legal fiction by which the army could restrain, feed, and clothe them. As soon as this legal fiction was removed, the army could no longer feed, clothe, and educate them on the military reserve. They would have to be turned over to the Indian Department, which had no restraining force or place to put them. It did not have influence enough with any Indian tribe to have them incorporated on a reservation. This legal fiction that covered the children born in captivity was solely in the interest of those Apaches.

I got the Kiowas and Comanches to permit them to occupy the military reserve that was to revert to them in case the land was no longer to be used for military purposes. So that by agreement, signed by the Kiowas and Comanches, the Apaches could be allotted land severally on the military reserve, which was enlarged by executive order so as to afford an allotment of 160 acres apiece—something more than fifty thousand acres.[4]

It was President Cleveland's idea to abandon the post and reservation when no longer needed for military purposes. His Washington advisor had reported to him that that time was near. The policy changed, however, in the time of General J. Franklin Bell as chief of staff, who caused the expenditure of more than a million dollars on Fort Sill as a School of Fire [for the Field Artillery, 1911], since which time there has been no thought of abandonment. When the time came to leave Fort Sill, I had a number of photographs taken of the plant and forwarded them with my last report to the War Department. I knew very well my policies would not be followed by my successors. Those fences and fields would disappear, and people would be apt to say, "Scott talks a great deal about his cornfields and so on, operated by Indian labor, but he has nothing to show for them, and he only imagined them." The photographs may be seen any day in the office of the Adjutant General in Washington.

Several days after my return to Chicago from Alabama the press announced the abandonment of nine military posts in different parts of the country, among them Fort Supply in Oklahoma.[5] Coming into the Pullman Building, I was told that General Miles wanted to see me and wished me to take the Apaches to Fort Supply. I hid out for a while to consider this and to consult the list of property at Fort Supply in the office of the chief quartermaster, which I wanted to have sent to Fort Sill for my use instead of having it sold at auction at Supply as this would materially help my appropriation of fifteen thousand dollars for the establishment of the Apaches. This accomplished, I was ready to be found.

The general asked how I would like to take the Apaches to Fort Supply, to take over the reservation as a cattle range and live in the abandoned post buildings. I told him I would not like it at all and based my objections on the size and shape of the reservation, which would not permit me to get more than a mile away from a border, making it impossible to keep clear of the whisky sellers. Those Apaches were homicidal monomaniacs who would kill anybody when intoxicated, having killed sixteen of their own people and wounded others in drunken clashes in Alabama. The general nevertheless painted quite an alluring picture of Fort Supply. He said he would send my

4. Utley, *Geronimo*, 252, 315–16, 316n9.

5. The army formally abandoned Fort Supply in 1895. Frazer, *Forts of the West*, 124–25.

Indian troop there and give me a doctor. I would in reality be a post commander, a pretty good position for a first lieutenant. I could occupy the post buildings and save my appropriation thereby. But the liquor question remained paramount in my mind.

The general got a little impatient with my stubbornness and ended by saying, "Well, you go out and look at Supply anyhow with Maus. I am going to New Mexico on a bear hunt. You and Maus go with me in my car as far as Newton, Kansas, and I will meet you afterward at Fort Sill."

He was going to New Mexico with Captain Leonard Wood of the Medical Department [U.S. Army] and with Frederick [Frederic] Remington, the artist. I asked him for the sixty-seven mules then at Supply, to be reserved from sale for me, with wagons, harness, tools, coffins, window sashes, and so on. He looked at me to see whether I really meant this, thinking it possible that I was trying to joke with him about the mules, but, seeing that I was really in earnest, he said, "All right."

It was at this time that I first saw Captain Wood and Remington but by no means the last.[6]

Remington told me that I was the most disappointing man he had ever seen. He had been hearing about me in the Indian country for ten years, and now meeting me at last he found me looking like a college professor. I asked him what he had expected me to look like, but he avoided specifying. Notwithstanding his disappointment at my appearance, we became excellent and enduring friends. He asked me to come and stay with him at New Rochelle [New York] for a month or two and tell him stories about the Indian country, to give him copy.

Going down on the train, we all had a discussion about uniforms over the cleared dining table. Remington, to illustrate his point, produced some large sheets of paper on which he drew pictures of the soldiers of European armies and left them on the table when we broke up, as of no more use to him. Later I thought I would go back and get one as a souvenir, but they were all gone. He drew with extraordinary facility.

Long before, Remington had had a judgment entered against him in Kansas, probably a remnant of his cowboy days, that Maus knew about.[7] When

6. Wooster, *Nelson A. Miles*, 197.

7. Remington's brief stint as a homesteader and the influence it had on his art career are documented in Taft, "Pictorial Record," 113–35.

we stopped, en route to New Mexico, for a few minutes at Kansas City, Kansas, Maus, impersonating a sheriff, called in from the platform in a gruff voice, asking if Mr. Frederick Remington were on board. Remington put for his stateroom, locked himself in, and would not come out as long as he was in Kansas.

I had heard from Fort Sill that the post commander had announced his intention of building a palisaded pen somewhere away from the post in which to corral the Apache prisoners of war, detailing a company of infantry out there as a guard over them for a month at a time. I asked General Miles if that were his idea of the way those Indians should be managed. He said, "Don't worry. I will send Maus there with you to start you right," showing that he had already abandoned the idea of our going to Supply—although he was sending us there to look at it anyhow—for he recognized the validity of my objections and had mentally given up the project.

Maus and I called together on the post commander in his office the morning after our arrival at Fort Sill and found him affability itself. He told us that he had picked out just the right place to locate the Apaches. Maus answered, "Excuse me, Colonel, the department commander directs that Lieutenant Scott shall locate those Indians." Every proposition our host advanced was met in the same manner. I felt so uncomfortable at hearing him knocked about in that fashion that I slipped out into the adjutant's office so that I would no longer hear. He drew it all down on himself, however, by impossible propositions. I was glad when he was ordered east soon after. He would have driven those Indians into running away had he remained in command.

The Apaches arrived in the beginning of winter, conducted by Lieutenant Allyn [K.] Capron [Jr.], Fifth Infantry, who had been with them at Mount Vernon. He was extremely anxious to transfer to the Seventh Cavalry, and I sympathized with his wish. He had made five applications that had all been refused by General Schofield, with instructions to stop making any more. I told him to make one more. We would all take hold of the wheels and make the wagon go. This time he was successful. He was transferred to my Indian Troop L, Seventh Cavalry.[8]

8. In 1898 the junior Capron became a Rough Rider in the Spanish-American War and was killed early. Theodore Roosevelt immortalized him with this quote: "In fact, I think he was the ideal of what an American regular army officer should be." Roosevelt, *Rough Riders*, 18–19, 95.

It was too late in the season for the Apaches to accomplish anything more than cut palisades for their houses. They were camped down in the brush out of the wind and wintered very comfortably for them. George [M.] Wrattan [Wratten], who had been their interpreter ever since their surrender, came with them to Fort Sill. I took some of the Kiowa Apaches to see them. That band had come from the north with the Kiowas before 1682 and had never been in Arizona. The Chiricahuas called them Half Apaches because they could understand half they said.

When the Chiricahuas arrived from Alabama, they brought only a few trunks and boxes with clothing and trinkets and had for livestock not even a dog or cat. Several hundred Kiowas and Comanches came to see them on arrival and tried to talk to them in the sign language. They had come from far west of the sign-talking country and thought those people crazy for making such foolish gestures. It was not until each side produced a Carlisle [Indian Industrial School, Carlisle, Pennsylvania] boy that the amazing spectacle was seen of three Indian tribes unable to communicate with each other except through the English language.

An old Comanche named Isa-tai came to the post afterward and asked if I had seen "all those people on the other side of the ocean."[9] I told him I had seen some of them. He asked if they were all as ugly as those Apaches. "Some white men are ugly, and some Comanches are ugly, but those Apaches are all ugly," wherein Isa-tai struck a greater truth than he was aware of, for the different branches of the Athabascan family as far north as the Arctic Circle are particularly ugly.

When General Miles had finished his bear hunt, he came down to look over the Apache situation. He acknowledged that Fort Sill, thirty-three miles away from the border of the reservation, was the proper place for them and ordered their location on the military reserve. When the Apaches had first arrived from Alabama, we were told that Eskimazin and his people had been left behind at Mount Vernon with no intimation as to their disposition, under guard of Captain [Hobart K.] Bailey's company of the Fifth Infantry. Several telegrams were handed General Miles while he was sitting on my porch. He would hand these to [Francis] Michler, his aide, without a word. Michler told

9. Isa-tai, whose name translates unfortunately to "Rear-End-of-a-Wolf" or "Coyote Anus," gained great acclaim within the Comanche tribe for having organized its first sun dance. Kincaid, "Isa-tai."

me later these were from the War Department, asking for a recommendation for the disposition of Eskimazin, the later ones rather insistent, saying, "You are delaying the concentration of the Fifth Infantry." But the general would not answer.

I went up to Chicago with him when he left in his car. At Kansas City, Michler brought me a message from Mrs. Scott at Fort Sill, saying a telegram had arrived there for me from the War Department with an offer of the five-year detail as military instructor at Girard College, Philadelphia, carrying with it a thousand dollars a year extra pay and a house to live in, which she had declined in my name without consulting me, well aware what my decision would be on account of my promise to stay with the Indians a certain time if permitted by the War Department. Mrs. Scott was very anxious to live for a while in Philadelphia with her parents. It was a source of grief to her to give up this opportunity, especially as she never saw her mother again.

Soon after I returned to Fort Sill from Chicago, a sergeant of the Fifth Cavalry from San Antonio brought up an Apache who had been left behind in Alabama in the hands of the civil authorities on a charge of murder. The sergeant told us that the Apache had come on a special train to San Antonio with Eskimazin and his people on their way to Arizona escorted by Captain Bailey's company of the Fifth Infantry. The general had finally come down out of his tree. He had not wanted to do it, but neither had he wanted to put aside my recommendation. He finally saw it was best.

Several years after, a troop of the First Cavalry that had escorted Eskimazin from the railroad to their agency came from Arizona to Fort Sill. Lieutenant [William H.] Osborne told us that those Apaches ran far ahead of the wagons, with the tears of joy streaming down their faces as they recognized the landmarks in their old country. The agent established them on their reservation, where they proved to be the most industrious, well-behaved, and progressive people he had, a notable example to the others. Eskimazin died soon after his return, and I felt glad that I had had something to do with allowing him to die in his own country, for he had been greatly wronged by the people of Arizona.

The Fort Supply property I had asked for was ordered sent to Fort Sill, including the sixty-seven mules, wagons, and coffins. I rested secure in the expectation of their arrival in due course but met a rude shock at El Reno, where Captain Glennan and I went up as witnesses before the civil court, when I learned that the quartermaster general of the army [Richard N. Batchelder] had ordered most of the mules and wagons sold at auction at every post, even at those far from the railroad, leaving them stripped of transportation in order to show an economical administration, this regardless of the necessities of the army. For this act he would have paid dearly had he not been retired before the Spanish War, which found the army without anything.

We met a man at El Reno who asked how many mules were to be sold at Fort Sill. He said that they were selling sixty-seven mules at Fort Supply, the auction to take place at eleven o'clock the next day. He had sent a man up there to buy them all. Glennan and I hurried down to the telegraph office, where I sent a telegram to General Miles, paying extra to deliver it to him wherever he might be, notifying him of the sale.

The sale took place next day at eleven o'clock as advertised. Seventeen mules had been sold when a telegraphic order arrived stopping the sale. I got fifty mules at Fort Sill. Some of these died of colic and other troubles. Some were drowned in Cache Creek, but I turned over fifty mules to my successor when I came to leave. I do not know how it happened, but I do know that none were bred there.

That mule train was put to hauling palisades, lumber, and shingles from the railway, sixty-six miles the round trip. Then it brought agricultural implements and a well machine, operated by a mule. It broke up seven hundred acres of land and operated mowing machines, rakes, and a hay baler. I had seen the maize corn of the Comanches grow up a dark green color, breast high, year after year, only to be struck by the hot winds from Mexico and turned to the color of dried tobacco, a total loss. I had heard of a Kaffir [kafir] corn, one of the varieties of sorghum from South Africa, a drought resistant, and brought the first Kaffir corn to that district. We raised three hundred thousand pounds one year and sold it to the government. We cut and hauled a thousand tons of prairie hay for the government and baled five hundred tons of it, all by Indian labor, built seventy-one dwelling houses and one storehouse, sank wells, some as deep as two hundred fifty feet, and fenced fifty thousand acres of the reservation to control our cattle. Those Indians performed an enormous amount of labor during the four years I remained with them. They kept their promise of good behavior to the extent that no complaint by an outsider was ever lodged against one of them. Their death rate diminished, their birthrate increased, and this was considered the most successful experiment with Indians ever entered into by our government.[10]

◆ ◆ ◆

When the Apaches first arrived, those who had known them in Arizona predicted their escape to Old Mexico. When I visited General [John R.] Brooke at Omaha, he said they would all run away before I got back to Fort Sill.[11] This was the common belief. I did not know myself but that, if they got intoxicated, they would be likely to commit some crime and run away to escape the consequences. They were fully capable of making their way west unseen. One of them, going east, had jumped off a car near Independence, Missouri, and was never heard of again until he turned up later, an outlaw in the Sierra Madre in Old Mexico. Some were found by their people and brought into Fort Sill who had run away from Carlisle and made their way out there, although they had never been there before.

I had a map drawn of the trail, with all its water holes over the seven hundred miles [from Fort Sill] to the Mescalero Agency [New Mexico], by a Mescalero Indian living with the Comanches who had traveled it several times. Copies of this map were sent to the department commander to enable him to cut off runaways with troops from the other end upon telegraphic notice that they had started.[12] I told them plainly on the first arrival that they had better not try to get away. The Comanches were my friends, not theirs, and would tell me at once where they were. I would open fire on them as soon as I saw them. I showed them twenty days' rations maintained in the stables where Chambers lived, with a pack outfit so that we could be on the road after them in half an hour. It would go hard with them if they should start. But there was never even any talk of it among themselves. I made a particular effort to attach Naiche, Toclany [Toclanny], and Kaahtenay to me personally.

10. Scott inserted a testimonial from his superior on his "remarkable progress in the improvement of the minds, characters, and condition of the Apaches," along with the robust vital statistics of the tribe. Wesley Merritt, Headquarters, Department of the Missouri, to the Adjutant General, Washington, D.C., Sept. 15, 1896, reprinted in Scott, *Some Memories*, 192.

11. The headquarters of the Department of the Platte, commanded by Brooke, was located in Omaha, Nebraska. His limited experience with Indians was largely confined to the Sioux Campaign of 1890–91. Jensen, Paul, and Carter, *Eyewitness at Wounded Knee*, 25–36.

12. A copy of Scott's map, among the papers of a departmental commander of the U.S. Army, turned up for auction in 2009. "Lot 288, Indian Wars Apache Map."

The Apache Kid was loose then in Old Mexico, as well as thirteen of the Chiricahua band that had refused to surrender with the others. They were committing depredations on both sides of the line and would come into the agency secretly now and then, steal a woman, and get away, pursued by the troops across deserts and mountain ranges without result. It seemed to me that that method was as certain to result in failure as hunting deer with a brass band. My Apaches were perfectly familiar with their strongholds, hid away in the high ranges of the Sierra Madre in Mexico. I submitted a plan to Colonel Lawton, inspector general, who put it before General Miles, who in turn approved it.

This plan was to go west on a hunting trip from Fort Sill, telling no one our destination, taking those three Apaches, whose families would be left behind in our power, taking also Capron, Clancy, and about fifteen officers and sergeants picked for such service, and boarding a train somewhere in the Southwest. Lawton agreed to have supplies and a packtrain waiting for us at Fort Bowie, Arizona. We would start out ostensibly to hunt, moving slowly down outside the foothills of the Sierra Madre in Old Mexico, chasing deer and small game, and turning loose at the same time those Apaches who had grudges against the Apache Kid and hated him intensely to examine the Apache trails and all their old strongholds in the mountains of Old Mexico until they found the outlaws, when they were to back out without being seen, join us on the prairie, conduct us to within a night's march of the stronghold, and guide us so that we could surround it before daylight. Both Lawton and General Miles said that this was the only plan with hope of getting them. I went on to Washington to arrange for it, but it was all spoiled by the attitude of the Mexican minister, who refused to allow us to enter Mexico unless on a hot trail within certain limits of the border, as laid down in the treaty with Mexico. The plan had to be given up, much to my chagrin, because I believed in its prospect for success. General Miles and Lawton, [Oscar J.] Charles, Capron, Clancy, and the three Apaches were greatly disappointed also, but General Miles could not change the Mexican minister, whose name was [Matfas] Romero, if my memory serves me rightly.

In a fight [1896] in Mexico, Squid [Sedgwick] Rice of the Seventh Cavalry killed Matsé [Massai], the Apache who had jumped off the train near Independence, Missouri.[13] Several of those thirteen Chiricahuas were killed by

13. Robinson, *Apache Voices*, 90–91, 96.

Mormons in the mountains. In 1913 General [Pancho] Villa told me that he knew where to find the survivors, but more important military matters prevent[ed] considering their capture, for there were then far worse outlaws on every side of us.

◆ ◆ ◆

In order to prevent the lapse of our cattle appropriation into the Treasury, with no certainty of getting it out, we were obliged to purchase our cattle before we were ready, before we could build a fence or raise winter feed for them. The first storms of winter drove them for twenty miles the first day, right down into the Comanche country, far from white supervision. The hungry Comanches liked beef. We would often have to drive them back in the teeth of a storm. I know of no better way to lose a herd quickly than to drive them on the open range in winter. We were confronted with the loss of the whole herd without feed or shelter.

We had been told many times never to sleep in the Apache camp if we did not want to have our throats cut and the Apaches to escape. Nevertheless, when the storms got bad, Capron and I would take turns sleeping in the camp. Whenever a black cloud was seen at night in the north, our horses would be saddled before daylight by Naiche or some of his Apache cowboys. We would then round up the cattle, throw them into the shelter of the woods and bluffs, and hold them there until the storm was over. This saved the greater part of the herd.

We had to turn cowboys ourselves to teach the Indians to rope and throw cattle and brand calves. All nature seemed to combine against us. It seemed that it would be a miracle if we could ever establish that herd. First, it was the Texas fever, then the cold and starvation, the heel fly, the screwworm, and anthrax. The Indian had to be taught to recognize these and to understand the manner of treatment. He had to see that the treatment was applied. We had to learn farming in order to teach it, had to teach carpentering, well sinking, teaming, and the care of mules. My accounts were well kept for me by First Sergeant Stecker.

Our first calf, born on the range, was long recognized among hundreds of others by its tail, broken when mobbed by the mules. The first bulls were pedigreed Herefords, with white faces, considered the best beef breed able to rustle for itself on the open range. The cows were seven-eighths Hereford. New pedigreed bulls were added from time to time until the experiment was abandoned. The Apache steers used to take the top of the market at

Kansas City. The herd yielded a revenue, when once established, of $25,000 a year. The first cattle cost $12,000. When the herd was finally sold out, it was known far and wide as the best herd of cattle in the Southwest and brought at auction $294,000.

I saw one day a cultivated-looking gentleman walking about Fort Sill, evidently a stranger with no place to stay since there was no hotel. I invited him to our house. No one knew his name or his business, and I did not ask him. He was invited to go about with me to see the Apaches at work. We struck the hay camp in the middle of the morning when everything was going full blast in every direction—mowers here, hay rakes there, stackers over there, making quite a little scene of Indian industry. My guest became somewhat indignant and accused me of framing up a scene to impress him. I told him that I did not even know who he was and knew no reason why I should take the trouble to impress him. It turned out that he was Francis [E.] Leupp, sometime afterward commissioner of Indian Affairs under President [Theodore] Roosevelt, then acting as an inspector of the Indian Rights Association. I soon convinced him that the Indian Rights Association had nothing whatever to do with me. I did not care a whoop with whom he was affiliated. He soon saw that he had made a mistake, recognized the scene was the ordinary daily routine, and never got over that picture of Indian industry. He got President Roosevelt to offer me the command of the Indian school at Carlisle when General [Richard Henry] Pratt resigned and upbraided me every time I saw him for not accepting.[14]

I had made application to the appointment of my First Sergeant Stecker, who had been trained for years with Indians and knew every one of the Kiowas and Comanches, as agent at Anadarko. Commissioner Leupp asked me, "Do you know what you have done?" I told him I knew of many things I had done but not what I had been caught at. He said, "You have just defeated Dr. Hugh Scott of Oklahoma City for the position of agent at Anadarko." This was the first time I had ever heard of Dr. Hugh Scott, but we became friends afterward in Washington and long received each other's mail.[15]

14. Leupp became something of a Scott convert after his 1894 inspection of the reservation. Leupp, *Notes of a Summer Tour*, 3–13. For more on Leupp, one of Roosevelt's "six friends," see Hagan, *Theodore Roosevelt and Six Friends*. Regarding Pratt, he was actually forced to retire in 1904. See Utley's introduction and annotation in Pratt, *Battlefield and Classroom*, xvii–xviii, 337n2.

15. The other Hugh Scott served as the private secretary of Frank Frantz, the last territorial governor before 1907 statehood. Perry, "Twenty-seven Years a State," 396.

Not long after the arrival of the Apaches at Sill they asked for a permit to go after mesquite beans, which they had not tasted since leaving Arizona. My friends told me that it was too risky to let them go for the nearest mesquite grove was west of the mountains, forty-five miles away, and they would get a good start toward running away. I gave them permission to leave after work Saturday noon if they would promise to be back ready for work at 7 A.M. Monday. They promised and were allowed to go. They had only a few horses to carry tentage and supplies and bring back the beans. They gathered some three hundred bushels of beans, traveled that ninety miles on foot, and were back ready for work Monday morning as they had promised. They never during four years broke a promise to me.

Arrangements were made with the Indian Department to put the Apache children in the Indian schools at Anadarko. The parents were assembled and told that the wagons would be ready in four days to take the children to school at Anadarko. I wanted them to start neat and clean, a source of pride to their parents. This was received in complete silence, and I asked Chihuahua if they had anything to say about it. Old Chihuahua got up and said, "Of course, we don't want our children to go away from us, but we have been here long enough to know that when you say the children will go to school in four days, they are going to go, and it is no use for anybody to talk about it."

During the school term those mothers would buy a little candy or other presents and trot the thirty-three miles on foot to Anadarko and back just to give it to the children. William H. Quinette, the post trader, my old friend for many years, used to say that the Apaches were more thrifty and knew how to manage their money better than any of the surrounding tribes. General Pratt often said that the Chiricahua Apaches were the brightest children that went to Carlisle.

Naiche was the hereditary chief and was the son of old Cochise, after whom Cochise County, Arizona, was named. He was a straightforward, reliable person. When he was in charge of the cattle herd, I could depend on him completely in every weather. He never disappointed me. Geronimo, like Sitting Bull of the Sioux, was an unlovely character, a cross-grained, sour, mean, selfish old curmudgeon, of whom, as of Sitting Bull, I never heard recounted a kindly or generous deed. When they surrendered, General Miles said Naiche was the wildest man he had ever seen, but I never heard of an improper act during the four years he was with me.

Old Chihuahua was called the Apache Chesterfield, from his polite manners. He wore an officer's blouse with major's shoulder straps and a derby hat. His manners were very courtly.

We raised the first season more than two hundred and fifty thousand watermelons and cantaloupes. Everybody had all the melons he could eat. The seed was new, the soil virgin, and the melons acquired such a reputation that they undersold all that were raised in that part of Oklahoma. I can see my daughter Anna, then about nine years old, behind the quarters, sitting in front of an Apache melon wagon, doing the bargaining, and making the change for the Apaches. Each man made for himself what he could in the sale, which taught him how to market his produce.

Every summer the officers of the garrison used to make purses for competitions between troops and Indians on the Fourth of July, which drew large and picturesque crowds. I built a grandstand by placing a number of large army wagons without bows, their tongues parallel, about six feet apart and covering them with floorboards. I put an awning and a railing about the platform with chairs that made quite a comfortable stand, pulling it down afterward in half an hour and returning the material where it belonged.

I remember there were thirty-two entries in one race. All got off at the first trial without any jockeying to gain an improper advantage. The losers took the decision of the judges without a murmur.

Geronimo, then sixty-seven years old, rode a two-mile race bareback and came in far behind on his worthless old plug. He had bet on his horse and expected to win, fortified in the belief of the efficacy of his medicine power. Those Indians were all inveterate gamblers, taking their losses without a whimper.

24

President Cleveland and the Indians

In 1892 the Cherokee Commission came to the Indian Territory to arrange for the purchase of the Indian lands for settlement by white people. Its members were charged with all sorts of irregularities in obtaining agreements. The Kiowas, Comanches, and Kiowa Apaches elected me to take a delegation of their tribes to Washington to prevent the ratification of the treaty by Congress. Some of the influential Indians were said to have sold out the interests of their people to the Cherokee Commission. Quanah Parker, chief of the Comanches, was in favor of ratification. He got permission to visit his children at Carlisle [in 1893?] and ran over to Washington without the knowledge of his agent and arranged for a hearing before the Committee on Indian Affairs of which Mr. [William S.] Holman of Indiana, often referred to as the Watch-Dog [Watchdog] of the Treasury, was chairman.

Quanah's appointment for a hearing was on the day we arrived in Washington, and my delegation attended the hearing. It was Quanah's appointment. He had it all his own way at first and held the sympathy of the committee, who wanted to open the land for settlement by the white man. The committee was about to close the hearing and go to lunch when I asked for my day in court. The chairman asked, "Who are you, and what are you, a white man, doing here?" I handed him my card, and he exclaimed, "Why, you are a soldier. How do you come here?" I told him I was there by order of the commanding general of the army. Quanah jumped up in a great rage and said he would not have any white man speak for him and his people.

I said, "Quanah objects to my speaking here for the Kiowa and Comanche people, but he is speaking only for himself and not for his people, who have not sent him here, and he does not represent their sentiment. If he has any credentials, as I know he has not, let him produce them. Here are my credentials, signed by the agent of the Kiowa and Comanche people, certifying to my election with this delegation to represent them in open council, and I would like to be heard," whereupon the committee agreed to hear me for an hour at 1 P.M.

We met and quarreled from 1 until 5 P.M., the delegate from Oklahoma the most conspicuous in the opposition in support of Quanah. We metaphorically kicked shins, pulled hair, gouged, bit, and scratched, catch-as-catch-can, no holds barred, all the afternoon. Quanah announced his intention of killing me before I could get back to Fort Sill. The committee reserved decision.

The Southwest from St. Louis down was determined to open the country, fraud or no fraud. In those days I used to be the enemy of the Indian Department and everybody in it, but three men I knew to be honest—James McLaughlin, J. George Wright, and Major [C. F.] Larrabee in the Indian Office. I set out to arrange an interview with President Cleveland through the War Department. I knew nothing of the tangled mazes in those days to be found in Washington—wheels within wheels and deep pits for simple people like me—but some of the wiser men in the War Department advised me to arrange my interview through the commissioner of Indian Affairs, Mr. [Daniel M.] Browning.

Ahpiatom, a Kiowa of my delegation, made a great impression among the senators and congressmen in the president's anteroom. He was beautifully dressed in soft yellow buckskin with long fringes and with his silver medal on his breast. He looked off down the Potomac like an eagle off a crag, paying no more attention to the senators handling his ornaments than if they had been ants crawling about his feet and despising their effeminate curiosity about his trinkets.

We went in with Commissioner Browning. When I had finished stating my case to the president, he jumped up from behind his desk, striking one hand into the other in emphatic indignation and exclaimed, "I will not permit it. I will see justice done to those Indians as long as I am in power!" And he did. Through the influence of President Cleveland and of Senator Matt[hew S.] Quay of Pennsylvania, who had a romantic interest in the Indian, as well as a wide knowledge of them and their history that filled me with amazement, the ratification of that agreement was prevented, against all the power of the Southwest, for seven years. But I later picked up a newspaper in Havana and read that it had been ratified, fraud and all.

Every now and then someone would send me a marked copy of the *Congressional Record* in which Mr. Dennis Flynn, the delegate from Oklahoma, would dance a fancy dance on my poor carcass, which pleased him and his constituents but did me no harm, although it did not conduce to pleasant relations. He came down to Havana on a congressional investigation and asked at the door of the palace who was upstairs, and, hearing my name, exclaimed with joy, "What! Colonel Scott from Oklahoma? Lead me to him." He seemed overjoyed to see someone he knew in that strange country, but I felt like throwing him out, for I do not like people who blow hot one minute and cold the next. I reflected, however, that that would not be tactful as it would make an unnecessary enemy for the governor general. So we made it all up.

I never applied in vain to President Cleveland or Senator Matt Quay for help in getting justice for the Indian. Clancy caught a soldier with a twenty-five-gallon keg of whisky selling drinks to the Apache Indians in violation of the law. I wanted to try the man by court-martial as the only way I could get him punished, but the judge advocate in Chicago decided that he would have to be tried in one of the civil courts in Oklahoma. On my way to Washington I stopped in Chicago to see the judge advocate about it. I was only a first lieutenant in those days, a football for everybody. I told the judge advocate that it was very necessary to stop whisky selling to Indians, who, as said before, were homicidal monomaniacs under its influence. I could not get the man punished in the civil courts. He ruffled up like an angry owl, snapping his eyes at me, and said, "Do you have the audacity to come here and say to me, sir, that the courts of the United States will not do justice?" I told him that was just what I had come to tell him since he did not seem to know about it, but he would not recede.

I explained the matter to President Cleveland, who took me into the old cabinet room upstairs in the White House, where the cabinet was then assembling. He called the attorney general, Judson Harmon, to whom he introduced me, saying, "This is Lieutenant Scott of the Seventh Cavalry, who will explain a case to you which I want you to prosecute without mercy." The case was called at El Reno, but the prosecuting attorney failed to subpoena the principal witness, and the case was thrown out of court. I did not have money enough to pursue it further, but it went far enough to frighten people from selling any more whisky to Apaches in my time.

While waiting with my delegation in the anteroom of the White House to see President Cleveland, a man asked what tribe of Indians those were from. I replied that they were Kiowas and Comanches. He said, "I used to fight the Comanches before the Civil War when I was in the dragoons in the Wichita Mountains."

I told him, "I know all about you then. You used to be at old Fort [Camp] Radziminski on Otter Creek near the Wichitas with Major George H. Thomas, later the 'Rock of Chickamauga.'"

He turned out to be Major [Charles D. A.] Leoffler, who had kept the door of the Cabinet Room since the time of Lincoln, whose orderly he had been. He said, "You are the only man alive now in Washington who knows there ever was such a place as Camp Radziminski," and seemed overjoyed at his discovery of me. Whenever I wanted to see any of the presidents after that, I had only to poke my head into the door of his office and ask, "Does old Major Radziminski live anywhere around here?" and the president would have to see me whether he wanted to or not, no matter who was waiting to see him in the anteroom. He came up later with his wife to see us at West Point, having stayed in our house last in attendance upon President Lincoln.[1]

Before going home I met a friend on F Street late one Saturday night who told me that R[obert] V. Belt had just been nominated for commissioner of Indian Affairs, which gave me a severe jolt. I considered how I could prevent his confirmation, concluding to try Senator Matt Quay first.

I found that the senator was sick in bed. He sent for me to come upstairs and asked how I was getting on. When I told him I was not getting on, he asked what my trouble was. I said, "R. V. Belt has been nominated commissioner of Indian Affairs."

He broke out, "What damned business is that of yours?" I told him that Belt had once been assistant commissioner, had learned the inside of the Indian Office, and had become counsel in claim cases against the Comanches aggregating two million dollars, with fees amounting to some three hundred thousand dollars to be got out of those Indians. The Senate was going to confirm him in a position to adjudicate on those cases himself.

The senator seemed disgusted with my meddling in political appointments. He turned over with a snort with his face to the wall as if to say, "Get

1. Lincoln visited West Point on June 24–25, 1862. Miers, *Lincoln Day by Day*, 3:123.

out. I am tired of you." I got out, believing that my shot had missed the mark. I would have to try somewhere else.

There was a man from Oklahoma, originally from Pennsylvania, who wanted to be assistant commissioner of Indian Affairs. He thought I had some influence with Senator Quay from Pennsylvania, which I could be induced to exert for him. He dogged me wherever I went. He asked my delegation to sign a petition for his appointment. When they asked what they should do about it, I told them to forget how to write their names, and they forgot. The man followed me into the room of General Miles's aides in the War Department on Tuesday and told me that R. V. Belt had been nominated as commissioner of Indian Affairs on Saturday. On the following Monday Senator Quay appeared in the office of the secretary of the Interior and told him that, if he did not withdraw that nomination, he would defeat its confirmation in the Senate. The secretary withdrew it. This caused great joy in the Indian Office, where Belt was much disliked. It was soon found out how it was accomplished. I got ready for trouble with Belt, but nothing ever happened. I never saw him and never heard from him at any time.

When one of the new agents was appointed at Anadarko for the Kiowa and Comanche Indians, Captain [Walter S.] Schuyler and I, passing through, stopped to call on him and make his acquaintance. He occupied most of our call by trying to find out from us the different ways an agent could obtain graft, which disgusted us extremely. His grafting during the next two years went beyond bounds. His actions were a demoralizing influence on his Indians, who were all enraged against him on account of the treatment received from him. He became intolerable to everybody. I wrote out a request for the Indians to present to the Indian Office for his dismissal, gave it to my cousin with a pen and bottle of ink, and told him to go in the buggy with I-see-o to every Kiowa and Comanche camp and witness himself the signature of all those who wanted to sign. They drove down two teams and followed some Kiowas clear up into the Cheyenne country to get their signatures. The agent had saved enough in two years on his salary of eighteen hundred dollars, as he said, to buy a new farm for himself and set his son up in a store and his son-in-law in a canning factory. The agent was subsequently discharged.[2]

2. The agent may have been George D. Day, nicknamed "Grinner" by the Kiowas. Mooney, "Calendar History of the Kiowa Indians," 1:408.

Shortly after President [William] McKinley was inaugurated, General Miles introduced me to a Mr. [A. C.] Tonner, who lived next door to the president at Canton, Ohio, and had come on to Washington with him to receive some vacancy as yet undetermined. In the meantime he had a desk in Secretary [of the Interior] Cornelius [N.] Bliss's private office. He later became the assistant commissioner of Indian Affairs and told me that they were going to send that discharged agent back to Anadarko. I told him that it would be only over my dead body and raised a fearful racket in Washington. After some two weeks Tonner told me that the administration felt that the ex-agent was too strong for them. They would have to do something for him, but, if I would shut up and go home, they would not send him to Anadarko, merely appointing his son-in-law agent for the Poncas. I answered that I was not holding any brief then for the Poncas, for whom I was very sorry, but that, if they would really promise not to send him to the Comanches, I would shut up and go home. The son-in-law was sent to the Poncas and went to the penitentiary in a year and a half.[3]

One reason why I was so averse to the return of the ex-agent to the Comanches was his action when the children in the Kiowa school began having measles. Instead of keeping them quarantined in the school and treating them rationally, he turned them all out, carrying the infection into every family. Shortly afterward he brought the Comanches, as well as the Kiowas, into the same camp at the agency for a payment.

The parents had no knowledge of the proper treatment of measles and put the children in water to allay their fever, with the consequence that the Kiowas lost three hundred children of measles in one month. The sight of so many mourning parents in one camp was heartrending. The women cut off their hair and scratched their faces, arms, bosoms, and legs. Some cut off the joint of a finger in mourning. The blood covered them and was allowed to remain without washing until worn off. The cries of mourning were heard in every lodge.

We had measles in our camp at Fort Sill, where Captain J. D. Glennan of the Medical Corps labored with them incessantly as did Lieutenant Quay, Sergeants Stecker and Clancy, and myself. Having authority to compel proper

3. The son-in-law of George Day was Asa Sharp, who married George Day's daughter Emma in Indian Territory. Asa C. Sharp and Emma Ethel Day, Apr. 19, 1893, in "Oklahoma Marriages, 1870–1930." Sharp's tenure as an Indian agent was marked by several "irregularities," pointed out at bruising length (191 pages) in "Leasing of Grazing Lands."

treatment, we lost no cases of straight measles. Our only losses were those complicated with such other diseases as whooping cough, for none of those children could stand two such diseases at once. We quarantined the camp, and our loss was very small. It was an unusual sight to see two lieutenants of cavalry sitting on the floor of an Indian lodge making poultices for Indian children.

The parents were so grateful to Captain Glennan for his tireless and skillful care that they brought me forty dollars as their first payment and asked me to buy him a horse. I told them he already had a horse and could not use any more horses and suggested a piece of silver, which pleased their fancy. This was presented to him with the inscription that it carried the gratitude of the Indians of Troop L [Seventh?] Cavalry for his services.

The Indian women used to nurse their children until they were three years old, when the milk would give out. The child would be weaned on jerked beef, as dry and hard as a piece of sole leather. This would cause intestinal disorders that led to the loss of many children. We got a cow for the camp and weaned the children on cow's milk with much better results.

25

End of the Plains

Unable to sleep one night in 1897 in Washington, I turned over all my affairs in my mind. I thought, "You have your coyote and bear dogs, your horses, your Indian interests, everything you want. You are freer than any junior officer you have ever seen out there. But you are not educating your children. Give away your dogs, get rid of your horses, say good-by to your Indians, and go somewhere where your children can be educated properly."

Since they had now outgrown the school facilities at Fort Sill, I went down to the War Department next morning and arranged for a station in Washington in either of two capacities. My choice of them was a detail in the Smithsonian Institution, the Bureau of [American] Ethnology under Major J[ohn] W[esley] Powell, director, of deathless memory, to write a book on the sign language of the buffalo Plains. Then I went back to make arrangements to leave Fort Sill with my family. My children were soon at school in Washington.

Before I left Fort Sill, Sergeant I-see-o came in, sat down by the fire, and asked if what he had heard was true. He had heard that I was going away from Fort Sill forever to live in the East. I said, "Yes, it is true." He turned his face away. I could see the tears run down his profile while he sat crushed in his chair without a word. I tried to comfort him, but he soon got up and went away unable to speak.[1]

1. I-see-o lived a long life, a Fort Sill fixture until his death on March 11, 1927. His tombstone reads, "Last Indian Scout on Active Duty," which was due in part to General Scott's later effort in making the old

I wound up my affairs, gave away the pack of coyote and bear dogs I had bred and trained so carefully, sold my horses, and bade farewell to all my Indian friends.

I had seen Dr. [C. D.] McMurdo leave for one of the great northern posts after a long and happy sojourn. He had looked all around at the landscape of mountain and plain for the last time to impress its memory on his mind before getting into the ambulance for the drive of thirty-three miles to the railroad. Now it was my turn to do the same thing. Loving every bit of it in sight, I got into the ambulance with real sorrow in my heart. After nine years of service, nine useful years of strenuous outdoor life on horseback, where we had been so happy, a life of usefulness to white men and red, now I was leaving it. I did not know it then, but it was the end of my happy Plains life without anxieties. I expected to go west again when my children were through with school, but the Spanish War changed all that. I was to become thenceforth a dweller in cities engaged in administrative work. This seemed the road to preferment. I traveled that road and am traveling on it yet.[2]

◆ ◆ ◆

I reported to the veteran ethnologist, Major J. W. Powell, director of the Bureau of Ethnology, who gave me a desk and told me that I knew my subject much better than he did. I could begin to record it in my own way. I soon obtained access to the Library of Congress and to the [U.S.] Geological Survey and began to search the records of the earliest Spanish, French, and English explorers of the West. I found an enormous quantity of literature carrying only small references to the sign language here and there, but it had all to be searched to glean out the little material in existence.

It has always been a deep mystery to me why those explorers did not better appreciate the value of the sign language to their enterprises. The famous explorers Lewis and Clark (1804–1806), who were the first white men to encounter many of the Indians of the Northwest, were directed by President [Thomas] Jefferson to make a comprehensive report of all they saw that

scout "a sergeant for life" in the U.S. Army. Swett, "Sergeant I-See-O," 350. He is buried in the Fort Sill post cemetery. See also Nye, *Carbine and Lance*, 309–11.

2. At this point Scott packed his memoir with laudatory letters from his superiors, including C. H. Carlton, J. P. Sanger, and Nelson Miles, the last acknowledging him for "successfully governing the worst tribe of Indians on the continent" (presumably the Chiricahua Apaches at Fort Sill). Scott, *Some Memories*, 209–15.

was new and interesting. They spent the winter of 1804–1805 among the three tribes [Arikara, Hidatsa, and Mandan], which inhabited the earthen lodges on the upper Missouri [and] which spoke three different tongues and received visitors from other tribes, speaking still other vocal languages. They saw the sign language used intertribally every day. Their man Drewyer [George Drouillard] learned enough of the sign language to interpret for them at different times. Yet their references to it in their report are so casual as to do nothing more than prove a knowledge of its existence. Every tribe on the Plains spoke it as an intertribal language with varying degrees of skill, but only three of the early travelers did more than allude to it.

The officers of our army lived with it all about them while serving on the Plains for a hundred years, but Captain [William] Philo Clark, Second Cavalry, was the only one I ever saw who acquired a reasonable degree of proficiency. I have seen many who had enough interest to learn maybe a dozen signs but not enough interest to learn to put them properly together. They never knew that the language had a syntax of its own.

I have often marveled at this apathy concerning such a valuable instrument by which communication could be held with every tribe on the Plains of the buffalo, using only one language, by which an officer could make himself independent of interpreters, render great service to his associates and to his government, acquire a commanding influence over whole tribes and districts, and which possibly might save his life.

I had hardly done more than locate some of the sources of history when our warship *Maine* was blown up in the harbor of Havana with the loss of two hundred American sailors. This event caused great resentment against Spain.[3]

3. The USS *Maine* sank on February 15, 1898. This abridgment of Scott's *Some Memories* ends on page 217.

Epilogue

In addition to the Spanish-American War, Hugh Scott encountered a series of distractions that kept him from his research and writing on the Plains Indian Sign Language, although the next decade and a half saw a remarkable rise in his professional fortunes. This late bloomer entered the period as a captain; he ended it as a major general. Ultimately, occasions arose that did allow for limited forays to Indian country, and Scott told of three episodes that taxed his troubleshooting skills in the remaining pages of his autobiography.

In the aftermath of the Spanish-American conflict, Scott excelled as a principal member of the staff of the military governor of Cuba. In 1903, the year his mentor Nelson Miles retired as commanding general of the U.S. Army, Scott himself became the military governor of the Sulu Archipelago in the Philippines. He saw considerable field service, engaged the local populations under both friendly and hostile circumstances, and early in his tenure received his first and only battlefield wounds during a brush with warring Moros. Both hands suffered severe injuries with parts of two fingers of his right hand shot off. (This disability failed to hinder the indefatigable sign talker, though, when he later needed to reemploy his sign language skills.) In 1906 he returned to the United States and became the superintendent of the U.S. Military Academy. The promotions came quickly—lieutenant colonel (March 1911), colonel (August 1911), brigadier general (1913), and major general (1915). His Progressive-era political leanings caused him no apparent hindrance during the presidencies of Theodore Roosevelt, William Howard Taft, and Woodrow Wilson.

In spite of his increasing administrative duties, Scott still made time to deal with problems in Indian country as they cropped up, particularly during the span of 1908–15. In retrospect, such assignments may be all the more surprising since on November 16, 1914, he himself had reached the position of U.S. Army chief of staff. Moreover, the European powers were mired in the early stages of the First World War, and the nation sat ill-prepared to enter that conflagration. Nevertheless, this man, who in the next three years would have an important hand in forming millions of men into an overseas army, may have been prouder of his single Indian company at Fort Sill and its achievements in uniform and post-military service than of his helping gather the mighty American Expeditionary Forces.

Sign Talker ends with three return visits to Indian country—to the Hopi tribe in 1911, the Navajo tribe in 1913, and the Paiute tribe in 1915.[1] There were others, but, for whatever reason, they were not recounted. These anecdotes seem a bit more mature, even mildly sardonic, as contrasted to the previous chapters; in their telling, an older, wiser, possibly world-weary Scott emerges. None of these groups used the Plains Indian Sign Language, but it no longer seemed to matter to the old soldier. His diplomatic skills, especially those with Indian peoples, had been honed to the point where he could make do quite nicely without.

◆ ◆ ◆

The Hopi Indians

In the autumn of 1911 the secretary of the Interior [Walter L. Fisher] called upon the secretary of war [Henry L. Stimson] to take over the case of the Hopi Indians of Arizona, with the request that troops be sent to coerce the so-called hostile element at Hotevilla [Hotvela or Third Mesa], who had defied their agent and refused to obey any of his directions, which were those of the Indian Department. The secretary of war directed me to report to the secretary of the Interior and carry out his instructions. I reported every day for

1. Scott, *Some Memories*, 471–77, 487–95, 533–41.

ten days, without being able to get any instructions for some reason unknown to me. Finally I was told to go to Holbrook, [Navajo County,] Arizona, where I would find troops from Fort Apache, take charge of them, and go to Keams Canyon, Arizona, about a hundred miles north to the Hopi and Navajo Agency, and cooperate with the agent.

I found the agent, Mr. Leo Crane, a very agreeable young gentleman, but recently appointed [in 1911], who was very anxious to do his duty. He had had some experience in the Indian Office in Washington but none in the field. He said he had received no orders to cooperate with me but would be glad to do anything for me he could. He told me that an old Hopi chief named Yukeoma [Yukiwma] was at the bottom of all the trouble, a fanatical old sinner, who opposed everything the government wanted to do. While he and his people called themselves peaceful, they had guns and had been known to use them against troops. This rebellion had occurred many times in the past for which troops had been brought here before in consequence of which there had been bloodshed.[2]

Yukeoma had been imprisoned at Alcatraz Island, California, Fort Huachuca, Arizona, Fort Wingate, New Mexico, and many times at Keams Canyon, but these confinements made no impression on him. He had been brought to Washington, but influence brought to bear upon him there was without a particle of effect. He had even been taken to the White House, where President [William H.] Taft gave him his orders in person. He was asked on return whether he had seen the president and replied that he "didn't know whether he had seen the president or not—he had seen a big, fat man they said was president, but he did not know who he was."

The point at issue now was the refusal of Yukeoma and his people to allow their children of school age to go to the agency schools. Although the agent had not received any orders yet to cooperate with me, I concluded to leave the troops at the agency, go over to the hostile town of Hotevilla with the surgeon [Henry F. Lincoln], a bright, young fellow who liked adventure and hoped we might find some at Hotevilla, a cook, a teamster, and an orderly, and try and see what was troubling Yukeoma. We took possession of the empty house of the field matron, who had left because of Yukeoma's unpleasantness.

2. Information on the 1911 episode can be found in part 2 of Whiteley, *Orayvi Split*—in particular, in chap. 26, "Yukiwma Goes to Washington, Returns to Hotvela, and Renews His Resistance (1911)." See also Jacobs, "Battle for the Children," 43, 45.

I sent for Yukeoma, who appeared with his staff. We all had dinner together, and I got him to tell us his troubles, which were many and various. Witches were at the bottom of nearly all of them. He had much to say of a return from the East of a party that had gone east at a time "tradition" tells of, at which time the "tradition" foretold his head was to be cut off, and everything foretold long ago was to come to pass. In the meantime no children could go to school as this would be in violation of the "traditions." He produced a "tradition" against everything he did not like, which meant everything the government wanted. He could manage to produce a "tradition" in short order against anything he had never even heard of before. He said President Taft and Secretary Walter Fisher were both witches. Every time a coyote would come near, it would be pointed out by him to me as a witch and identified as either Taft or Fisher, secretary of the Interior.

The old man would come over and eat with me every day and would bring over now and then a Hopi watermelon. He was very fond of canned pears and would take a can or so back with him. He related the migration legends of the Hopi clans and their ancient settlement, which I asked the doctor to write down. This went on for ten days without making a dent in Yukeoma's resolution to persist in rebellion. He was the only Indian I have ever seen who could not be influenced by reason, sympathy, and kindness. Of course, the children must go to school with or without his resistance, but I was perfectly willing to wait a month or two months rather than have to kill him or any of his people.

The doctor and I had him under observation for ten days, during which we both came to the same conclusion separately that he was really a lunatic, "gone" on the subject of witches. There was no use wasting any more time trying to bring a crazy man around. So I sent word to the troop commander to come over with the agent and empty wagons for the children, to surround the village before dawn, taking possession of every strategic point and allowing no gathering anywhere for resistance.[3] The people woke up to find every place occupied, with no opportunity to get together. I then provided the agent with a guard of troops and told him to search the houses with his own men.

3. Frank B. Edwards, a first lieutenant in the Twelfth U.S. Cavalry, was the troop commander and was stationed at Fort Apache. Whiteley, *Orayvi Split*; Post Return, Fort Apache, Ariz., Oct. 1911, Returns from U.S. Military Posts, RG 94, NARA.

The old man came over in a fury, having felt from our feeding him and our listening to everything he said, that he had softened my heart about taking the children, but he was never told anything that would give him a right to any such impression. Our talk had been mainly about other things. But opposition excited him vastly. He was now in an impotent fury and informed the agent and myself we were both witches like Taft and Fisher. I did not try to punish him, for that in my belief was a matter for the Indian Department. I was there only to get the children. He frequently invited us to cut off his head, confident probably that we would not accept the invitation, but I could see from the lack of care he had bestowed on it that it would prove of no value to me.

When the children were rounded up, they were put in the wagons. We made our respectful compliments to Yukeoma, and all left for the mission at Oraibi [Orayvi].

I had been vastly entertained at Hotevilla by the Hopi ceremonies and customs. We were there in the winter solstice when they were engaged in turning back the sun. We white men have no gratitude for what the Hopi do for us twice every year. The sun travels back and forth between the Tropic[s] of Capricorn and Cancer, and the Hopi sun priests watch this carefully. They and their ancestors have been engaged in this practice for a long time. The Hopi have been a stationary people who were never wanderers like the Plains people, who traveled with the buffalo, here today and gone tomorrow. Oraibi antedates the discovery of America by Columbus. During the hundreds of years of its life those sun priests have noted the movements of the sun—or apparent movements—and when the sun rises at a certain marked place on the horizon, the priest announces that it is eight days from Soyaluna—time for the ceremonies to begin. Most of these take place down in a kiva, or ceremonial chamber underground, entered by a hatchway by means of a ladder. The hatchway is so covered as to allow a sunbeam to strike the wall of the kiva in a certain place. The beam travels back and forth during the year, and on the day of Soyaluna it has almost reached its furthest limit. Then the old men are to be found down in the kiva, turning a wheel with all their might. This turns back the sun to travel toward the other tropic. If the sun were not turned back in this way, the Hopi believe, it would go straight off, and we would die in darkness and cold.

The Hopi are the most intense ritualists I am acquainted with. They heap ritual upon ritual, and the ritual seems endless and without purpose.

I suppose the underlying thought of most of their ritual was lost ages ago. In any event it tires me out completely. I suffer it as long as I can get any meaning from it. Dr. Walter Fewkes, director of the Bureau of Ethnology, is the only person I know of with patience to continue researches into this ritual. He knows all there is to know about the Hopi.[4]

I had long been acquainted with the Spanish history of that country and remembered about the [Pueblo] revolt of 1680, when the Spaniards were driven out of what is now New Mexico and Arizona with the loss of many men. They did not come back for about fifteen [twelve] years, when the country was reconquered "for the faith" by Diego [de] Vargas, as he has recorded on Inscription Rock [at El Morro National Monument, New Mexico]. Some of the churches were destroyed, and their *curas* [priests] killed. I was anxious to know what memory of it was retained by the Hopi and asked if there had ever been a church here. One of them said, "Yes, it was right there and was torn down. There is the priest's bathtub yet. He took a bath in it every time it rained."

This was a stone with a concave surface, not injured from incessant bathing, for it rains there not much oftener than once in eighteen months. If cleanliness is next to godliness, that priest must have been far from heaven. I asked what had become of the priest. The answer was, "We threw him off that rock." That answer seemed so definite that I asked no more questions.

When we went down into a kiva a short time afterward, I was amazed to see the rafters were of pine logs, twenty inches in diameter, with large diamond figures carved on them. I asked my hosts where those logs had come from. The answer was prompt and decisive, "Out of that church," destroyed, as I have remarked, in 1680.

"But," I said, "there was never any forest like that around here. Where did they come from to make the church?"

"Off that mountain," my informant replied, pointing to San Francisco Mountain [San Francisco Peaks] near Flagstaff, Arizona, a hundred miles away.

4. Jesse Walter Fewkes, the director of the Bureau of Ethnology from 1918 to 1928, published extensively on the Indians of the American Southwest. See Hough, "Biographical Memoir of Jesse Walter Fewkes," 261–83, which includes a bibliography.

I felt a little dazed at this and asked, "You had no horses or cattle then. How were they transported?"

The answer was, "We carried them by hand." It only occurred to me to wonder, then, why they had not thrown the priest off the rock before carrying logs a hundred miles for his church. What manner of man was that priest who was able to induce these wild Indians to carry those logs without force! How filled with zeal he must have been for the glory of God and the salvation of those souls so far away in that vast wilderness! There used to be real men in those days.

I went out to see the Snake Dance at Walpi [Arizona] in 1921 with my old friends Slocum and John A. Johnston of Washington and, while inspecting the agency at Keams Canyon, ran across my old friend Yukeoma in jail there for the 'nth time.[5] I reproached the agent for Yukeoma's appearance. He appeared half starved and naked. The agent said he could not help it. The Indian had been given plenty of warm clothing but would not wear it and would not eat the food given him. I sent for him to come to the agency office, where he sat upon the agent's swivel chair, his knees doubled up to his chin and his bare feet in the chair, looking like a dried up little old chimpanzee. He received me with affability as an old friend who had misused him, but he was willing to let bygones be bygones. I asked him whether, should I interest myself in procuring his return to his home, he would promise to obey the agent. He said, "No! No!"—no more and no less.

I looked at the little monkey with what amounted almost to stupefaction. This was the result of twenty years of effort by the great American nation or, rather, the Indian Bureau to make that dried up little monkey obey.

But the Indian recognizes no law outside his natural desires. The characteristics of his race—lawlessness, the freedom of the Plains, and instincts based on age-old traditions—are too strongly inherent in him for him to be taught obedience in one generation.

I advised the agent [Crane] to keep the children without allowing them any vacation at home or he would have all the trouble to do over again. Then after waiting a few days to see whether Yukeoma was going to make any effort to retake the children, we started to march back to the railroad and went to San Antonio to take over the colonelcy of the Third Cavalry.

5. This is the same Slocum of the Fort Meade oysters story.

The Navajo Menace Dispelled

When we reached Fort Huachuca, Arizona, a telegram was received relating to a difficulty at Beautiful Mountain with the Navajo Indians on their reservation. I was directed to go to Gallup, New Mexico, where a squadron of the Twelfth Cavalry from Nebraska would arrive. I should go north with it as escort, meet the veteran inspector of the Interior Department, Major James McLaughlin, and settle the matter.[6]

A bad situation had been developing there due to the distance of the Indians from the agency and the agent [W. T. Shelton], allowing his power to be used by the Navajo police to even up their private grudges. At a previous settlement in 1908 he had asked me what criticism I had to make on his management. I told him then he did not get about enough among his people to give them his personal touch. Here he was in trouble again, allowing the police to manage his business.

A policeman had arrested a Navajo woman during the absence of her family and had taken her into the agency, where she was locked up. Her husband returned and found his enemy had carried off his wife. He gathered his sons and went into the agency to see the agent and recover his wife. The agent was away at Farmington [New Mexico], but he met his wife outside and took her up on his horse behind him. A policeman caught his bridle in order to stop him, and some of the agency employees ran out for the same purpose. He struck the policeman over the head with his quirt, broke away, took his wife home, and fortified himself at Beautiful Mountain in a very difficult position on a high terrace, which only one man could climb up to at a time. He secured great Navajo support. They all had food and water and plenty of high-powered rifles with ammunition. The leaders had declared their intention to sell their lives as dearly as possible.

The situation was very dangerous since there were thirty thousand Navajos on the reservation. The mountains were covered with snow. A winter campaign might involve the whole tribe in one of the most difficult and little known sections of the country, among those great canyons that run down into the Grand Canyon of the Colorado. No one could predict when such a

6. The "we" was elder son Captain David Hunter Scott, Fifth Cavalry, and younger son Lewis Merrill Scott, a mining engineer. Troops A, B, C, and D of the Twelfth Cavalry, commanded by John W. Craig, came from Fort Robinson, Nebraska. Buecker, "In the Old Army," 19, 22n26.

campaign would end. The cost would run far into the millions, to say nothing about the suffering and bloodshed on both sides.

We were met at the hotel in Gallup by Father Anselm Weber, the Catholic missionary to the Navajo, and [Henry] Chee Dodge, the most prominent Navajo, who were deeply impressed by the trainloads of soldiers, horses, mules, wagons, and supplies rolling into Gallup, one after another, and believed that I had come to kill every Navajo I could find. They had come to soften my hard heart.

I enjoyed their trepidation for a while, but it would have been too cruel to let them go in that frame of mind. I sent them off happy, saying that, if any shooting was done, it would only be after it had been begun by the Navajo themselves. I explained the troops had been sent at the request of the agent to the secretary of the Interior [Franklin K. Lane]. I had not been consulted about sending them at all. Moreover, I did not want them considering their presence a useless expense and annoyance to the troops.

I made what arrangements for the troops were possible, having wood, hay, grain, and water put on their campsite, but they arrived in a hard, cold rain to camp in the mud. I felt sorry for them and their stock exposed to the weather. I hired an automobile to take me and my aide ahead of the troops and told the commander [John W. Craig] I would go ahead of him in the machine, traveling much faster than he could in the deep mud. I wanted him to stop at the last water, a little trading store twenty-five miles away, until he got further instructions. I expected to be back there with the principal men as prisoners before he could reach there with his command.

The United States marshal [Andrew H. Hudspeth] wanted to go with me, but I was afraid his presence would be injurious. He had, however, acted with unusual good sense and right feeling, for the agent had urged him to gather a large posse of armed men and attack the Indians in their stronghold. Realizing the consequences of such an act on his part, he had declined to do it and was supported in his position by federal judge [William H.] Pope at Santa Fe. I told the marshal, however, that he must stay with the troops. I would bring the prisoners to him.

My son and I started north the next day, but the machine stuck in the mud and had to be dug and hauled out so often I discharged it about twelve miles out when the cavalry came along. We changed to horses and told the chauffeur he could go back.

We camped that night at the Navajo school at Tonachi, twenty-five miles out, where the chauffeur asked me to try him again as the roads were better from there on, and he was given another trial. We made better time to the Navajo store near the Two Gray [Grey] Hills, where the troops had been ordered to stop. As we approached the store, my heart fell heavily at the sight of Major McLaughlin and the agent, coming out to see who was coming in the machine. I had thought that they were at the agency whence their last telegrams had come, but here they were. They had been working on this case for several months. It had arrived at such a stage they felt they ought to call for troops. If I took them over with me to the Indians, I would be severely handicapped in the beginning, but how to leave McLaughlin behind without hurting his feelings, a friend for more than thirty years? I did not know.

We all went in and sat around the fire discussing matters for an hour without my seeing any way to leave them behind. The agent was especially insistent that I should have the troops over, saying the Navajos had been talked to again and again for several months, each time getting more and more outrageous. Now they were clear out of bounds and would certainly kill me—as the Modocs killed General [Edward] Canby in a somewhat similar situation—if I went over without troops.[7] I told them I had to give the Indians a chance first. I could not go over and shoot them all without giving them an opportunity and would have to go. The troops had their orders already to halt here until called for.

The agent broke out anxiously, "You aren't going to make us go over with you, are you?!"—thus falling into my hand like ripe fruit. I said not at all. I would go over first and send for them if it became necessary. I was gone with my aide within five minutes in the machine.

I had looked at my son [Hunter] for a few minutes wondering if it would be best to risk us both—one in a family was enough—but I reflected no one had ever wrapped me in cotton wool when I was young.[8] I would not wrap him, for it would go far toward killing him to be left behind.

We reached a little Navajo trading post near Beautiful Mountain late that afternoon. It was kept by a Mormon named [Frank] Noel whose premises were so full of women and children we had to sleep in a tent in the yard. He was in great fear of losing his store and family in case of hostilities. The hostiles, as they were called, saw the arrival of the machine from their lookout

7. In 1873 members of the Modoc tribe assassinated General Edward R. S. Canby during a seemingly peaceful council. Murray, *Modocs and Their War*, 180–89.

8. The phrase "wrapped in cotton wool" means to have been overprotected.

and sent their scouts that night to prowl around outside. We saw them listening at windows and their shadows pass over the tent walls.

A courier was sent out to the hostiles next day for them to come in to the store for a conference. This was refused at first, but further messages brought them in the second day, seventy-five of them, heavily armed. They crowded in and filled the store so it was difficult to get a gangway for me to enter. The white men at the store urged me to make them leave their arms at home, but it was hard enough to get them to come as it was. A demand for them to disarm would cause deep suspicion of a trap and probably defeat my whole plan as they would probably refuse to parley. My son went in behind the counter with the trader, while I had a gangway made and three chairs and a bench placed in the center, my back against the counter.

Old Bizoshe, the father, was old and stiff in his ways. Those that knew him said nothing could be done to influence him, that everything had been tried in vain, that the old man was hard as iron, and the eldest son was of such mentality no one could deal with him at any time. It was just running unnecessary risk, the white men said, to try to effect the impossible.[9]

I sat the old man near me with some ceremony. The large crowd of armed Indians jammed into the store and listened with perfect silence after they had once settled down. I said, "My brother, I hear that you are in trouble out here. Troops have been sent for you, but I have told them not to come any nearer than the Two Gray Hills unless sent for, for I thought we could come to an agreement here among ourselves. You and I are too friendly for anything of that sort, and now I want you to tell me what is the matter."

He poured out his troubles in a perfect stream. I let him go until he was through, listening to him without interruption. Then I told them I was too tired to talk any more that day. They would find a hogan (Navajo hut) out in the yard and plenty of food so they could rest, too. I would talk to them again in the morning. An Indian cannot be hurried. He needs time to gather and assort his impressions and allow them to soften him. They could have the rest of the day and all night for the purpose of consideration. I had telegraphed the agent to have some food ready for me, but he had failed to do so. When questioned, he said he did not believe in giving Indians food. I had to

9. More on Bizoshe (or Bi-joshii), his eldest son, Little Singer, and the Beautiful Mountain uprising can be found in McNitt, *Indian Traders*, 347–58.

make myself personally responsible for the food at the store rather than let the Indians get under the influence of anybody else. Hunting for food might have resulted in ruining the whole project. The account was paid afterward by the department. Father Weber came in with Chee Dodge and stayed with us.

The nights were quite cold. When old Bizoshe came in after dinner to learn from the trader what we were talking about, I established him at the fire in an easy chair with tobacco and began to hunt for his weak spot. I found he was a historian and asked him, "Where did the Navajos come from first?"

That was enough to launch him on the history of the trials and tribulations of the Navajo. He told us they had come up out of the underworld through a hole in the La Plata Mountains of Colorado. The Pueblos of the Rio Grande came up out of the same hole but on the opposite side, which argues for a long stay of the Navajos in that country. When he went out later, I told Hunter, "It's all right. We've got him bagged. He is coming our way when the time comes."

They all crowded into the store next morning with their arms. Chee Dodge acted as interpreter. I felt them out a little from time to time to see how soft they were, decided to risk a direct demand, and asked the old man, "What are you going to do?"

He answered, "I am going to do just what you tell me to do." Each one in their turn said the same thing.

I then said, "Very well. The marshal has warrants for you (Bizoshe) and three sons. The wagons will be here this afternoon, and I want you to get in them and go with me to Gallup. You will have to answer for your conduct to the judge at Santa Fe. We will start tomorrow morning."

They said they would like to go home to make arrangements for the care of their stock during their absence. They were told they could go on one condition—that they must promise to return in time to leave on the wagons a little after sunrise. I was urged not to let them go lest they run clear away and start trouble among the other Navajos, but I allowed them to leave. The wagons did not get in when expected, and it was obvious they must have a night for rest after that long drive, so our start was put off another day.

The eldest son said his child was sick. He would like to go back and spend the night with it. He made the same agreement as the day before. Having left all their horses at home, they had to do all their traveling back and forth on foot, six miles in and out. He was back as promised, but, when the others got into the wagon, he refused to go, saying his child was too sick to leave. We looked each other in the eye for a minute, and I told him, "You go and get into that wagon." He got into the wagon.

We drove up to the camp and were soon surrounded by the soldiers who had come all the way from Nebraska to fight "those wild Navajos" and wanted to see what they looked like. The Indians, not understanding the language, became uneasy lest they intended some damage. I told them to go and get their dinner in the store and stay there until I came for them. The rear guard of the troops had to stay back with some belated wagons. I got back before their arrival at this camp, making good my word. The marshal, hearing the glad tidings of our arrival, hurried up to see his prisoners, but, finding them all gone, thought I had allowed them to escape. He became wrathy, but he was soon pacified.

We changed teams here and started on a long, cold drive for the Navajo school, where we spent the night and went to Gallup next day. The old man was very frail. He had no idea how to ride in a side-seated ambulance. The weather was very raw and cold. I had to hold a blanket around him all the ninety miles into Gallup lest he get pneumonia. They were given a good supper and a warm place to sleep in the jail. It was explained that we would have to separate here. Father Weber and Chee Dodge would go to Santa Fe with them. I turned them over to the marshal and bade them be of good cheer. The old man hugged me to his breast, making a rather affecting scene when we parted. I sent a letter to the judge by Father Weber, saying he would probably find the four Navajos had been as sinned against as sinning, if not more so. If he intended to imprison them at Santa Fe, the expiration of their sentence would find them there with no money, unable to speak the language, and without transportation home. Thus they might be thrown on the charity of the town, whereas, if their sentences expired at Gallup on the edge of their reservation, their people could come for them on horseback and take them home safely. The judge gave them thirty days in Gallup.

We started back toward El Paso.[10]

10. President Woodrow Wilson highly praised Scott: "I instinctively knew that you were the right man to send, and the result has justified my expectations perfectly. . . . You have done a great public service." Woodrow Wilson, the White House, Washington, D.C., to Brigadier General Hugh L. Scott, El Paso, Tex., Dec. 16, 1913, reprinted in Scott, *Some Memories*, 633.

Arrest of the Paiutes

On one Sunday morning in February 1915, Mr. Lane, secretary of the Interior, accompanied by Mr. Cato Sells, commissioner of Indian Affairs, came out to the house of the chief of staff at the top of the hill at Fort Myer,

General Scott in council with Paiute Indians, Utah, 1915. From Scott, *Some Memories of a Soldier*, between pages 528 and 529. Editor's collection.

Virginia, the secretary in something of a fury over the criticisms he had read in the newspapers while coming from California.

They said that there had been a battle near Bluff [in San Juan County], Utah, between some Paiute Indians and the United States marshal of Utah [Aquila Nebeker] with a large posse in which the latter was worsted with loss of life on both sides. The secretary said he had no one he could send to settle the matter, which was still fraught with danger, and wanted to know if I could help him and go out myself.

I demurred a little at this, saying, "You have just sent some very stiff letters to Germany and England. There is no peace in Mexico, and I don't know whether the secretary of war wants to have his principal assistant wandering about in the snow and sagebrush of Utah at a time like this. It all depends on his wishes." Secretary Lane said he would go at once to Secretary [Lindley M.] Garrison.

The latter brought up the question on his arrival at the office the next morning, saying Secretary Lane had asked to have me go west and settle the matter. Secretary Garrison had asked if he could not send someone else, but Secretary Lane had asked, "Who can that person be?"

Secretary Lane had told the secretary of war that the Paiutes were related to the Utes of Colorado and had intermarried with the Navajo tribe, which contained some thirty thousand Indians, many living close to the great canyons that run down into the Grand Canyon of the Colorado. A war with them would be a long-drawn-out, expensive affair of which no one could predict the end.

Secretary Garrison asked if I would mind going. I told him I would be very glad to go if he wished it. He then said I had better go and asked how large a body of troops I wanted to take. I told him I did not want to take any.

"What!" he said, loud enough to be heard out in the corridor, "don't want any?"

I said I wanted to take Colonel [Robert L.] Michie as an aide and Sergeant [Paul R.] Randolph, my orderly.[11] It was soon arranged for me to see

11. The Paiute troubles and Scott's exploits received extensive national newspaper coverage, which provided details of the places and people involved in the fracas. Sample articles include "Scott As a Mediator," *Washington Post*, Mar. 8, 1915; "Gen. Scott Captures Outlaw Indians," *New York Times*, Mar. 21, 1915; "Scott Brings in the Piutes," *Boston Daily Globe*, Mar. 21, 1915; "Scott Reports Success," *New York Times*, Mar. 22, 1915; "Scott Nips Piute War," *Washington Post*, Mar. 22, 1915; "Gen. Scott Tells How He Ended Piute War and Took 27 Prisoners," *Washington Post*, Mar. 23, 1915; and "How Gen. Scott Won the Hostiles," *New York Times*, Mar. 25, 1915.

the assistant attorney general, Mr. Charles Warren, who ordered the United States marshal at Bluff to take no further steps until my arrival, when I would give him further orders. We left that night for Denver. I had told Secretary Lane that in case I should go west I would want two things. He had said, "I will arrange for anything you ask." I wanted to have food for the Indians lest they fall under the influence of someone else while searching for food. Moreover, I wanted old Bizoshe, the Navajo whom I had arrested at Beautiful Mountain several years before, sent to Bluff, Utah. I had never seen the Paiute Indians, and Bizoshe could introduce me in a way the president of the United States himself could not.

After the affair was over, I got a letter from the clerk at the Navajo Agency, who had been sent out fifty miles to notify Bizoshe. Bizoshe replied after some reflection, "I am an old man, and that is a far country (more than one hundred miles of rough traveling) and a country of strangers, but my brother wants me, and I will go." He started at once for Bluff with his two sons in a wagon.

Our train got stuck in the snow in the middle of Nebraska, and the delay caused us to miss our train out of Denver. We utilized the delay consequent to waiting for another train by conferring with the United States District Attorney [Harry B. Tedrow] and the marshal of Colorado [Dewey C. Bailey or Samuel J. Burris], who told us what the Paiute fight had been all about. It appeared that the trouble in Utah began over the murder of a Mexican in Colorado with which a Paiute named Stenegat, or Hatch, was charged.[12] He had run off to join his Paiute relatives in Utah near the Mormon town of Bluff.

The Colorado authorities made application to those of Utah for Hatch's extradition for trial. The matter had run along for a long time without result, and the demand had been lately renewed. Several posses had gone to Bluff to make the arrest and had returned empty-handed, considering it too dangerous to attempt. Then the marshal of Utah, under the pressure from Colorado, gathered about seventy-five gunmen as a posse and had gone down to Bluff. Being afraid to negotiate with the Indians, he had surrounded the camp of a portion of the band before dawn. The Indians awakened to find themselves surrounded by an armed band of strangers and concluded that they were being attacked by a large band of cowboys with whom they were

12. His name usually appeared in the newspapers as Tse-ne-gat, sometimes as Everett Hatch.

constantly at war over the occupation of the range. A clash resulted. Each side accused the other afterward of firing first. The truth will never be known. The posse gave no warning of their approach or intention. Blood was shed on both sides, the posse was defeated, and some of its scattered members were lost for days, wandering somewhere back of Monticello [the county seat of San Juan County, Utah].

Six Indian boys of eighteen or twenty years gave themselves up at once to the marshal without fighting, not knowing what it was all about. These were shackled and put in a room under guard. One of the young men, who could understand a little English, heard something that made him think they were going to be killed. He tried to escape by breaking the window. He was shot and killed half in and half out of the window, which was entirely unnecessary because he was unarmed and could have been taken back into the room without danger to anybody. In reality, he was murdered, which was supposedly justified on the plea that he was attempting to escape. The others, shackled, were taken under heavy guard to Salt Lake City before our arrival. They were entirely innocent.

Michie and I with Randolph left the Denver & Salt Lake Railway at Thompson's [now Thompson Springs in Grand County], Utah, and made our way south 180 miles as best we might—one stage over comparatively smooth country as far as Moab, a little Mormon town, in an automobile. The next morning at four o'clock we crowded into a two-horse mail hack built to carry three men and a driver. There were five of us, together with our bedding rolls, the mail, and express. The weather was bitter cold in that high altitude. We rode cramped up in that open stage until eight o'clock at night. Next day we had to go on in a sleigh. We had to get ahead to avert further bloodshed.

The marshal reported at Bluff and asked for orders. I told him to send home those seventy-five gunmen immediately. He expostulated [or, in other words, reasoned earnestly] at this, saying the Paiutes would capture the town. I told him that that was no longer his responsibility but mine. I would take care of the town. The gunmen must go. Bizoshe also reported with his two sons and asked what I wanted of him.

I told him the Paiutes were said to be twenty-five miles down the San Juan River. I wanted him to go with me and bring them back. He demurred strongly at this, saying, "I am afraid, and my two sons are afraid." Then he began a legend of the first Paiute's meanness and said they had all been mean ever since. I ridiculed him half an hour for refusing to believe that a

Navajo and a marshal could be afraid of a Paiute who lived mainly on roots and grasshoppers. He succumbed finally to the ridicule and said he would go, provided it were promised that, when we were both killed, we would be buried together, side by side. Colonel Michie agreed to attend to this, and the matter was soon settled.

Bizoshe had made no request for compensation for the services of his two sons, himself, and four horses but had come away willingly, serving as a friend. I asked the marshal before leaving Bluff if he would do me a favor. He said he "would be charmed at the opportunity." I inquired what he had been paying the members of the posse. He replied five dollars a day and expenses. Then I asked him to put Bizoshe and his two sons on his payroll from the time of their departure from home until their return, which was done. They were each paid quite a sum, which the old man well earned.

The Paiutes were reported to be at Mexican Hat, a city of one building twenty-five miles down the San Juan from Bluff.[13] We drove down there accompanied by Mr. [John] Wetherill from Kayenta, a gentleman who knew those Indians well. We located at Mexican Hat in the only building, a store about twenty feet square. The trader's wife was at Kayenta about fifty miles away, so we were given his bedroom, while he slept on his counter. Information came to us that the Paiutes had left for a stronghold at Navajo Mountain about a hundred miles west toward the Grand Canyon. We searched the neighborhood for hostile Indians without result until Mr. Wetherill brought in a Paiute from Kayenta, where he had gone to trade. I induced him to stay a night and sent him the next day with a message for his people, asking them to come in and see me, and with food and blankets for them.

Several days went by without any occurrence. Finally he returned, saying the Paiutes would be in next day. They came in a few at a time after hiding among the hills watching our camp with a glass lest some trap be laid for them. We gave them more food and blankets and made them all comfortable. Next day they told us their troubles. I allowed them to simmer all night. I felt them out gently next morning and decided to risk a refusal. But when the question was put point-blank, "What are you going to do?" they said, "We are going to do just what you tell us to do."

The whole tribe agreed to surrender and go to Salt Lake City on the one condition that I should go with them. This I readily promised but said the

13. The U.S. Census of 2010 listed a population of thirty-one for the San Juan County village.

marshal only wanted four—"Old Poke" [Polk], "Posey," and one other besides Hatch—who would have to be tried for murder in Colorado. We soon started for Bluff, Colonel Michie going ahead to procure food and a warm place for the prisoners to sleep.

The Mormons at Bluff had said they knew those Indians and would not believe they were coming with me until they saw them. The Mormons were having a good deal of fun, behind our backs, of course, all down that 180 miles from the railway, over those "swivel chair men from Washington" thinking they could do anything with these Indians. The whole countryside was expecting an attack by Indians and would not believe anything else. Some time afterward Mr. [Matthew K.] Sniffen of the Indian Rights Association told me they had informed him they had been ready to wager a thousand dollars that nobody could get them.

We started up toward the railway next day, taking the marshal with us, to whom I was most polite, desiring his influence at Salt Lake City. At first we were all crowded in the mail hack with our property. Later we got a few horses. My problem was to prevent those four Indians from being legally murdered. White men had been killed, and the trial would be in the hands of white men, possibly prejudiced against the Indian, whose land incidentally was wanted. There would be a cloud of white witnesses, although I believed that the white man had been the aggressor. This could only be proved by Indian witnesses, whose word would not be taken against that of white men.

We telephoned ahead to Bluff asking for a warm room and food. Every time they asked, "Don't you want a jail?"

We replied, "No."

When they asked, "Don't you want a guard?" we replied, "No! We want a warm room and food."

An automobile came out on a short piece of good road to take me into Moab. Everybody was curious to see those "bloody Indians" and asked where they were. Old Poke was pointed out sitting in the hack. I said the others were coming along on horseback. Several persons said to me, "We know those Indians better than you do. You'll never see them again." I replied I was willing to risk it. It was not long before they came jogging in on their horses.

The next twenty-five miles brought us to the railroad, which they had never seen before, and I had to go and pull them off the track at the approach of a train. Here Buffalo Bill Cody telegraphed us from Denver that a dinner was to be given for us by the governor of Colorado [George A. Carlson] and three hundred citizens of Denver. A similar invitation by telegram came from the governor of Utah [William Spry] at Salt Lake City, which was accepted as affording an opportunity to gain friendship for the Paiutes. The general manager of the Denver & Salt Lake Railway telegraphed he was sending his special car and came with it himself to take us in.

I told the marshal en route that the Utah papers had been giving him pretty rough treatment over being defeated by the Paiutes. He had lost a great deal of face at home, but in order to help him get some of it back I said I would turn the prisoners over to him and let his townsmen see him conducting them into the streets to jail. Michie and I were not known in Salt Lake City. We would jump off the rear end of the train and go quietly up the hotel without being seen by anybody. This pleased him immensely.

I made an appeal for the prisoners that night at the banquet, which was published all over Utah, and went next morning to see the United States District Attorney [William W. Ray] and asked him, "What sort of a case have you against the Paiutes?" He said he had a very strong case of murder against them. They had resisted the offices of the law and killed some of them.

"Let us talk about that a little," I said. "Who served the subpoena on them?"

He had to go out and ask the marshal about that and returning said, "Nobody."

"Did anybody tell them they were marshals?" I asked.

"No."

"Did they have uniforms to indicate they were marshals?"

"No."

"Then where is your case?" I asked.

"I reckon I haven't got any," he said.

Going to say good-by to the marshal, he carefully locked the door, put his chair near mine, and whispered, "What do you want done with those Indians?"

I whispered back, "Let them go," and so it was. They were all sent home except Hatch, who was tried for murder at Denver and acquitted. It was not long before they were back among their own tribe.[14]

14. Scott was quoted after the acquittal as saying, "I'm glad. I never thought he was guilty." "Gen. Scott, Veteran Indian Fighter Dies," *Winners of the West*, May 30, 1934. The trial of Tse-ne-gat is covered at

Peace continued there for seven years, notwithstanding constant effort to get the Indians away from the land where they and their ancestors had been born. Old Poke and Hatch died in their beds in 1923. The papers later recorded another difficulty with the Paiutes and various posses. I offered to go again and try to save the lives of those Indians but was told it was not an important matter, though I would be asked to go should it become important. It resulted, however, in the killing of Posey and some of his band [in 1923]. Later the Indian Department took sane measures for the prevention of such warfare that I had recommended seven years before without result. I feel certain that, if I had not gone in person with those Indians to Salt Lake City, some of them would have been legally murdered by trial and conviction, with one side only represented. I am never afraid of what the Indian will do in such flare-ups—if I can reach him in time. I am always afraid of what the white men do—legally.

◆ ◆ ◆

How sweet it is to look backward over the years and remember the gratitude of those simple, sincere, and humble people, both red and white, for the salvation of the women and children of that countryside is worth far more than any military glory that might have been won in bringing about their subjugation and punishment by force of arms.

some length in Parkhill, *Last of the Indian Wars*. Again, Scott received praise from President Wilson: "The whole country admires the way in which you handle these difficult and delicate matters, and I wanted to express . . . my own feeling of deep appreciation and genuine admiration." Woodrow Wilson, White House, Washington, D.C., to Gen. Hugh L. Scott, Chief of Staff, War Department, April 2, 1915, reprinted in Scott, *Some Memories*, 634.

Appendix

Joseph at Grant's Tomb

The following pair of vignettes involves Chief Joseph of the Nez Percé tribe, the famed Indian leader who appears in chapters 9 and 11 of this memoir. The original document survives as a five-page, double-spaced typescript, nestled among the handwritten drafts and typed sections that together formed the manuscript of *Some Memories of a Soldier*.[1] This particular section fell prey to the editor's pen and did not make the book, perhaps because the events recounted here did not fit neatly within the chapter's chronology or elsewhere. Scott's publisher advised, "May I suggest that you follow rather strictly the chronological order of your years, as that makes the story much clearer to the reader?"[2] Only one solitary, heavily edited line from the entire story appeared in Scott's book (in this book, see p. 83: "No Indians ever . . ."), which may have been where Scott intended its placement. The document is presented here in its entirety.

◆ ◆ ◆

1. Scott Papers, Library of Congress, boxes 103–108. Joseph's 1897 and 1903 visits to Washington, D.C., are briefly recounted in Pearson, *Nez Perces in the Indian Territory*, 297–98; and West, *Last Indian War*, 311, 313–14.

2. W. Morgan Shuster, the Century Co., New York, N.Y., to Hugh Lenox Scott, Princeton, N.J., Mar. 7, 1927. Scott Papers, Library of Congress.

Shortly before the dedication of the tomb of General Grant in New York during the McKinley administration, General Miles sent for me and told me to go down to the office of the commissioner of Indian Affairs where Joseph, chief of the Nez Percé, then was in the old Atlantic Building on F Street and induce him to go over to New York and take part in the great procession. Joseph had come over from Colville, Washington, about some business of his own and had been invited by Gen. O[liver] O. Howard to march in the division of the great parade he would command, but Joseph refused point-blank, saying he would not stay in the same part of the country with General Howard and was going right back to Colville. He charged General Howard with being the author of his misfortunes, had for him a most bitter hatred, and did not want to breathe the air of the same country with him.

Col[onel] W. F. Cody (Buffalo Bill) was then with his Wild West Show on Staten Island, and he sent a special emissary to Washington to induce Joseph to ride with him in the parade. The commissioner of Indian Affairs [W. A. Jones] had made several efforts to persuade him to go, but he would listen to nobody, determined to go back right away to Colville.

I found the commissioner trying again to influence him without success. I asked him to let me have Joseph for a little while in a room by ourselves. I told him General Howard had nothing to do with him. He need not speak to him if he should meet him if he did not want to. Cody would keep him with him, treat him well, and see that he was well taken care of. He would see New York and ride in a great parade. Cody would see that he had a good horse, and he would see a great sight, greater probably than he would ever see again. He agreed to go.

The *Harper's Weekly* of that time had a picture of the parade, showing Joseph riding with Buffalo Bill in the staff of Gen. Grenville [M.] Dodge, grand marshal of the parade.[3] Cody was so pleased that he telegraphed me in Washington that, if I would go over to Staten Island, he would take care of me and pay all my expenses for a month.

On that visit to Washington I happened to be in General Miles's office when Joseph came in and acted as his interpreter in the sign language in his conversation with the general around whom he had thrown his arms, holding him tight to his breast as I have seen Geronimo do also. They all loved

3. *Harper's Weekly*, May 8, 1897, 460. See also *New York Times*, April 21, 24, 1897. The grand march to mark the dedication of Grant's Tomb occurred on April 27.

the general, although they had met defeat from him. It seemed to make no difference. He knew how to treat them generously and to maintain their respect and affection.

After Joseph had gone out, I said to the general, "I think he is the best of all of them." The General replied, "I think he is."

In February 1903 Joseph came again to Washington with some of his young men—fine, stalwart, upstanding Nez Percés—and, hearing that I was in town, hunted me up in the office.[4] I told General [Leonard] Wood something about him, also that he had better come in and see him as I considered him the most important Indian of his time. After he had talked to Joseph for a while, he said, "Roosevelt would like to see him." Soon a telephone message came for me to take Joseph over there, where President Roosevelt made him the same speech I had just made to General Wood a little while before and he had passed it on. General Wood came in while we were still talking, and the president said to Joseph, "I invite you to my Army and Navy reception." Then swinging around and pointing his finger at me said, "You bring him." Continuing the conversation, he said, "When Wood goes to the Philippines, I want you to come over to fence and box with me." Wood and I had it all arranged that [Frank R.] McCoy and I were going over to the Philippines with him, and this showed our plans to be in danger. I rolled a piteous eye on Wood, who responded by saying, "I was in hopes Scott would go the Philippines with me." The president said, "Oh! All right then. You go ahead, and, if anybody stops you in the War Department, you come to me." I breathed somewhat easier after having grated a little on that bar.

I took Joseph and four other Indians to the reception, who were dressed in all their buckskin and war bonnets, together with my daughter Anna and a friend of McCoy's, for he was on duty at the White House that night and could not look after her. I felt very conspicuous with all that paint and feathers and would have liked much to put it off on someone else, but I was accustomed to obeying the orders of the president. There was no way to avoid it.

As we passed in the line before President and Mrs. Roosevelt, the former told me to take Joseph behind the line, a place reserved for the most distinguished guests. I established him there in a good place with his interpreter

4. At this time Scott was between foreign assignments, having arrived in Washington in May 1902 from Cuba. Scott, *Some Memories*, 273.

and took myself and [the] girls out of the limelight. Everybody wanted to shake hands with Joseph: Senator [Redfield] Procter [Proctor], Admiral [George] Dewey, Miss Alice Roosevelt, Mr. and Mrs. Alexander Van Rennselaer [Van Rensselaer] from Philadelphia, etc., etc., and many others. The morning papers declared that Joseph had been the main feature of the evening.[5]

General Miles sent for me the next morning and said, "I want you to do me a favor." I answered that it had always been the other way, and I would be charged to be able to please him. He said, "I see by the papers that you were at the White House last night with Joseph." I am persona non grata over there, and I want you to ask the president for one of those large silver medals for Joseph," which I proceeded forthwith to do. The president asked, "How do I get them?" I told him they came through the Treasury Department. "Then go out, and tell Loeb to get one for Joseph, and give him the proper address to send it," which [William] Loeb promised to do.[6]

When I came back from the Philippines on leave in 1906, I read that Joseph had died and wondered if he had gotten his medal in time. I asked Loeb, who replied that "he had sent it if he had said he would." I told him that was not enough for me, for he had a great deal more confidence in himself than I had in him.

One of my cousins was president of the Women's Club in Princeton at that time, and she told me that Mr. Ed[ward S.] Curtis, the great artist of Indian scenery from Seattle, was coming to lecture to the club that day. She was a widow and told me to go to the train to meet Mr. Curtis, give him his lunch, and produce him at the club in proper time. Being used to doing as I am told, I did it. Mr. Curtis threw some portraits of Indians on the screen, among others, Red Cloud, Spotted Tail, and Joseph. I asked afterward if he had known those Indians personally. He said he had known Joseph and was at Colville when he died. I asked if he had seen him with a silver medal. He said he had and knew the Indian that got it at the potlatch, which revived my confidence in Loeb and made me rejoice that Joseph had gotten the medal before he died.[7]

5. The formal reception occurred on February 12. *Washington Post*, Feb. 13, 1903.

6. William Loeb, Jr., was Roosevelt's personal secretary.

7. Joseph died on September 21, 1904, and the potlatch or ceremonial giveaway of his personal property occurred in June 1905. The latter event coincided with the dedication of a monument at his Nespelem, Washington, grave. Howard, *Saga of Chief Joseph*, 367–70.

No Indian in our history had made war more skillfully, more stoutly, or more humanely. The last time I ever saw him was that night at the White House when he seemed quite broken (Feb. 1903) and dazed. When asked a question, he would look helplessly at his interpreter to answer for him. I thought he was suffering from tuberculosis. He had forgotten his use of the sign language, in which he was very skillful in 1877, although he lived beyond the Rocky Mountains and outside of the sign-talking area where the inter-tribal language was the Chinook Jargon, [of] the Columbia [River]. The Flat-heads, Nez Percé, and several other tribes occasionally would make yearly journeys across the mountains to the buffalo Plains to make meat and robes and carry back great quantities. They were at war with all but the Crows over there and had to learn the sign language to use on the Plains. This yearly journey to and from the Plains made him well acquainted with the trail, which they had travelled since before the time of Lewis and Clark and usually went down the Yellowstone through where Livingston, Montana, now is, from which I diverted them in 1877 with ten men, throwing them nearer to General Miles at [the] Tongue River, enabling him at the end to capture them within a day's travel of safety across the British line, as treated elsewhere.

Bibliography

Manuscript Collections

Library of Congress, Washington, D.C.
Hugh Lenox Scott Papers
National Anthropological Archives, Smithsonian Institution, Washington, D.C.
Ethnographic Notes. General Hugh Lenox Scott. Manuscript 4641.
National Archives and Records Administration, Washington, D.C.
Post Returns, Fort Apache, Arizona, Fort Sill, Oklahoma Territory. Returns from U.S. Military Posts, 1800–1916. Records of the Adjutant General's Office, 1780s–1917. Record Group 94.

Unpublished Materials

Ferrell, Robert H., Indiana University. Personal communication with the editor, May 13, 2005.
Harper, James William. "Hugh Lenox Scott: Soldier-Diplomat, 1876–1917." PhD diss., University of Virginia, 1968.

Government Publications

Adams, Charles E. "Report of Kiowa, Comanche, and Wichita Agency." Kiowa, Comanche, and Wichita Agency, Anadarko, Okla., Sept. 16, 1890, to the

Commissioner of Indian Affairs. In *Fifty-ninth Annual Report of the Commissioner of Indian Affairs to the Secretary of the Interior, 1890*. 186–89. Washington, D.C.: Government Printing Office, 1890.

Bell, William Gardner. *Commanding Generals and Chiefs of Staff, 1775–1995: Portraits and Biographical Sketches of the United States Army's Senior Officer.* Washington, D.C.: Center of Military History, 2005.

Heitman, Francis B. *Historical Register and Dictionary of the United States Army from Its Organization, September 29, 1789, to March 2, 1903*. 2 vols. Washington, D.C.: Government Printing Office, 1903.

Holabird, S. B. "Report of the Quartermaster-General." Quartermaster-General's Office, Washington, D.C., Oct. 9, 1886, to Wm. C. Endicott, Secretary of War. In *Annual Report of the Secretary of War for the Year 1886*. Vol. 1, 321–565. Washington, D.C.: Government Printing Office, 1886.

"Leasing of Grazing Lands in the Ponca, Otoe, and Missouria Indian Reservations, Oklahoma." In *Letter from the Secretary of the Interior, Transmitting, in Response to Resolution of the Senate of December 19, 1899*. Senate Executive Documents, No. 217, 56th U.S. Cong., 1st Sess. Washington, D.C.: Government Printing Office, 1900.

Lincoln, W. L. "Reports of Agents in Montana." Fort Belknap Agency, Montana, Aug. 1, 1879. In *Annual Report of the Commissioner of Indian Affairs to the Secretary of the Interior for the Year 1879*. 98–100. Washington, D.C.: Government Printing Office, 1879.

Mallery, Garrick. "Sign Language among the North American Indians Compared with that among Other Peoples and Deaf-Mutes." In *First Annual Report of the Bureau of Ethnology of the Smithsonian Institution for 1879–1880*. 263–552. Washington, D.C.: U.S. Government Printing Office, 1881.

Merritt, Wesley. "Report of Brigadier-General Merritt." Headquarters, Department of the Missouri, Fort Leavenworth, Kans., Sept. 12, 1889. In *Report of the Secretary of War Being Part of the Message and Documents Communicated to the Two Houses of Congress at the Beginning of the First Session of the Fifty-first Congress*. Vol. 1, 163–67. Washington, D.C.: Government Printing Office, 1889.

———. "Report of Brigadier-General Merritt." Headquarters, Department of the Missouri, St. Louis, Mo., Sept. 11, 1890. In *Report of the Secretary of War Being Part of the Message and Documents Communicated to the Two Houses of Congress at the Beginning of the Second Session of the Fifty-first Congress*. Vol. 1, 195–99. Washington, D.C.: Government Printing Office, 1890.

Miers, Earl Schenck, ed. *Lincoln Day by Day: A Chronology, 1809–1865*. Vol. 3, *1861–1865*, edited by C. Percy Powell. Washington, D.C.: Lincoln Sesquicentennial Commission, 1960.

Mooney, James. "Calendar History of the Kiowa Indians." In *Seventeenth Annual Report of the Bureau of American Ethnology to the Secretary of the Smithsonian*

Institution, 1895–96. Vol. 1, 141–444. Washington, D.C.: Government Printing Office, 1898.

———. "The Ghost-Dance Religion and the Sioux Outbreak of 1890." In *Fourteenth Annual Report of the Bureau of Ethnology to the Secretary of the Smithsonian Institution, 1892–93*. Pt. 2. 653–1136. Washington, D.C.: Government Printing Office, 1896.

New York (State) Legislature. "Proceedings of the Fourth Annual Encampment, United Spanish War Veterans." In *Documents of the Assembly of the State of New York, One Hundred and Thirty-fourth Session, 1911*. Albany: J. B. Lyon, 1911.

Raynolds, William F. *Report on the Exploration of the Yellowstone River*. Washington, D.C.: Government Printing Office, 1868.

Sherman, W. T. "Report of the General of the Army." Nov. 10, 1876. In *Report of the Secretary of War Being Part of the Message and Documents Communicated to the Two Houses of Congress at the Beginning of the Second Session of the Forty-fourth Congress*. Vol. 1, 23–40. Washington, D.C.: Government Printing Office, 1876.

Terry, Alfred H. "Report of Brigadier-General Terry." Record of Events, Headquarters, Department of Dakota, Fort Snelling, Minn., Oct. 8, 1883, to the Adjutant General, Military Division of the Missouri, Chicago, Ill. In *Annual Report of the Secretary of War for the Year 1883*. Vol. 1, 106–19. Washington, D.C.: Government Printing Office, 1883.

U.S. Congress. *Report of the Secretary of the Interior, Being Part of the Message and Documents Communicated to the Two Houses of Congress at the Beginning of the First Session of the Fifty-second Congress*. Vol. 2. Washington, D.C.: Government Printing Office, 1892.

Newspapers

Boston Daily Globe, 1915
Harper's Weekly, 1897
Kansas City Star, 1913
New York Times, 1871, 1897, 1915, 1928, 1934, 1935, 1937
Washington Post, 1908, 1915
Winners of the West (St. Joseph, Mo.), 1934

Books and Articles

Anderson, Harry H. Foreword to *The Crazy Horse Surrender Ledger*. Edited by Thomas R. Buecker and R. Eli Paul, ix–xv. Lincoln: Nebraska State Historical Society, 1994.

Bonney, Orrin H., and Lorraine Bonney. *Battle Drums and Geysers: The Life and Journals of Lt. Gustavas Cheyney Doane, Soldier and Explorer of the Yellowstone and Snake River Regions*. Chicago: Swallow Press, 1970.

Bray, Kingsley M. "'We Belong to the North': The Flights of the Northern Indians from the White River Agencies, 1877–1878." *Montana: The Magazine of Western History* 55 (Summer 2005): 28–47.

Britten, Thomas A. *American Indians in World War I: At Home and at War*. Albuquerque: University of New Mexico Press, 1997.

Brown, William Carey. "Hugh Lenox Scott." In *Sixty-seventh Annual Report of the Association of Graduates of the United States Military Academy at West Point, New York, June 11, 1936*, 97–102. Newburgh, N.Y.: Moore Printing Company, 1936.

Buck, Solon J. "The Upper Missouri Historical Expedition." *Mississippi Valley Historical Review* 12 (Dec. 1925): 385–91.

Buecker, Thomas R. "In the Old Army: Harry K. Hollenbach at Fort Robinson, 1911–1913." *Nebraska History* 71 (Spring 1990): 13–22.

———. *Fort Robinson and the American West, 1874–1899*. Lincoln: Nebraska State Historical Society, 1999.

Carroll, John M., ed. *Custer's Chief of Scouts: The Reminiscences of Charles A. Varnum*. Lincoln: University of Nebraska Press, 1987.

Catlin, George. *The Manners, Customs, and Condition of the North American Indians*. 2 vols. London: Published by author, 1841.

Clark, William P. *The Indian Sign Language*. Philadelphia: L. R. Hamersly, 1885.

Coffman, Edward M. *The Hilt of the Sword: The Career of Peyton C. March*. Madison: University of Wisconsin Press, 1966.

———. *The Regulars: The American Army, 1898–1941*. Cambridge: Belknap Press of Harvard University Press, 2004.

———. *The War to End All Wars: The American Military Experience in World War I*. Lexington: University of Kentucky Press, 1998.

Corwin, Hugh D. "Delos K. Lonewolf, Kiowa." *Chronicles of Oklahoma* 39 (Winter 1961–62): 433–36.

Cox-Paul, Lori A., and James A. Wengert, eds. *A Frontier Army Christmas*. Lincoln: Nebraska State Historical Society, 1996.

Cullum, George W. *Biographical Register of the Officers and Graduates of the U.S. Military Academy, at West Point, New York, since Its Establishment in 1802*. Cambridge: Riverside Press, 1901.

Davis, Jeffrey E. *Hand Talk: Sign Language among American Indian Nations*. Cambridge: Cambridge University Press, 2010.

Davis, Richard Harding. *The West from a Car-Window*. New York: Harper, 1892.

Davis, William C. *Jefferson Davis: The Man and His Hour*. New York: HarperCollins, 1991.

Frazer, Robert W. *Forts of the West: Military Forts and Presidios, and Posts Commonly Called Forts, West of the Mississippi River to 1898*. Norman: University of Oklahoma Press, 1965.

Friesen, Steve. *Buffalo Bill: Scout, Showman, Visionary*. Golden, Colo.: Fulcrum Publishing, 2010.

Graham, W. A. *The Custer Myth: A Source Book of Custeriana*. Harrisburg, Pa.: Stackpole, 1953.

———. *The Reno Court of Inquiry: Abstract of the Official Record of Proceedings*. Harrisburg, Pa.: Stackpole, 1954.

Greene, Candace S. *One Hundred Summers: A Kiowa Calendar Record*. Lincoln: University of Nebraska Press, 2009.

———. *Silver Horn: Master Illustrator of the Kiowas*. Norman: University of Oklahoma Press, 2001.

Greene, Jerome A. *Nez Perce Summer, 1877: The U.S. Army and the Nee-Me-Poo Crisis*. Helena: Montana Historical Society Press, 2000.

———. *Stricken Field: The Little Bighorn since 1876*. Norman: University of Oklahoma Press, 2008.

———. *Washita: The U.S. Army and the Southern Cheyennes, 1867–1869*. Norman: University of Oklahoma Press, 2004.

———. *Yellowstone Command: Colonel Nelson A. Miles and the Great Sioux War, 1876–1877*. Lincoln: University of Nebraska Press, 1991.

Hagan, William T. *Theodore Roosevelt and Six Friends of the Indian*. Norman: University of Oklahoma, 1997.

Hagedorn, Hermann. *Leonard Wood: A Biography*. 2 vols. New York: Harper and Brothers, 1931.

Hanson, James A. *Little Chief's Gatherings: The Smithsonian Institution's G. K. Warren 1855–1856 Plains Indian Collection and The New York State Library's 1855–1857 Warren Expedition Journals*. Chadron, Neb.: Fur Press, 1996.

Hardorff, Richard G. *Washita Memories: Eyewitness Views of Custer's Attack on Black Kettle's Village*. Norman: University of Oklahoma Press, 2006.

Harper, James W. "Scott, Hugh Lenox." In *Dictionary of American Military Biography*, edited by Roger J. Spiller. Vol. 3, Q–Z, 969–72. Westport, Conn.: Greenwood Press, 1984.

Harrington, John P. "The American Indian Sign Language." *Indians at Work* (Sept. 1938): 24–32.

Hedren, Paul L. *After Custer: Loss and Transformation in Sioux Country*. Norman: University of Oklahoma Press, 2011.

———. "The West Loved Oysters Too!: A Look at That Time in America When Those Briny Bivalves Were All the Rage, Even beyond the Missouri River." *Montana: The Magazine of Western History* 61 (Winter 2011): 3–15.

"Honoring Their Grandfather: Chief Satanta's Descendents Seek the Return of His Shield." *American Indian Ritual Object Repatriation Foundation News and Notes* 2 (Spring/Summer, 1995): 1–3.

Hough, Walter. "Biographical Memoir of Jesse Walter Fewkes, 1850–1930." In *National Academy of Sciences Biographical Memoirs*. Vol. 15, 261–83. Washington, D.C.: National Academy of Sciences, 1932.

Howard, Helen Addison. *Saga of Chief Joseph.* Lincoln: University of Nebraska Press, 1978.

Hoxie, Frederick E. *Parading through History: The Making of the Crow Nation in America, 1805–1935.* Cambridge: Cambridge University Press, 1995.

Hutton, Paul A. *Phil Sheridan and His Army.* Lincoln: University of Nebraska Press, 1985.

Jacobs, Margaret D. "A Battle for the Children: American Indian Child Removal in Arizona in the Era of Assimilation." *Journal of Arizona History* 45 (Spring 2004): 31–62.

Jensen, Richard E., ed. *Voices of the American West.* Vol. 1, *The Indian Interviews of Eli S. Ricker, 1903–1919.* Lincoln: University of Nebraska Press, 2005.

———, R. Eli Paul, and John E. Carter. *Eyewitness at Wounded Knee.* Lincoln: University of Nebraska Press, 1991.

Kehrberg, Richard. "Scott, Hugh Lennox [*sic*]" In *The United States in the First World War: An Encyclopedia,* edited by Anne Cipriano Venzon, 532–34. New York: Garland, 1995.

Kime, Wayne R., ed. *The Sherman Tour Journals of Colonel Richard Irving Dodge.* Norman: University of Oklahoma Press, 2002.

Krausnick, Gertrude. "The Columbia River Historical Expedition." *Minnesota History* 7 (Sept. 1926): 242–48.

Krouse, Susan Applegate. *North American Indians in the Great War.* Lincoln: University of Nebraska Press, 2007.

Lawrence, Elizabeth Atwood. *His Very Silence Speaks: Comanche—The Horse Who Survived Custer's Last Stand.* Detroit: Wayne State University Press, 1989.

Lee, Robert. *Fort Meade and the Black Hills.* Lincoln: University of Nebraska Press, 1991.

———. "Warriors in Ranks: American Indian Units in the Regular Army, 1891–1897." *South Dakota History* 21 (Fall 1991): 263–316.

Leiker, James N., and Ramon Powers. *The Northern Cheyenne Exodus in History and Memory.* Norman: University of Oklahoma Press, 2011.

Leupp, Francis E. *Notes of a Summer Tour among the Indians of the Southwest.* Philadelphia: Indian Rights Association, 1897.

Libby, Orin G. *The Arikara Narrative of Custer's Campaign and the Battle of the Little Bighorn.* Norman: University of Oklahoma Press, 1998.

Mackintosh, John D. *Custer's Southern Officer: Captain George D. Wallace, 7th U.S. Cavalry.* Lexington, S.C.: Cloud Creek Press, 2002.

McChristian, Douglas C. "Custer's Avengers." *Greasy Grass* 8 (May 1992): 2–10.

McCormack, J. Michael. "Soldiers and Sioux: Military Life among the Indians at Fort Totten." In *Fort Totten: Military Post and Indian School, 1867–1959,* edited by Kathleen Davison, 3–23. Bismarck: State Historical Society of North Dakota, 2010.

McCoy, Tim, and Ron McCoy. *Tim McCoy Remembers the West.* Lincoln: University of Nebraska Press, 1988.

McDermott, John D. *A Guide to the Indian Wars of the West.* Lincoln: University of Nebraska Press, 1998.

McNitt, Frank. *The Indian Traders.* Norman: University of Oklahoma Press, 1962.

Meadows, William C., ed. *Through Indian Sign Language: The Fort Sill Ledgers of Hugh Lenox Scott and Iseeo, 1889–1897.* Norman: University of Oklahoma Press, 2015.

Methvin, J. J. "Ahpeahtone, Kiowa: A Bit of History." *Chronicles of Oklahoma* 9 (Sept. 1931): 335–37.

Miller, Jr., Edward A. *Lincoln's Abolitionist General: The Biography of David Hunter.* Columbia: University of South Carolina Press, 1997.

Momaday, N. Scott. *Three Plays.* Norman: University of Oklahoma Press, 2007.

Mooney, James. *The Cheyenne Indians.* Memoirs of the American Anthropological Association. Vol. 1. Lancaster, Pa.: American Anthropological Association, 1905–1907.

Murray, Keith A. *The Modocs and Their War.* Norman: University of Oklahoma Press, 1959.

Nichols, Robert Hastings. "Hodge, Charles." In *Dictionary of American Biography.* Vol. 9, *Hibben–Jarvis,* edited by Dumas Malone, 98–99. New York: Scribner, 1932.

Nye, W. S. *Carbine and Lance: The Story of Old Fort Sill.* Norman: University of Oklahoma Press, 1942.

Parkhill, Forbes. *The Last of the Indian Wars.* New York: Crowell-Collier Press, 1961.

Parkman, Francis. *The Conspiracy of Pontiac and the Indian War after the Conquest of Canada.* 2 vols. Boston: Little, Brown, 1929.

Paul, R. Eli, ed. *Autobiography of Red Cloud: War Leader of the Oglalas.* Helena: Montana Historical Society Press, 1997.

———. "Counting Indians." *Wild West* 18 (Dec. 2005): 27.

Paullin, Charles O. "Scott, Hugh Lenox." In *Dictionary of American Biography.* Vol. 11, pt. 1, *Supplement One to December 31, 1935,* edited by Robert Livingston Schuyler, 651–52. New York: Scribner's, 1944.

Pearson, J. Diane. *The Nez Perces in the Indian Territory: Nimiipuu Survival.* Norman: University of Oklahoma Press, 2008.

Perry, Dan W. "Twenty-seven Years a State." *Chronicles of Oklahoma* 12 (Dec. 1934): 393–401.

Powers, Thomas. *The Killing of Crazy Horse.* New York: Knopf, 2010.

———. "Warrior Petraeus," *New York Review of Books* 60 (Mar. 7, 2013): 39–43.

Pratt, Richard Henry. *Battlefield and Classroom: Four Decades with the American Indian, 1867–1904.* Edited by Robert M. Utley. New Haven: Yale University Press, 1964.

Ricketts, Palmer C. *History of Rensselaer Polytechnic Institute, 1824–1914.* New York: Wiley, 1914.

Robinson, Sherry. *Apache Voices: Their Stories of Survival as told to Eve Ball.* Albuquerque: University of New Mexico Press, 2000.

Roosevelt, Theodore. *The Rough Riders.* New York: Scribner's, 1921.

Scott, Douglas D., P. Willey, and Melissa A. Connor. *They Died with Custer: Soldiers' Bones from the Battle of the Little Bighorn*. Norman: University of Oklahoma Press, 1998.

Scott, Hugh Lenox. "Early History and Names of the Arapaho." *American Anthropologist* 9 (July 1907): 545–60.

———. Foreword to *Caspar Collins: The Life and Exploits of an Indian Fighter of the Sixties*, by Agnes Wright Spring, 11–12. New York: Columbia University Press, 1927.

———. "Kado or Sun Dance of the Kiowa." *American Anthropologist* 13 (July 1911): 345–79.

———. "The Sign Language of the Plains Indian." In *Archives of International Folk-Lore Association*, edited by Helen Wheeler Bassett and Frederick Starr, 206–20. Chicago, 1898. Reprinted in D. Jean Umiker-Sebeok and Thomas Sebeok, eds. *Aboriginal Sign Languages of the Americas and Australia*. Vol. 2, *The Americas and Australia*. New York: Plenum, 1978.

———. *Some Memories of a Soldier*. New York: Century, 1928.

Scott, Kim Allen. *Yellowstone Denied: The Life of Gustavus Cheyney Doane*. Norman: University of Oklahoma Press, 2007.

Scott, William Berryman. *Some Memories of a Palaeontologist*. Princeton: Princeton University Press, 1939.

Seton, Ernest Thompson. *Sign Talk: A Universal Signal Code, without Apparatus, for Use in the Army, the Navy, Camping, Hunting, and Daily Life*. New York: Doubleday, Page, 1918.

Smith, John David. "Let Us All Be Grateful that We Have Colored Troops that Will Fight." In *Black Soldiers in Blue: African American Troops in the Civil War Era*, edited by John David Smith, 1–77. Chapel Hill: University of North Carolina Press, 2002.

Southwell, Kristina L., and John R. Lowett. *Life at the Kiowa, Comanche, and Wichita Agency: The Photographs of Annette Ross Hume*. Norman: University of Oklahoma Press, 2010.

Spring, Agnes Wright. *The Cheyenne and Black Hills Stage and Express Routes*. Glendale, Calif.: Arthur H. Clark, 1949.

Swett, Morris. "Sergeant I-See-O, Kiowa Indian Scout." *Chronicles of Oklahoma* 13 (Sept. 1935): 341–54.

Taft, Robert. "The Pictorial Record of the Old West: Remington in Kansas." *Kansas Historical Quarterly* 16 (May 1948): 113–35.

Thoburn, Joseph B. "Horace P. Jones, Scout and Interpreter." *Chronicles of Oklahoma* 2 (Dec. 1924): 380–91.

Thrapp, Dan L. *Encyclopedia of Frontier Biography*. Vol. 3, *P–Z*. Glendale, Calif.: Arthur H. Clark, 1988.

Ursula, M. "Sources for the Study of Oklahoma Catholic Missions: A Critical Bibliography." *Chronicles of Oklahoma* 16 (Sept. 1938): 346–77.

Utley, Robert M. *Custer: Cavalier in Buckskin*. Norman: University of Oklahoma Press, 2001.

———. *Geronimo*. New Haven: Yale University Press, 2012.

Viola, Herman J. *Diplomats in Buckskins: A History of Indian Delegations in Washington City*. Washington, D.C.: Smithsonian Institution Press, 1981.

Waggoner, Josephine. *Witness: A Húŋkpapȟa Historian's Strong-Heart Song of the Lakotas*. Edited by Emily Levine. Lincoln: University of Nebraska Press, 2013.

Wagner, Arthur L. *The Service of Security and Information*. Kansas City, Mo.: Franklin Hudson, 1893.

Wagner, Frederic C., III. *Participants in the Battle of the Little Big Horn: A Biographical Dictionary of Sioux, Cheyenne and United States Military Personnel*. Jefferson, N.C.: McFarland, 2011.

West, Elliott. *The Last Indian War: The Nez Perce Story*. Oxford: Oxford University Press, 2009.

White, Virgil D, ed. *Index to Indian Wars Pension Files, 1892–1926*. Vol. 1, *A–K*. Waynesboro, Tenn.: National Historical Publishing, 1987.

Whiteley, Peter M. *The Orayvi Split: A Hopi Transformation; Part II: The Documentary Record*. Anthropological Papers of the American Museum of Natural History 87. New York: American Museum of Natural History, 2008.

Who Was Who in America: A Companion Volume to "Who's Who in America." Vol. 1, *1897–1942*. Chicago: Marquis, 1943.

Wolff, David A. *Seth Bullock: Black Hills Lawman*. Pierre: South Dakota State Historical Society Press, 2009.

Wooster, Robert W. *Nelson A. Miles and the Twilight of the Frontier Army*. Lincoln: University of Nebraska Press, 1993.

Online Sources

Anderson, H. Allen. "Big Bow." In *Handbook of Texas Online*. Austin: Texas State Historical Association, 2010. Available at https://tshaonline.org/handbook/online/articles/fbi39.

———. "Lone Wolf." In *Handbook of Texas Online*. Austin: Texas State Historical Association, 2010. Available at https://tshaonline.org/handbook/online/articles/flo09.

Collections Search Center. National Museum of Natural History. *Smithsonian Institution*. Available at http://collections.nmnh.si.edu/search/anth/?irn=8419876.

"Find a Grave Index." Database. *FamilySearch*. 2015. Available at https://familysearch.org/ark:/61903/1:1:QV2Z-4P23.

Haley, James L. "Red River War." In *Handbook of Texas Online.* Austin: Texas State Historical Association, 2010. Available at https://tshaonline.org/handbook/online/articles/qdr02.

Harper, James W. "Scott, Hugh Lenox." *American National Biography Online.* Oxford: Oxford University Press, 2000. Available at http://oxfordindex.oup.com/view/10.1093/anb/9780198606697.article.0600587.

Hendrickson, Jr., Kenneth E. "Wichita Falls, TX." In *Handbook of Texas Online.* Austin: Texas State Historical Association, 2010. Available at http://www.tshaonline.org/handbook/online/articles/hdw02.

"Historical Expeditions" [Great Northern Railway]. *Streamliner Memories: Memorabilia from the Silver Age of Passenger Trains.* Streamlinermemories.info.

Hosmer, Brian C. "Parker, Quanah." In *Handbook of Texas Online.* Austin: Texas State Historical Association, 2010. Available at https://tshaonline.org/handbook/online/articles/fpa28.

Kincaid, Gaines. "Isa-tai." In *Handbook of Texas Online.* Austin: Texas State Historical Association, 2010. Available at https://tshaonline.org/handbook/online/articles/fis05.

"Lot 288, Indian Wars Apache Map Drawn by Hugh L. Scott, 7th Cavalry." *American History Auction.* Cincinnati: Cowan's Auctions, June 24, 2009. Available at http://cowansauctions.com.

Military Record of Colonel Hugh L. Scott, U.S. Army, Superintendent U.S. Military Academy, West Point, New York. Washington, D.C., 1906. Available at Hathi Trust Digital Library, http://catalog.hathitrust.org/Record/009609839.

"Oklahoma Marriages, 1870–1930." *FamilySearch.* Available at https://familysearch.org/ark:/61903/1:1:V28X-WKQ.

"Robert King's Oklahoma and Indian Territory U.S. Marshals and Deputy U.S. Marshals." *Oklahoma Outlaws and Lawmen History Association.* Available at http://okolha.net.

Scott, Hugh Lenox. *Some Memories of a Soldier.* New York: Century, 1928. Available at HathiTrust Digital Library, http://catalog.hathitrust.org/Record/000314756.

Index

Page numbers in italics indicate illustrations.